Michele Sibiloni

# Fuck it



Edition Patrick Frey
n.197

All the animals come out at night…

Street-walkers, good-time girls, vagabonds, village fools, rastas, pimps, drunken expats, drunken locals, drunken everybody, underpaid guards, overworked bouncers, old-timers, orphans, urchins, beggars, hoodlums, hustlers, grasshopper vendors, all kinds of cops, NGO workers and back-alley exorcists.

Some Peace Corps blogger once described Kabalagala – Kampala's most deliciously sleazy bar district – as 'Tijuana on acid'. He went on to describe how some girls in a bar tried to seduce both him and his girlfriend, while showing them pictures of their kids on their smartphones. He was shocked and sickened. An altogether different type of safari from a mollycoddled 4×4 cruise through Queen Elizabeth Park, a far cry from a charity trip to the village to fit out Mama and Papa Okello with a new water pump.

We can't blame the Peace Corps worker for being surprised, as Uganda has successfully presented itself to the international community as a responsible, progressive site for aid and development for nearly three decades now. In 1986 the country emerged from an 8-year civil war, following a 7-year dictatorship, following 70 years of exploitative colonial rule. It was the epicentre of the AIDS pandemic, though you wouldn't guess that from the outrageous promiscuity of its urban dwellers. While presenting a façade of burgeoning bourgeois culture and righteous religious values, Kampala enjoys one of the wildest nightscapes in Africa.

The rich, pungent variety of images in this book will elicit a range of reactions: pity, disgust, uncertainty, titillation – natural responses to such beautiful horrors.

Broken eggs, bruised legs, torn skirts, laughing lads, crested cranes, packs of dogs and a wide-eyed man with a gun in his hand. The stories told by these grimy vignettes are at once a cartoon strip and an archive of the ephemeral, an African symphony and a Third World catastrophe, a naughty grope and a guilty giggle.

This is the *noir*: the fallen angels of debauchery and desperation. This is the future: brazen young things with money to burn – all poolside parties and bleach-blonde hair. This is the past: *askaris* with arrows, women with burdens, military junta in open jeeps. This is contradiction: a city of Puritan alcoholics, prostitutes giving love for free, perverted aid workers, developing that arse. This is a disgrace: a security guard on $1/day, a corrupt ruling class passing laws on morality, a white man who's pissed his pants.

These are nocturnal adventures, in the dark, with no moral compass. The undomesticated beasts of today's Africa, red of lip and claw, getting high and savaging tourists in uncontrollable packs of avaricious lust.

Amazonian warrior queens, fierce and inscrutable, with sharp tongues and sharper knees for ripe white balls. Prostrate poverty-stricken tragedies, abused victims of a merciless global economy. Life, love and laughter.

Lap it up with hungry eyes or flick through with bored detachment. If it makes you feel better, weep bitter tears of helplessness onto the pristine pages. The occupants don't really care whether you pity or desire them. Their lives, on the long, warm nights, go on regardless.

David Cecil

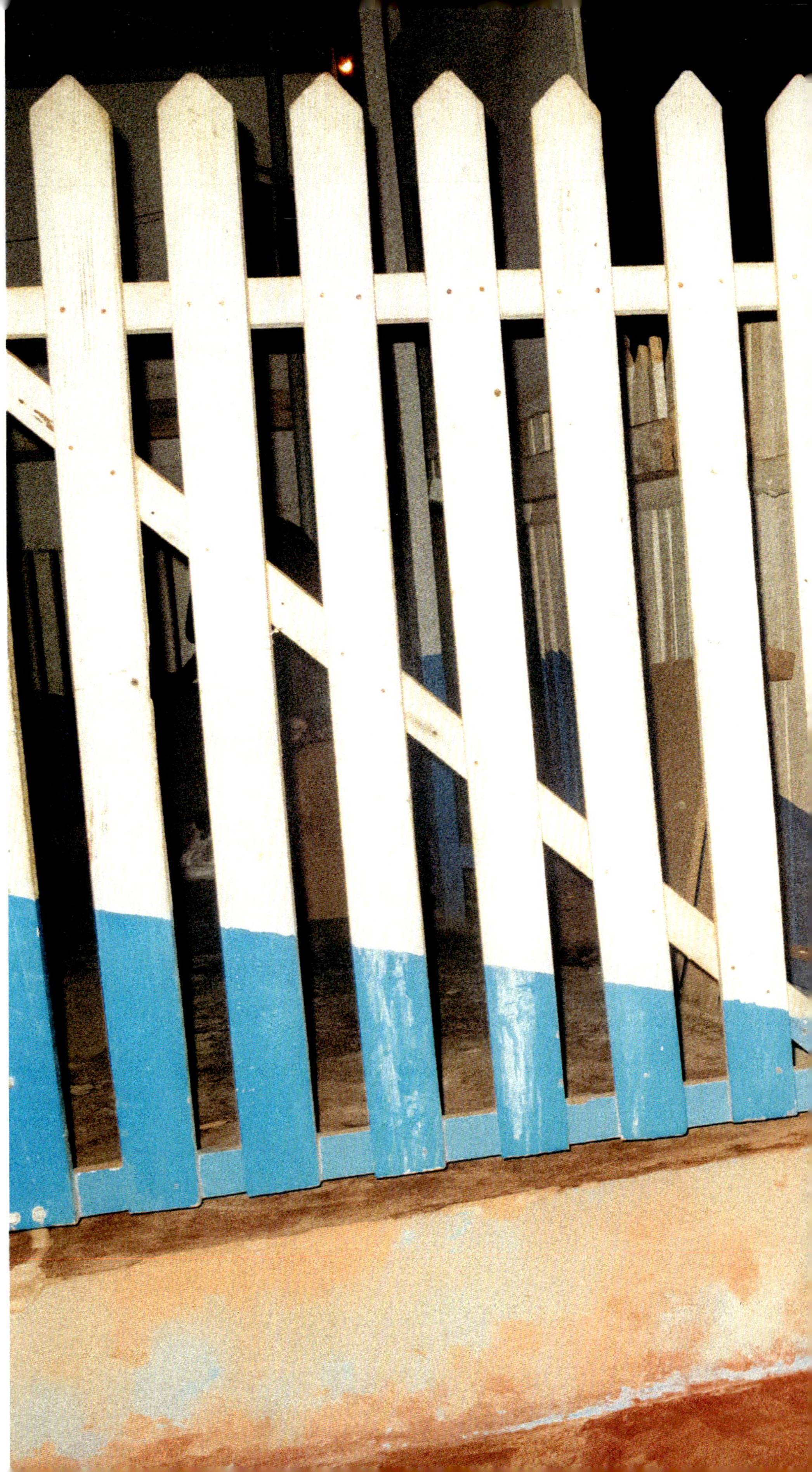

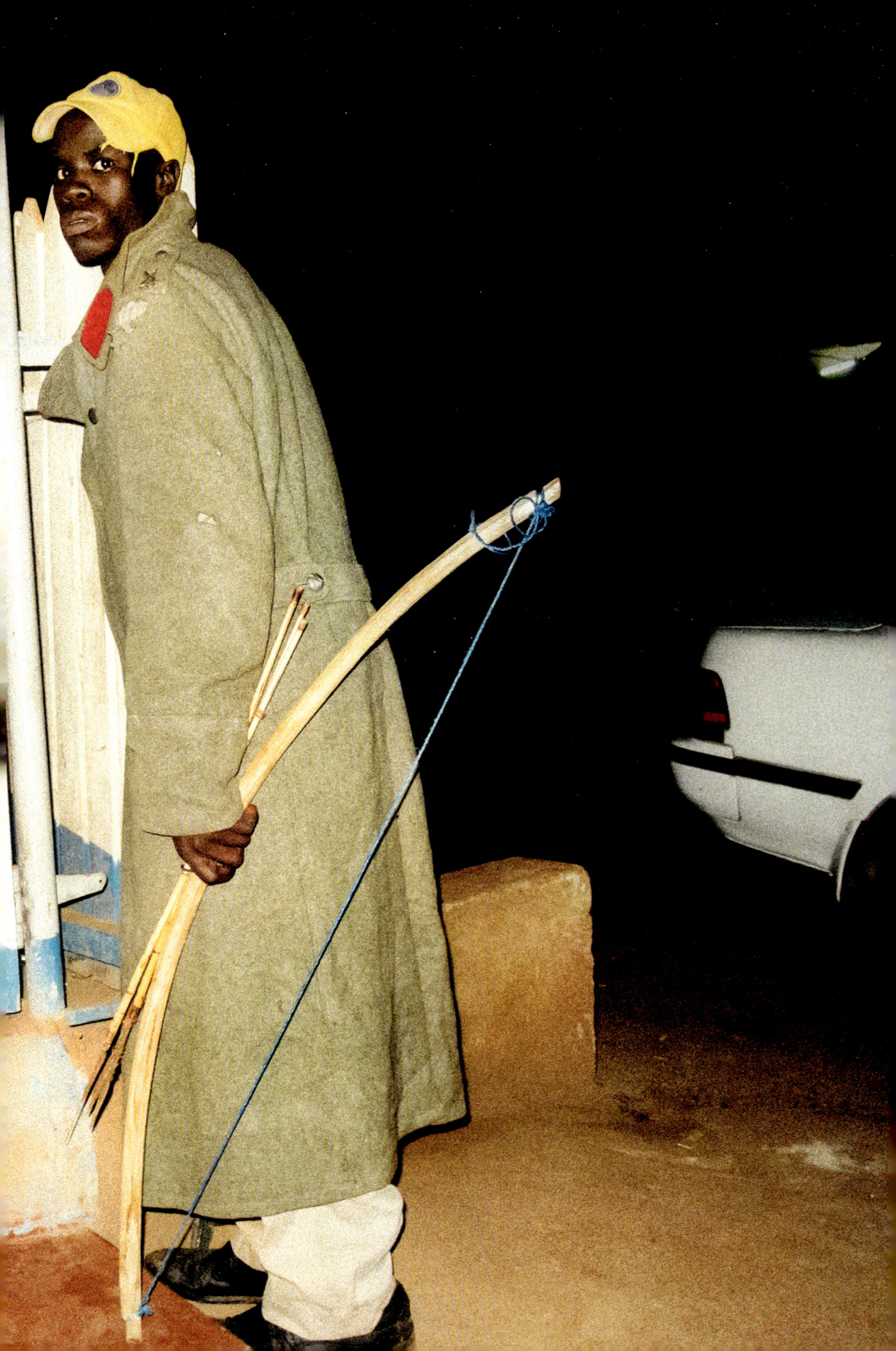

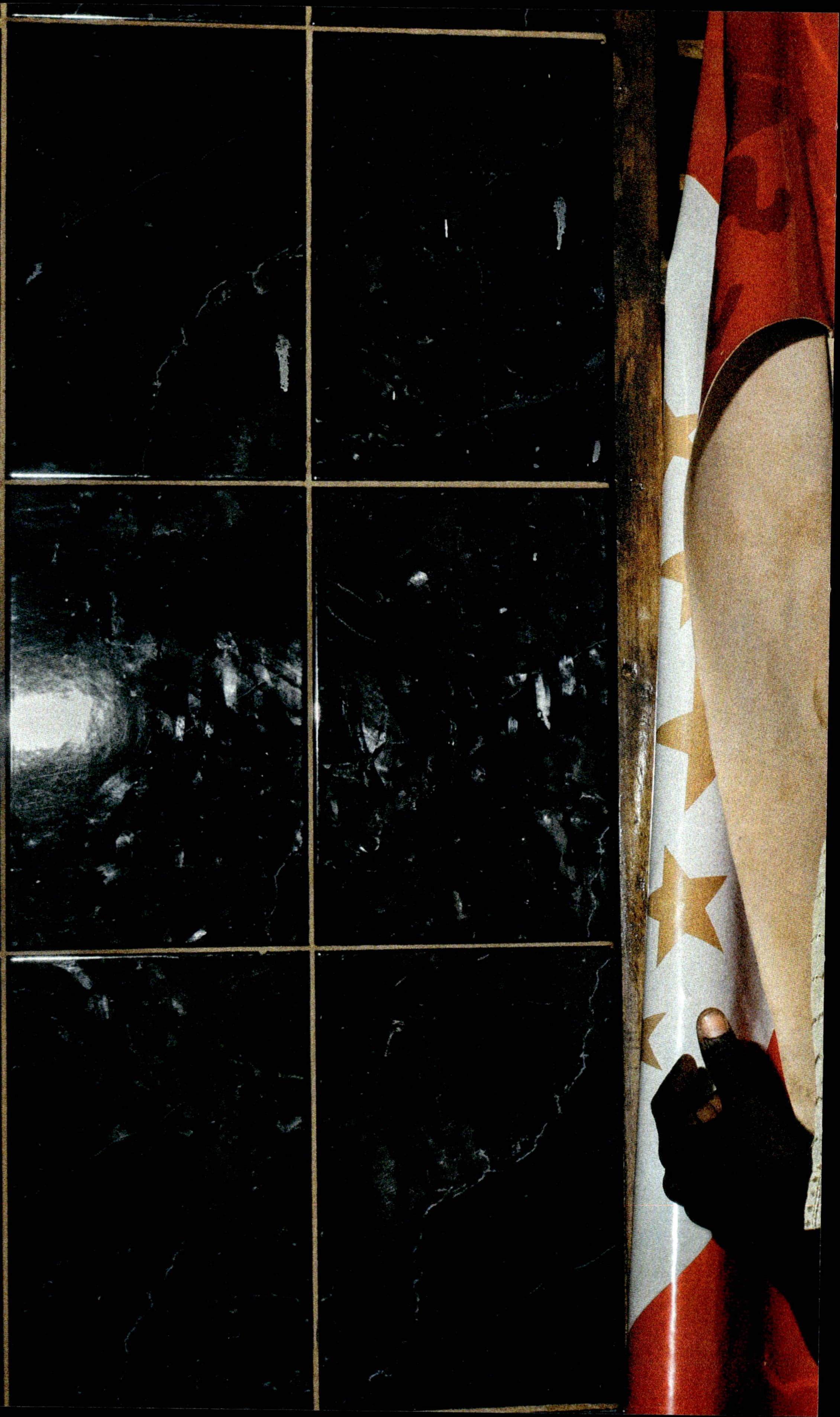

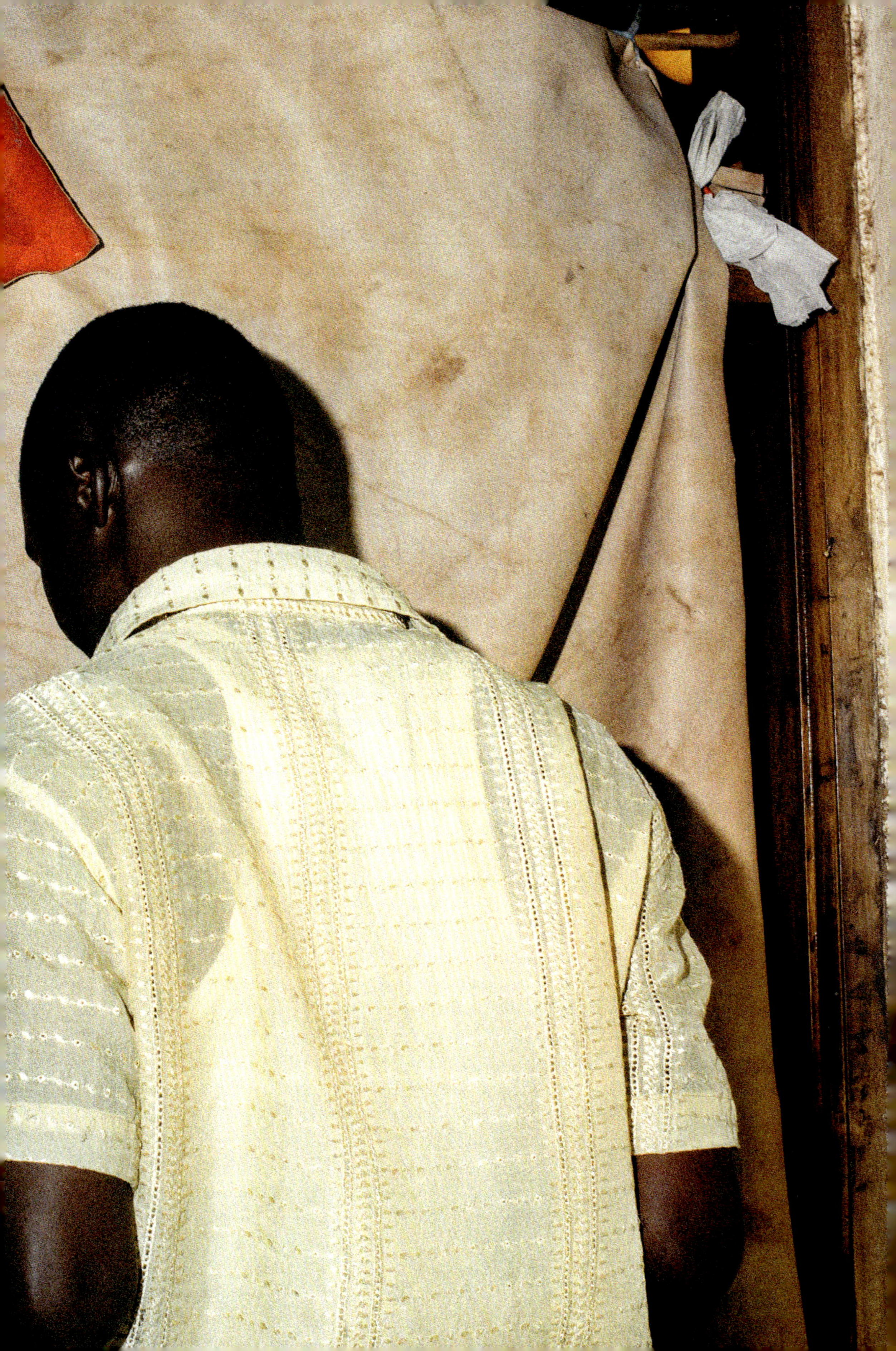

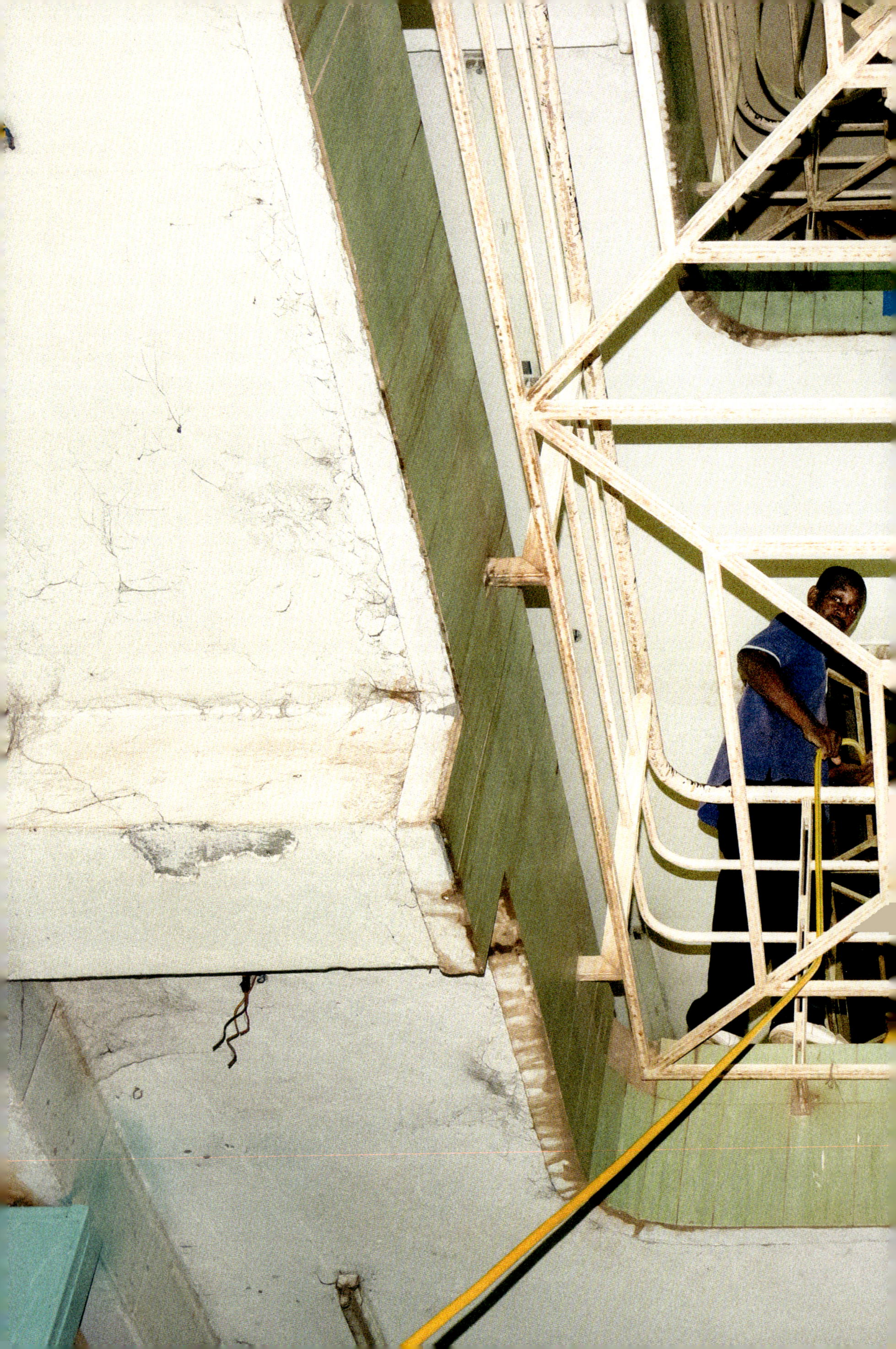

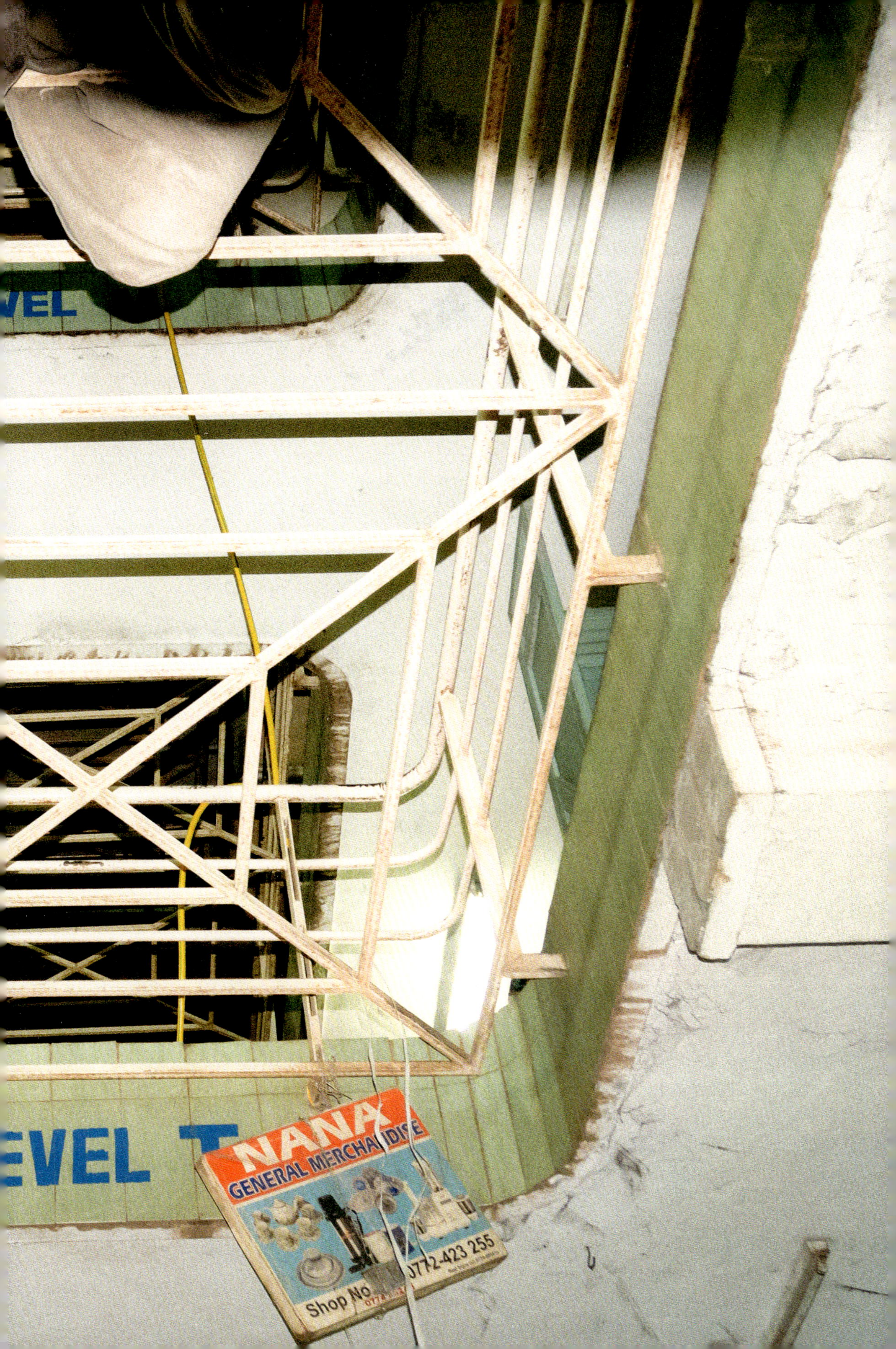
NANA
GENERAL MERCHANDISE
0772-423 255
Shop No

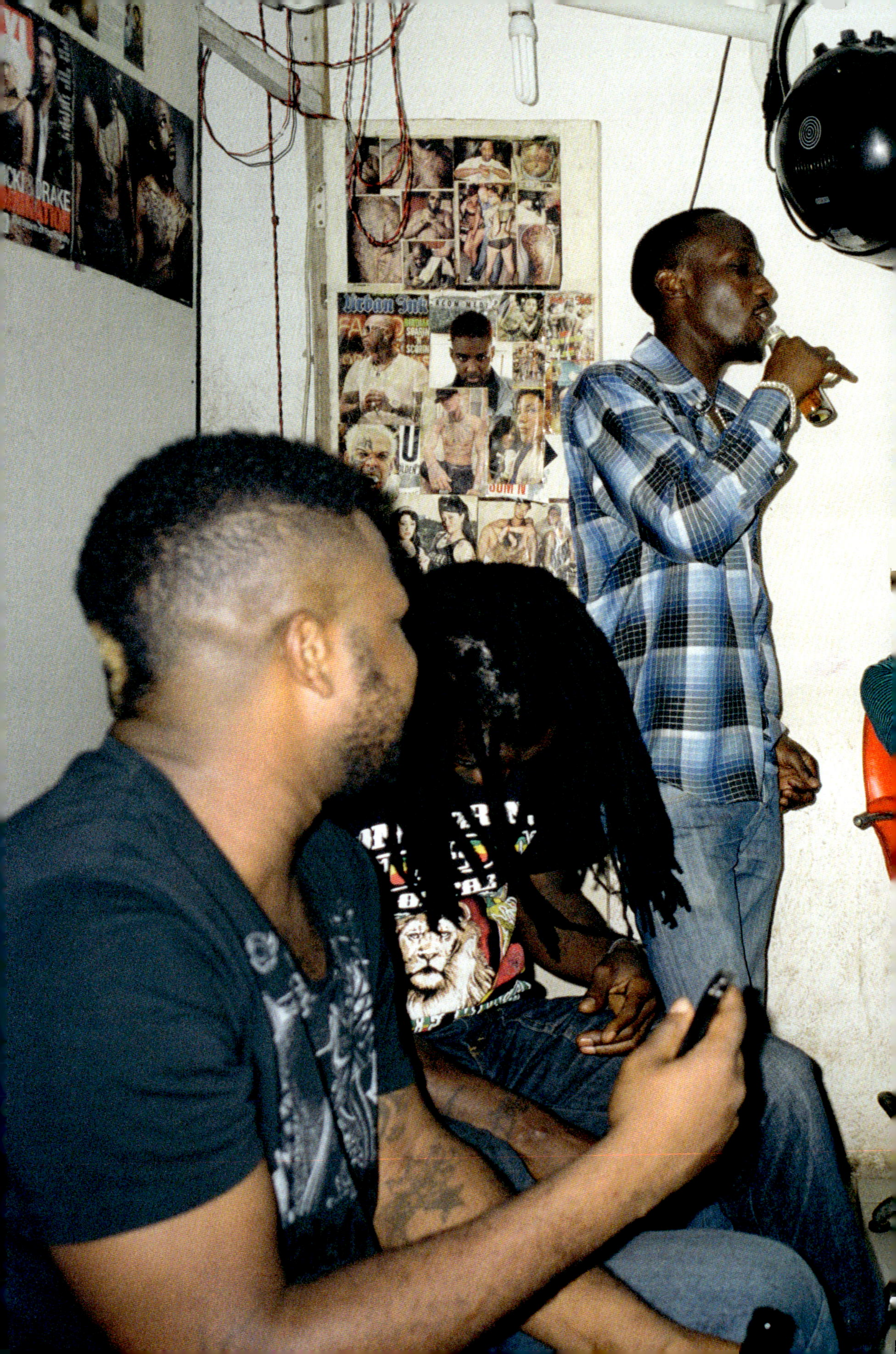
Urban Ink

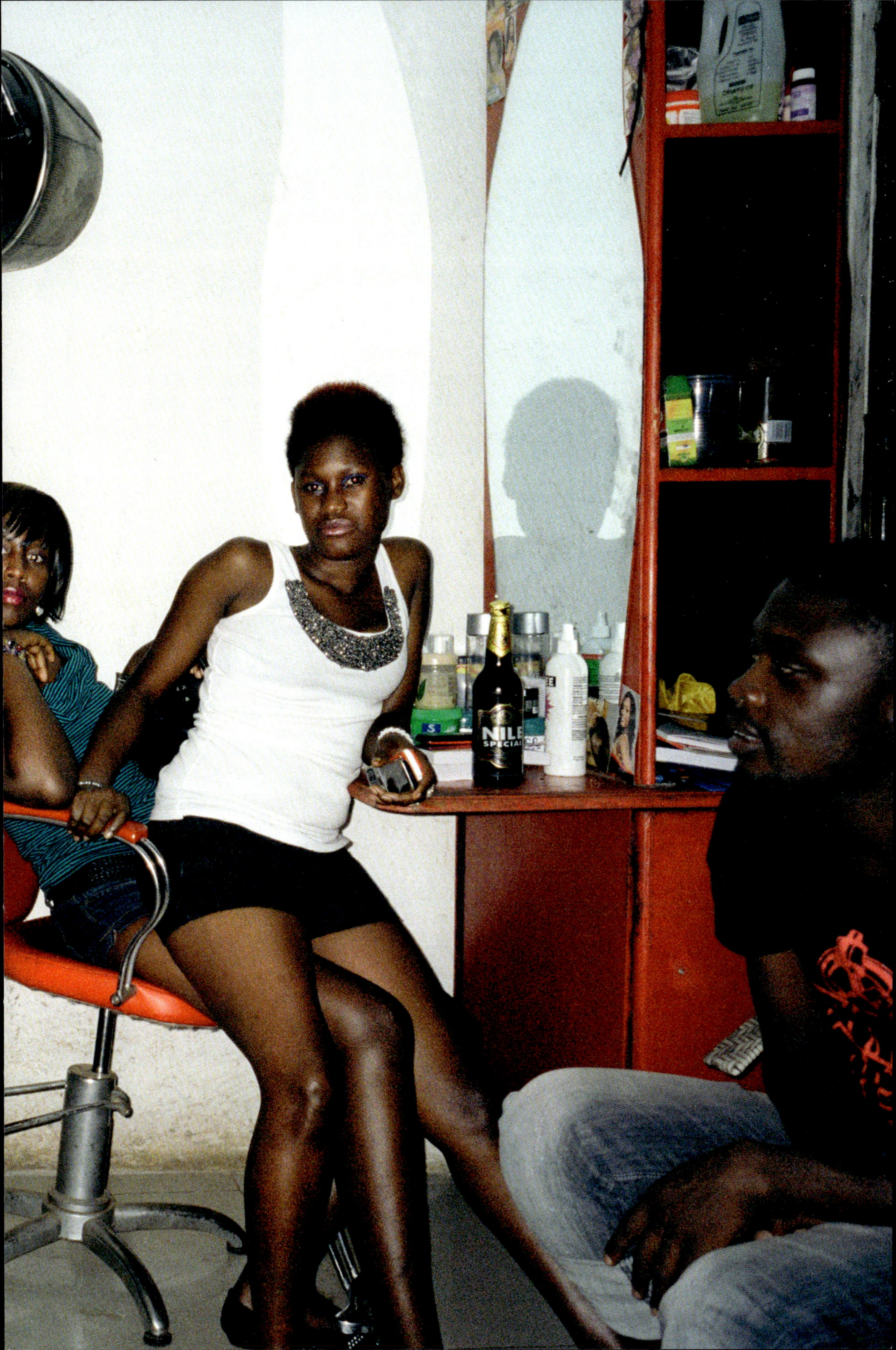
NILE
SPECIAL

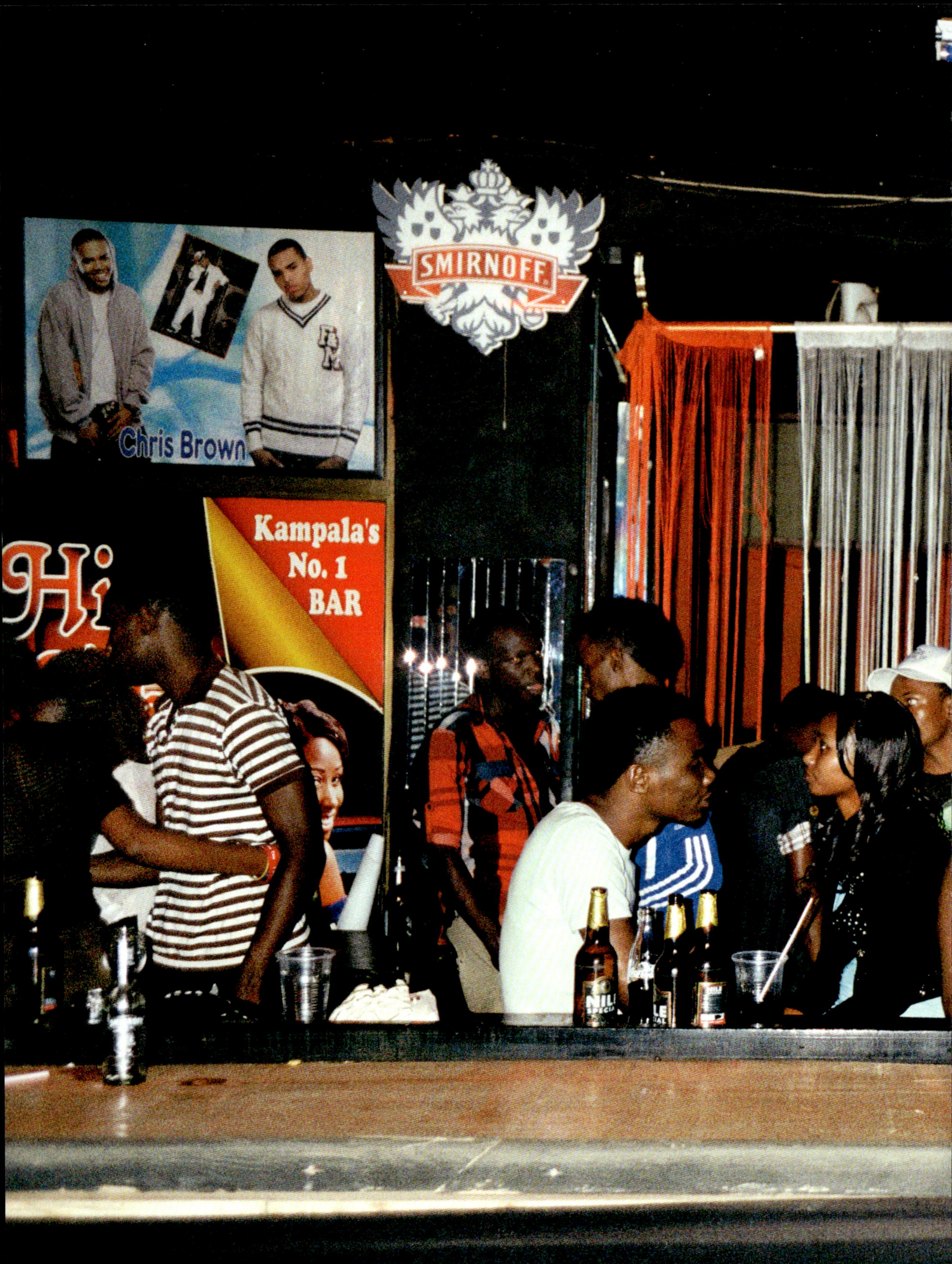
SMIRNOFF
Chris Brown
Kampala's
No. 1
BAR

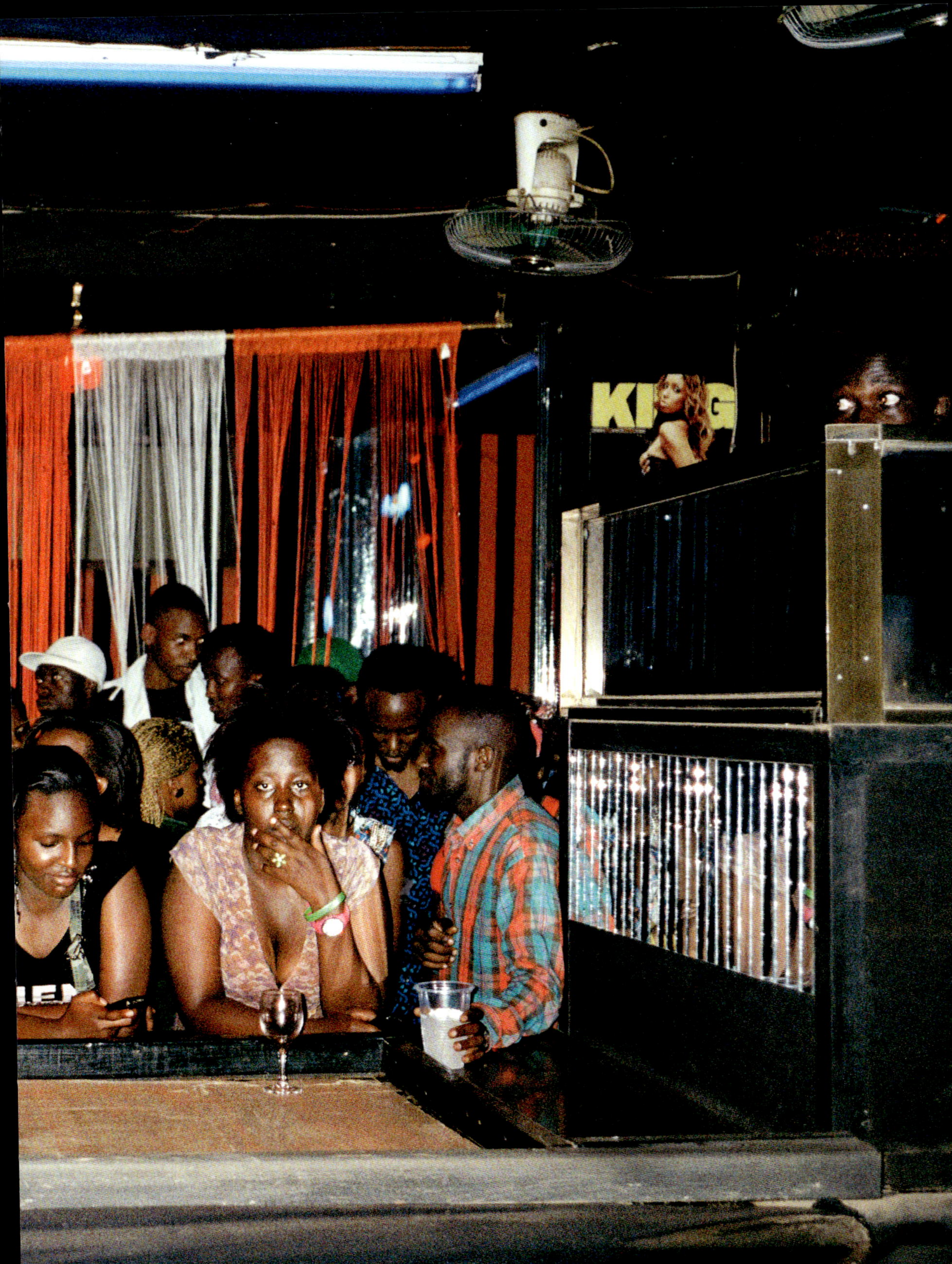

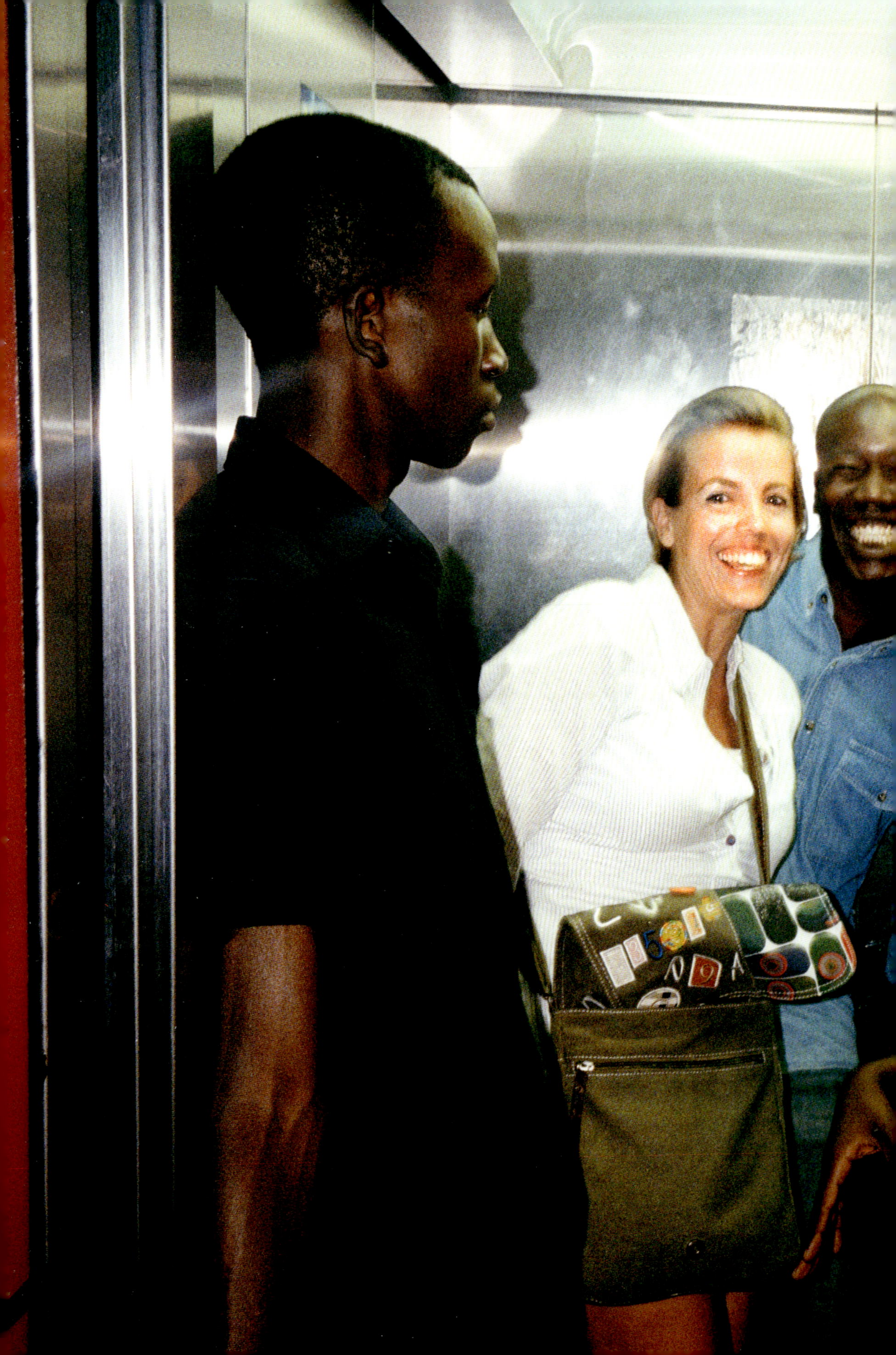

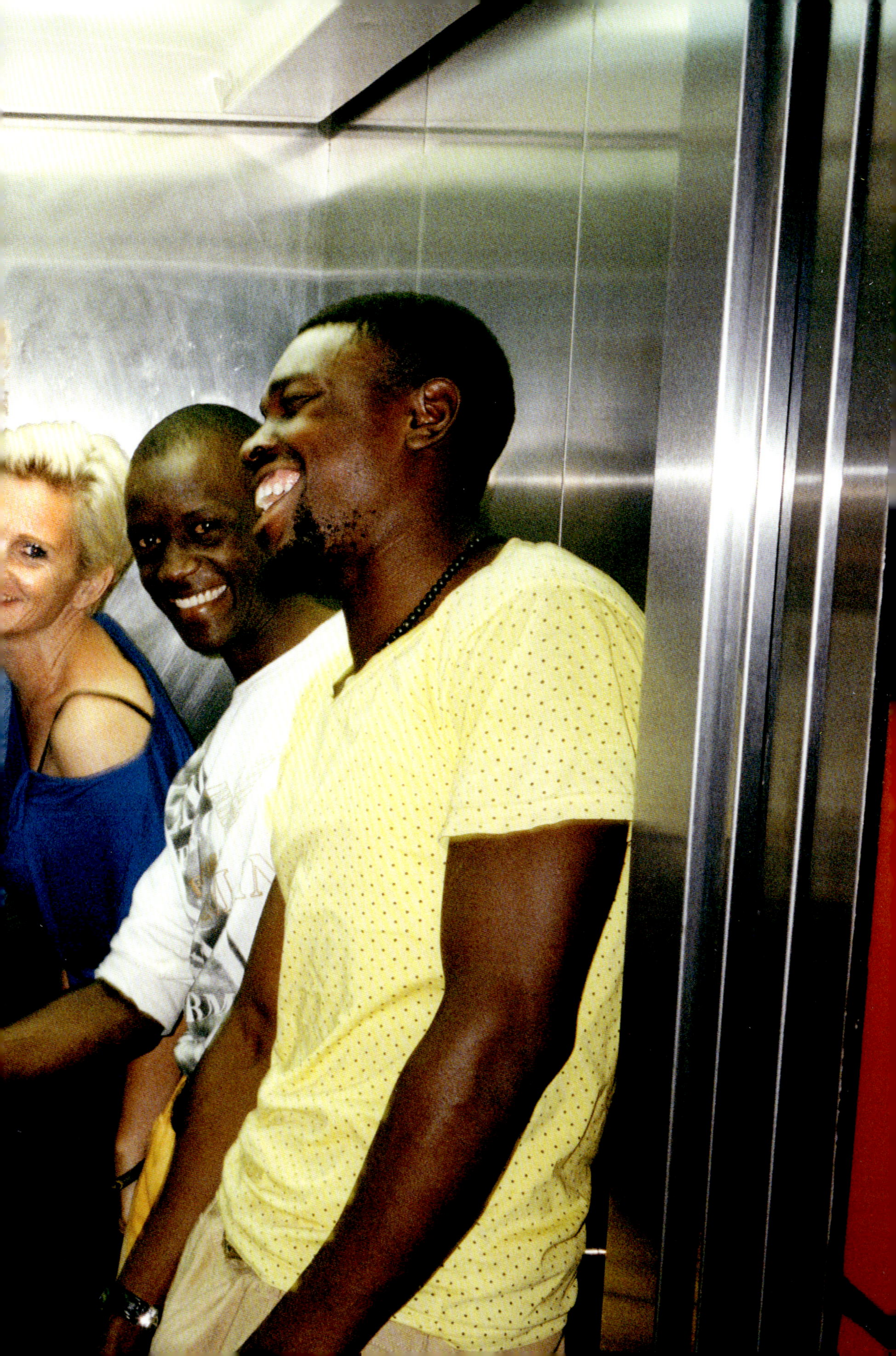

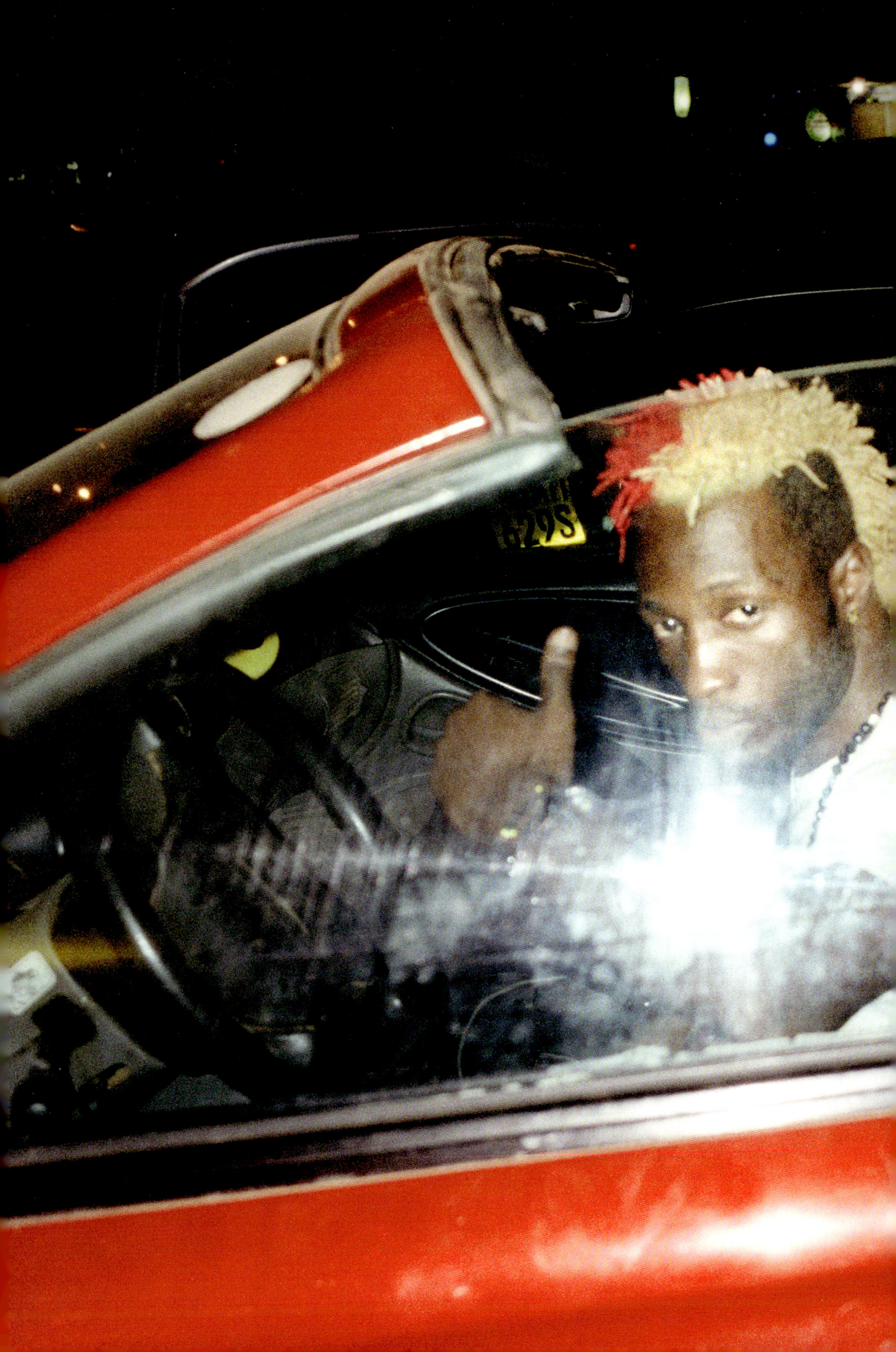

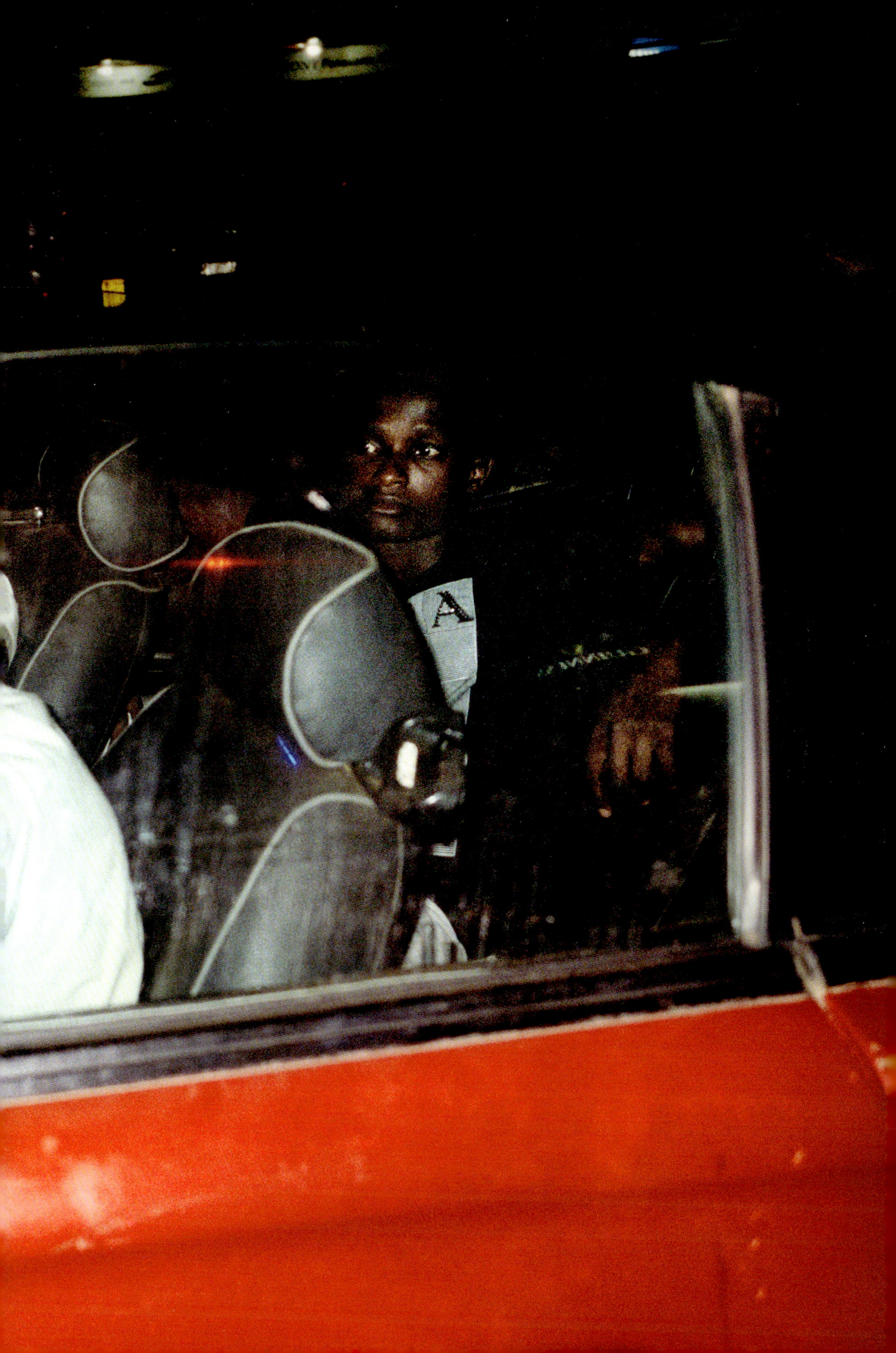
A

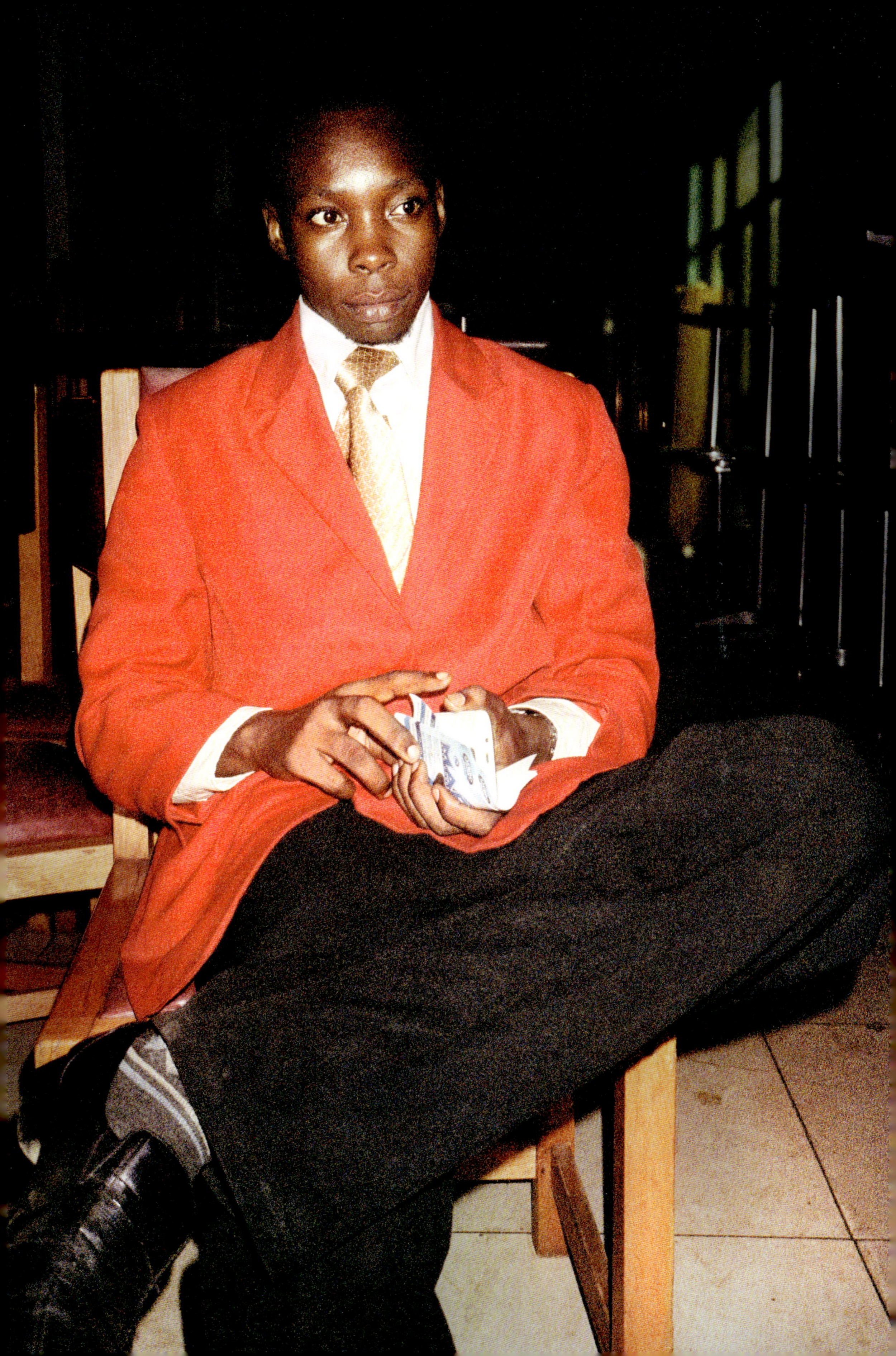

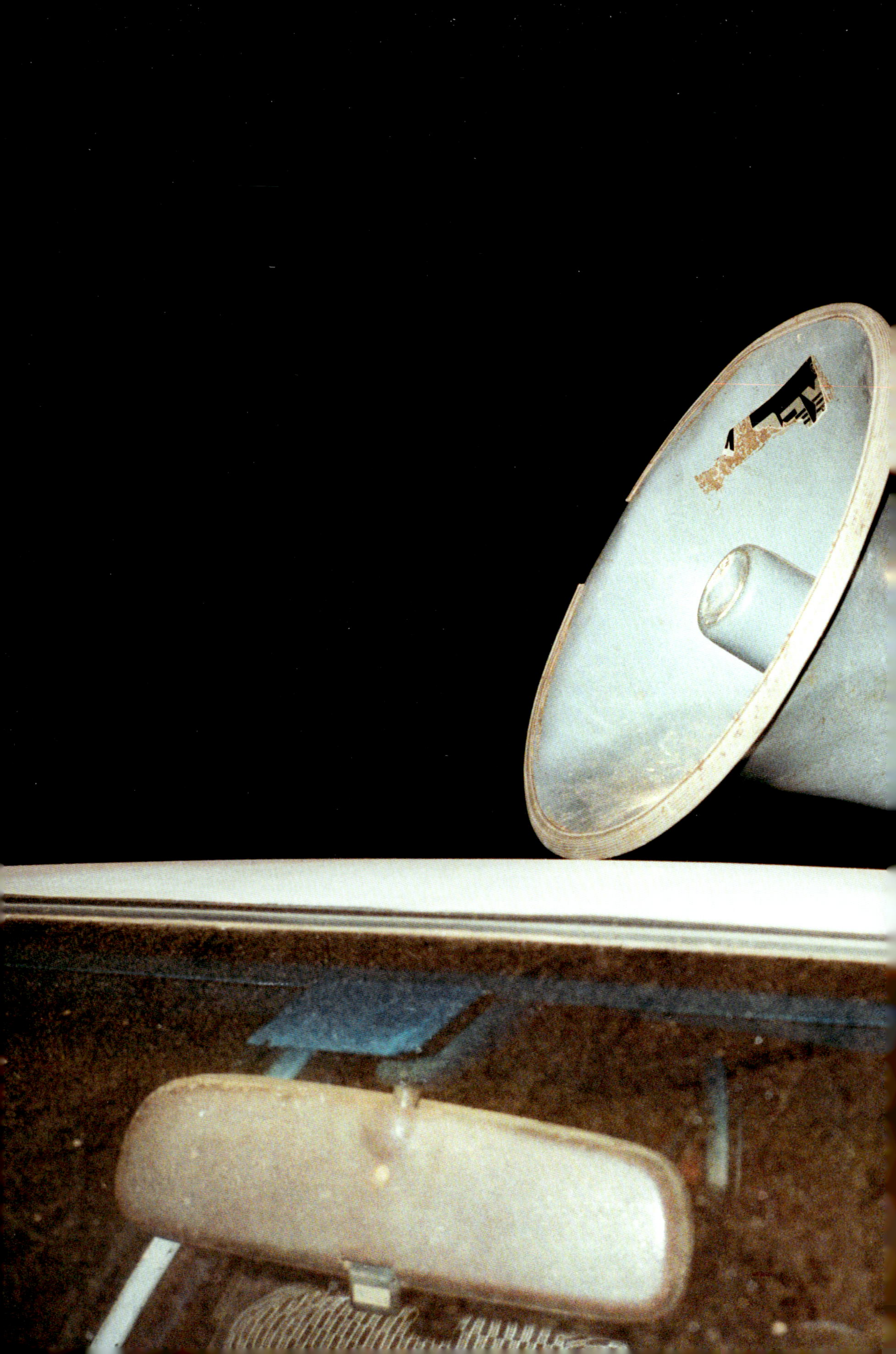

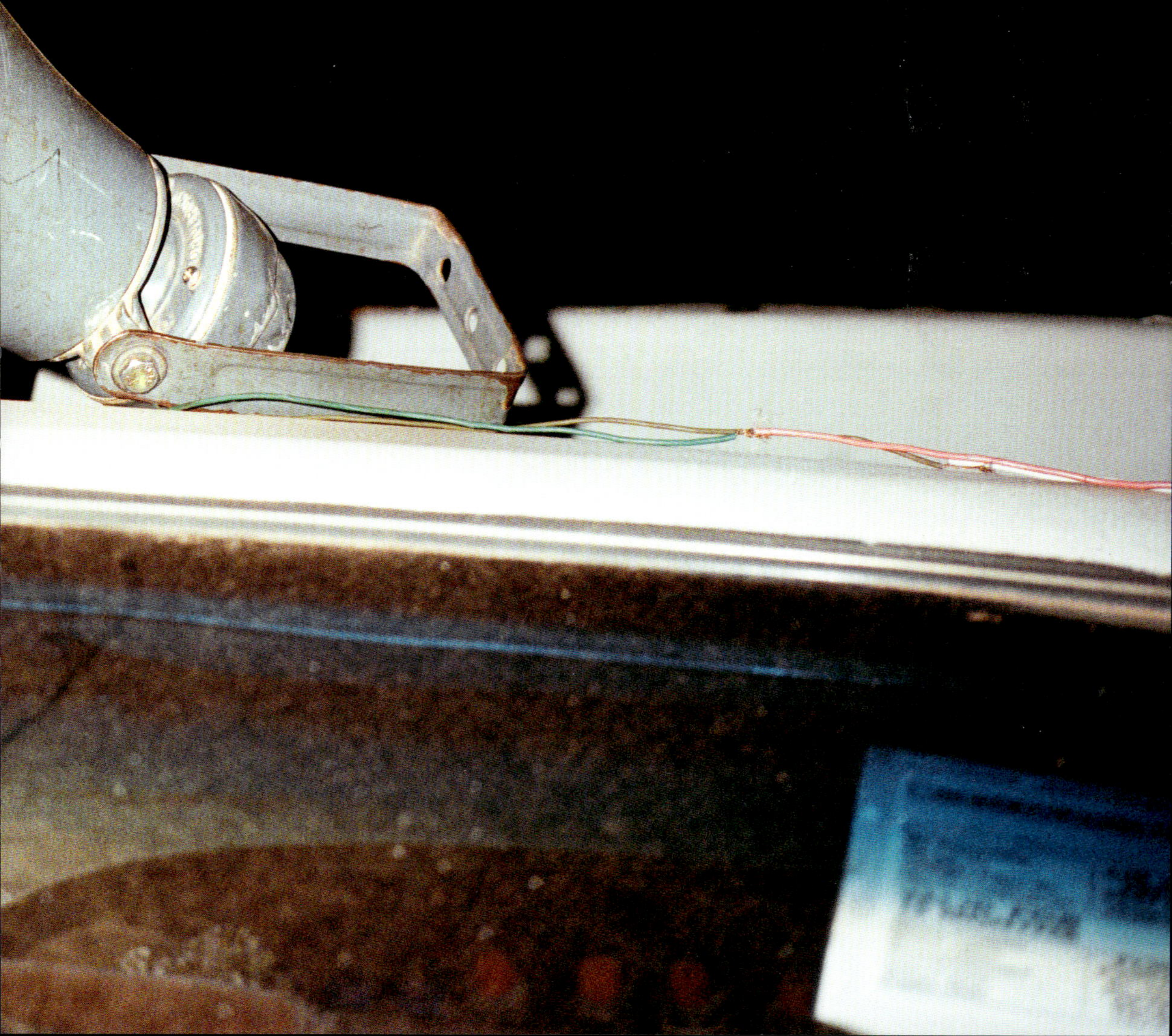

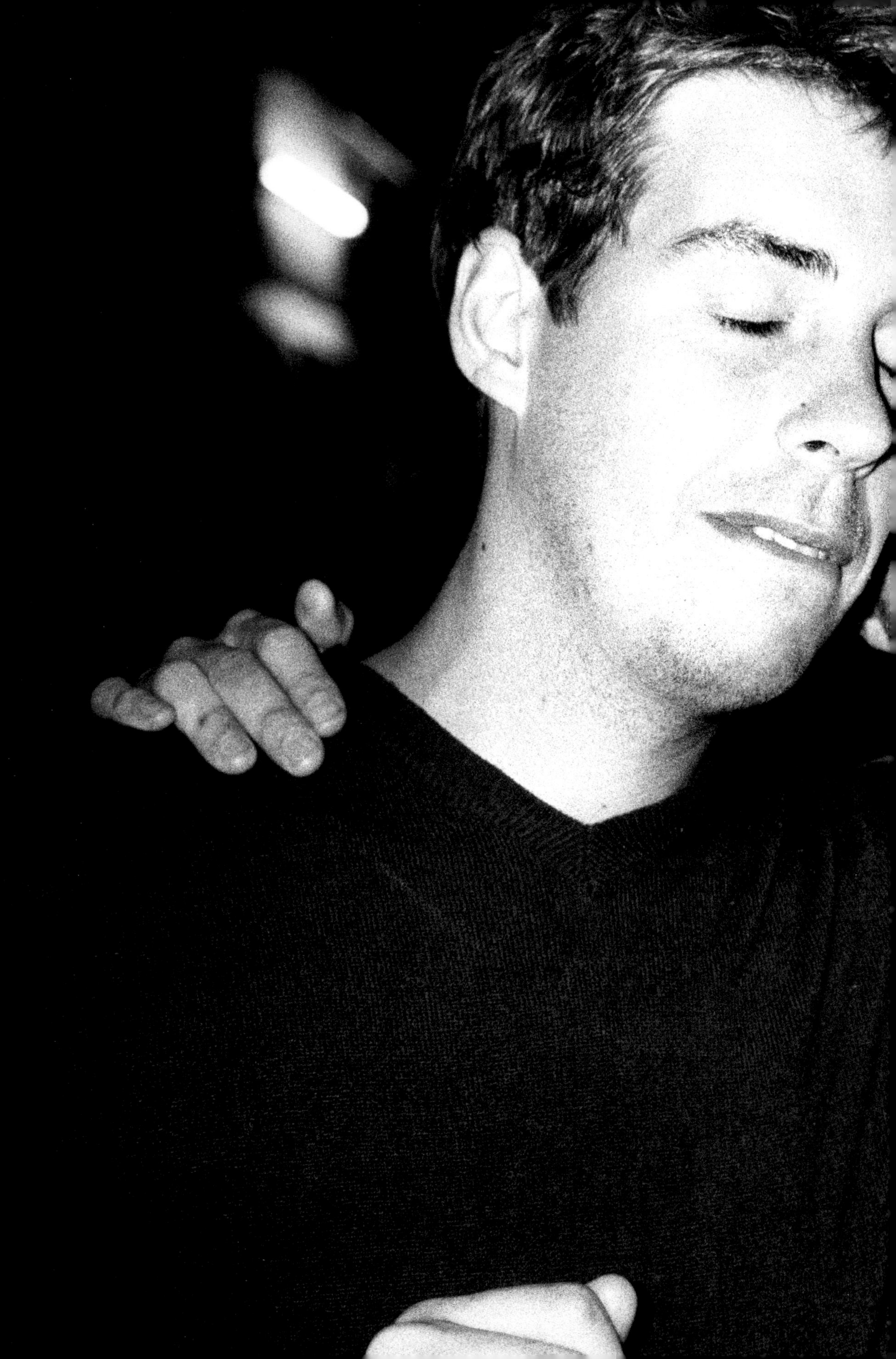

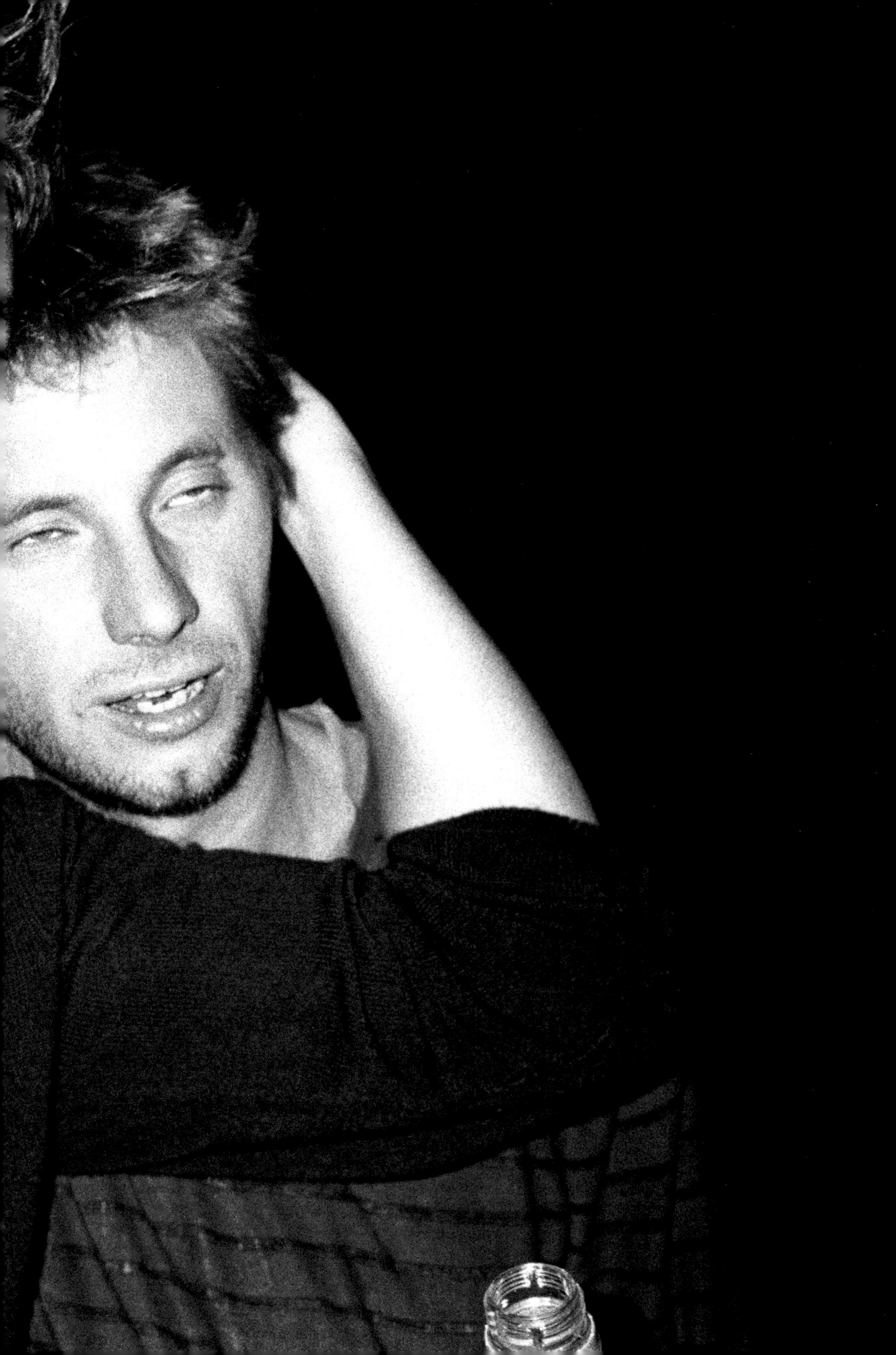

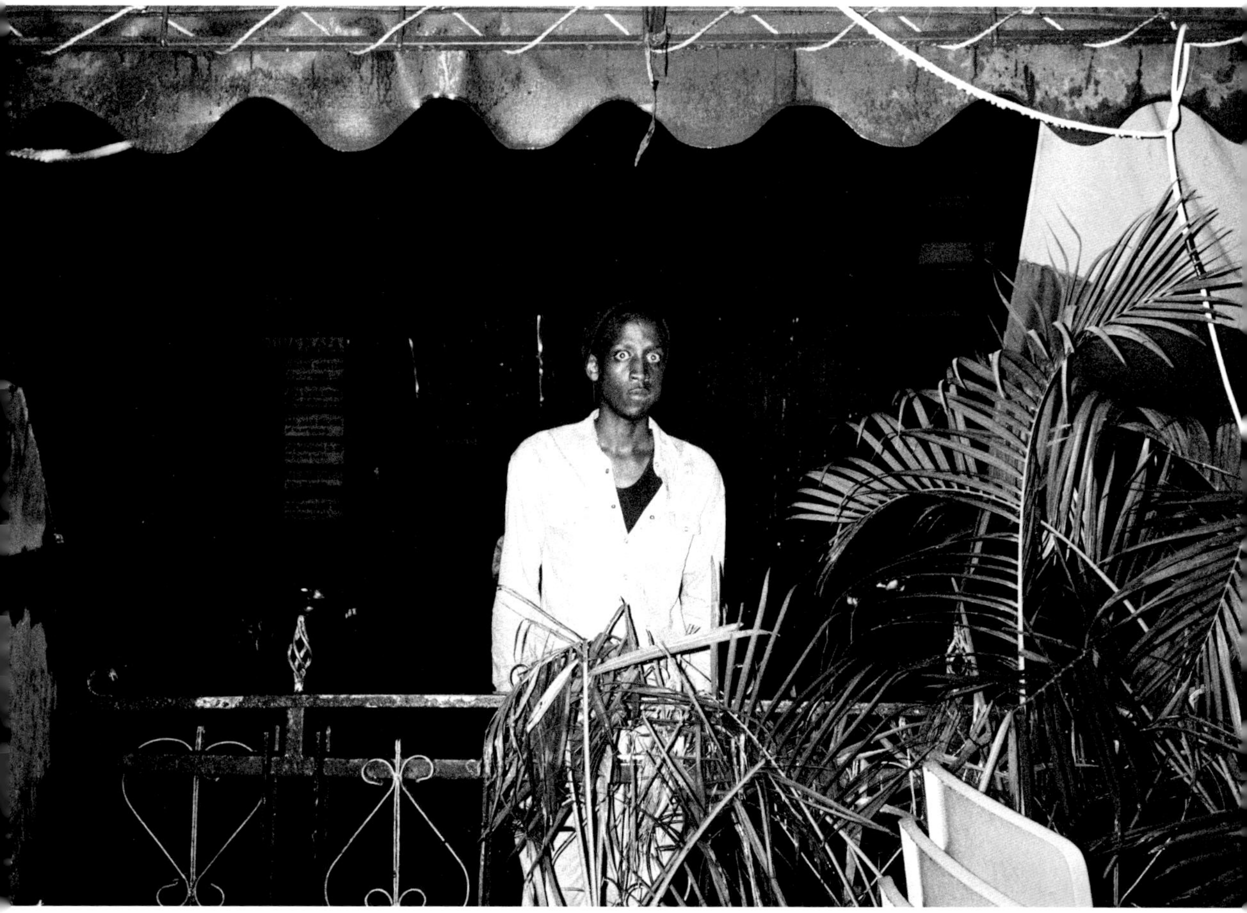

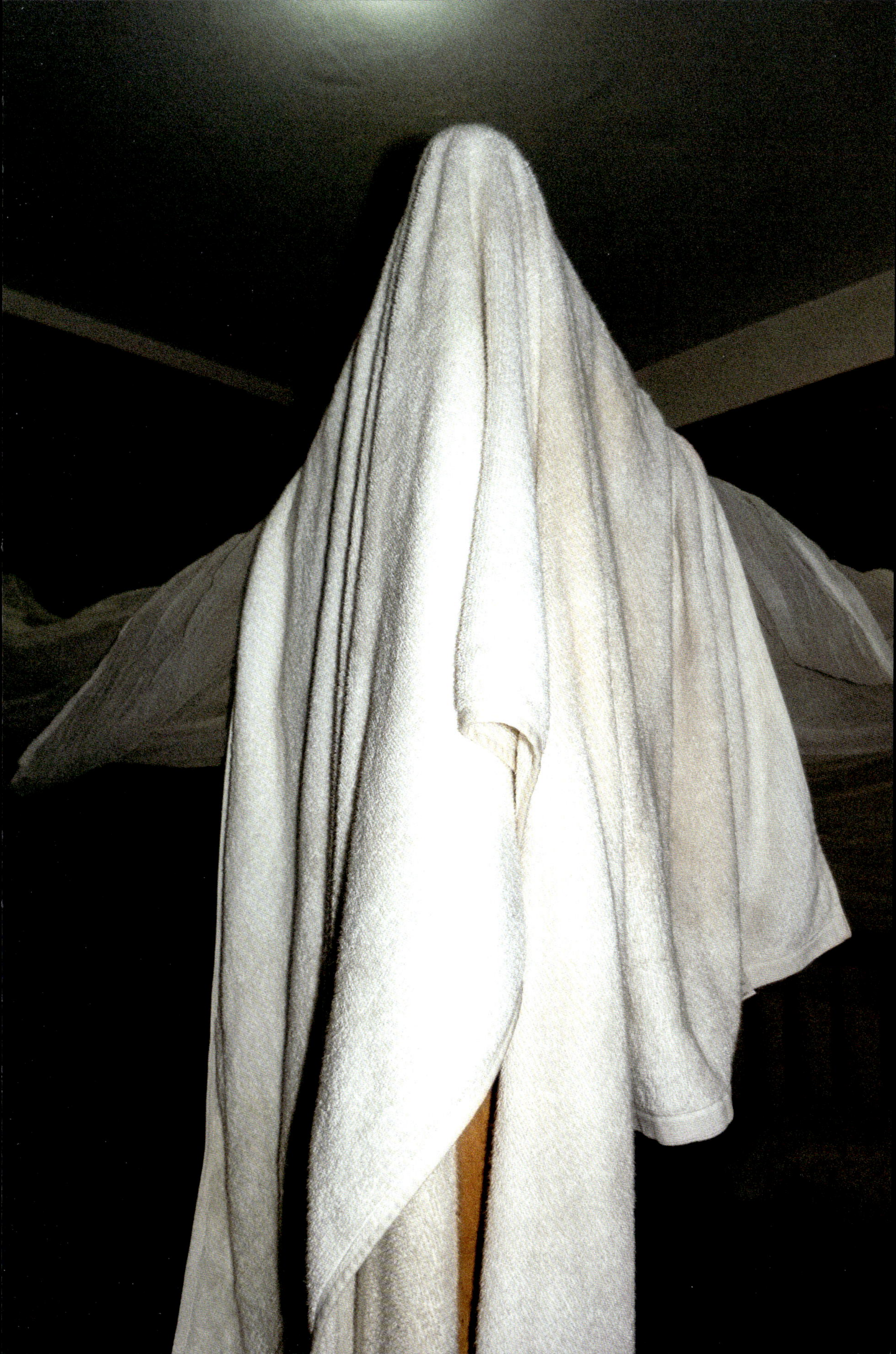

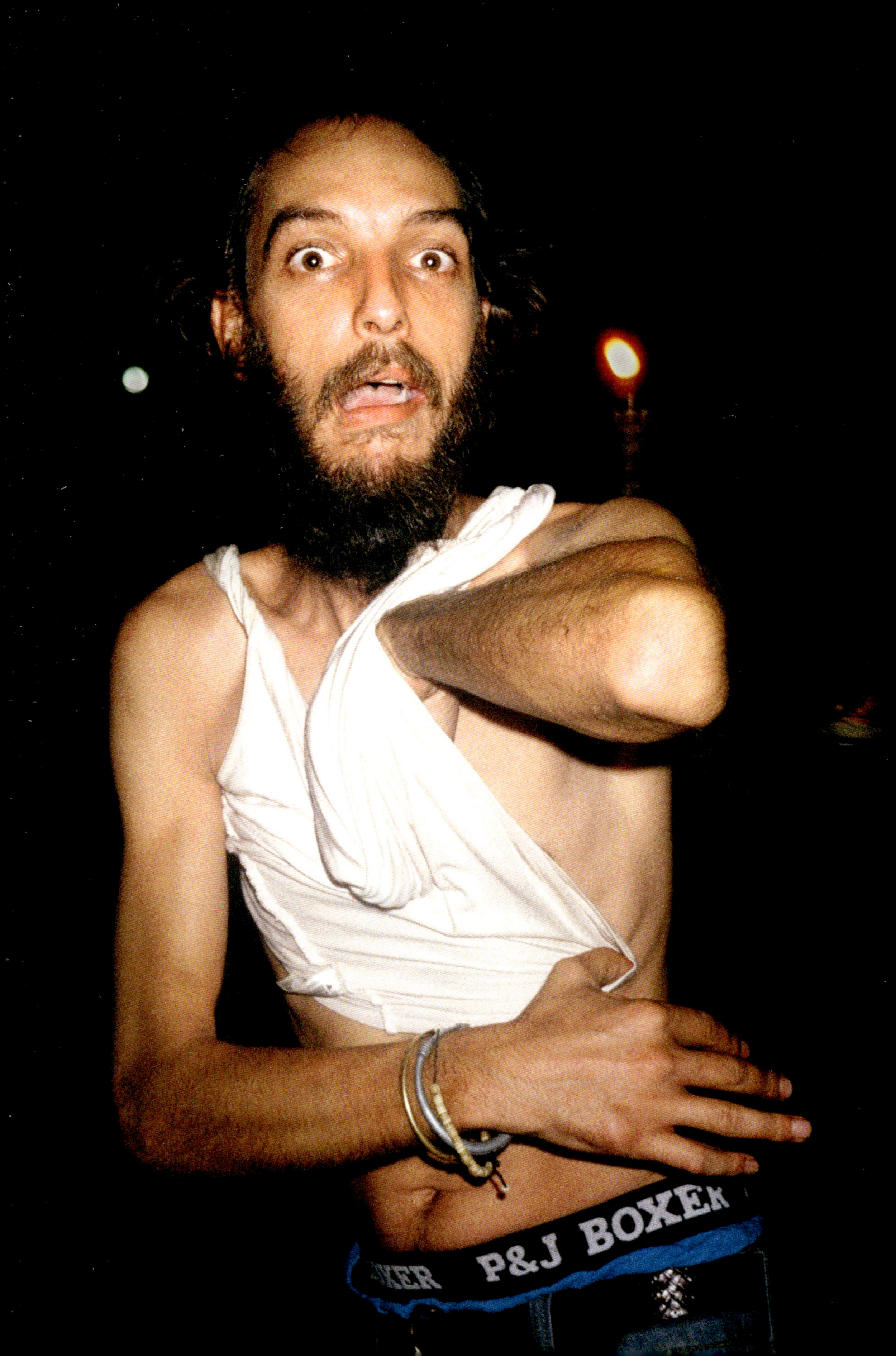
P&J BOXER

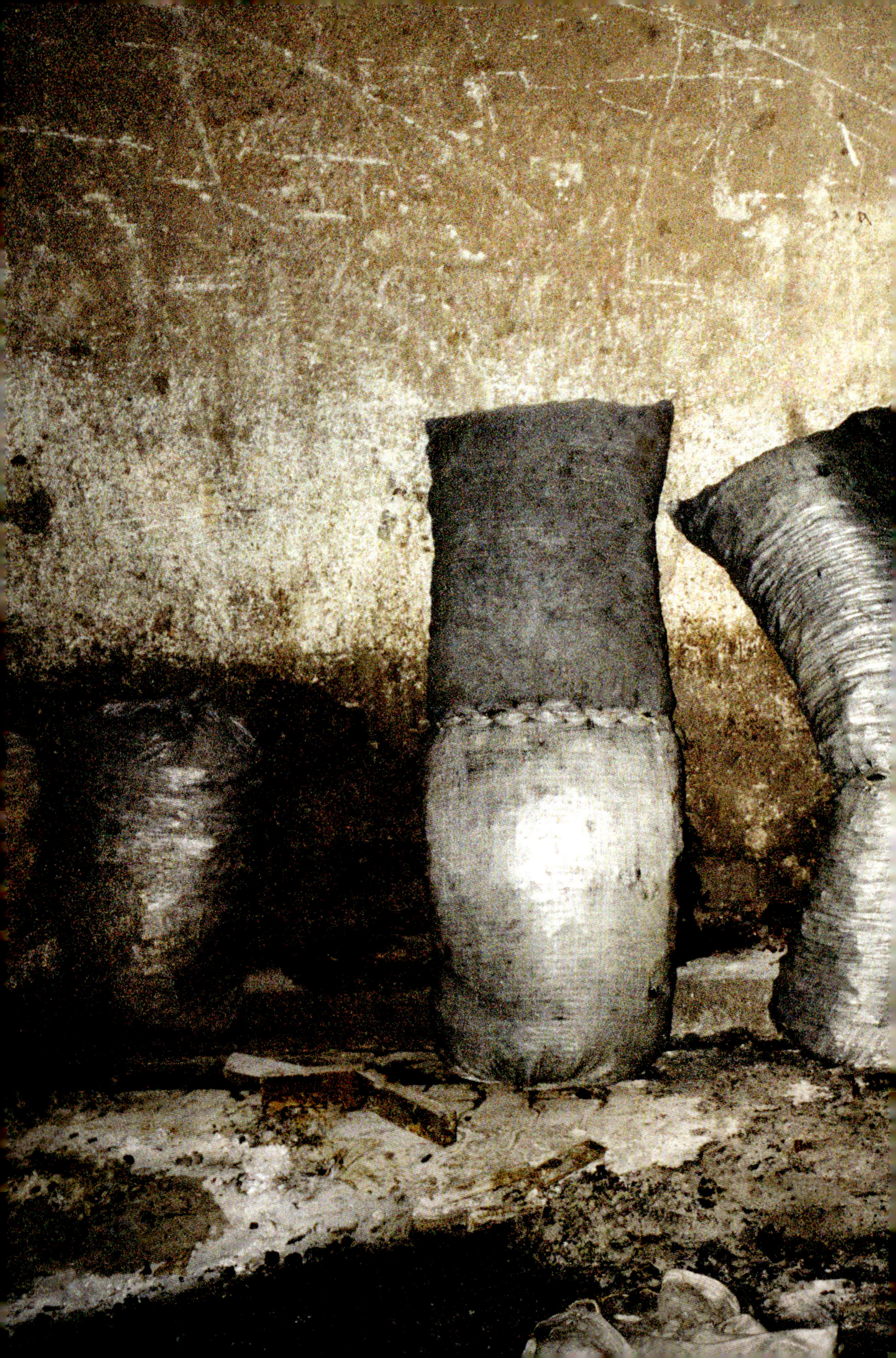

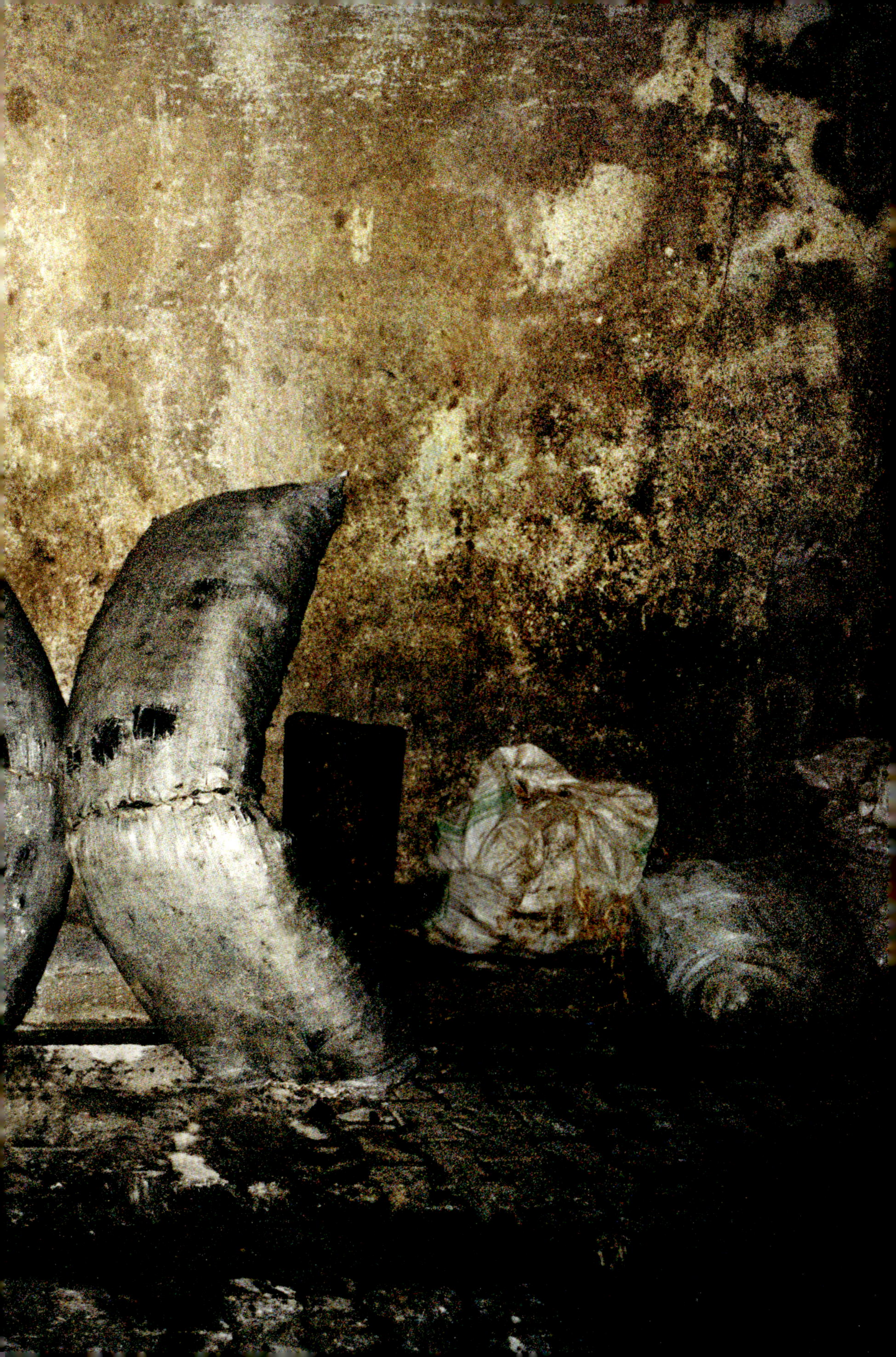

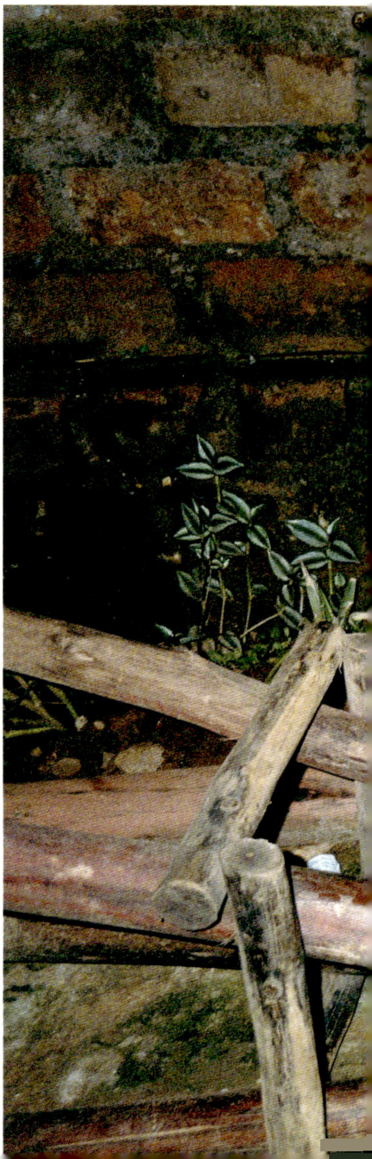

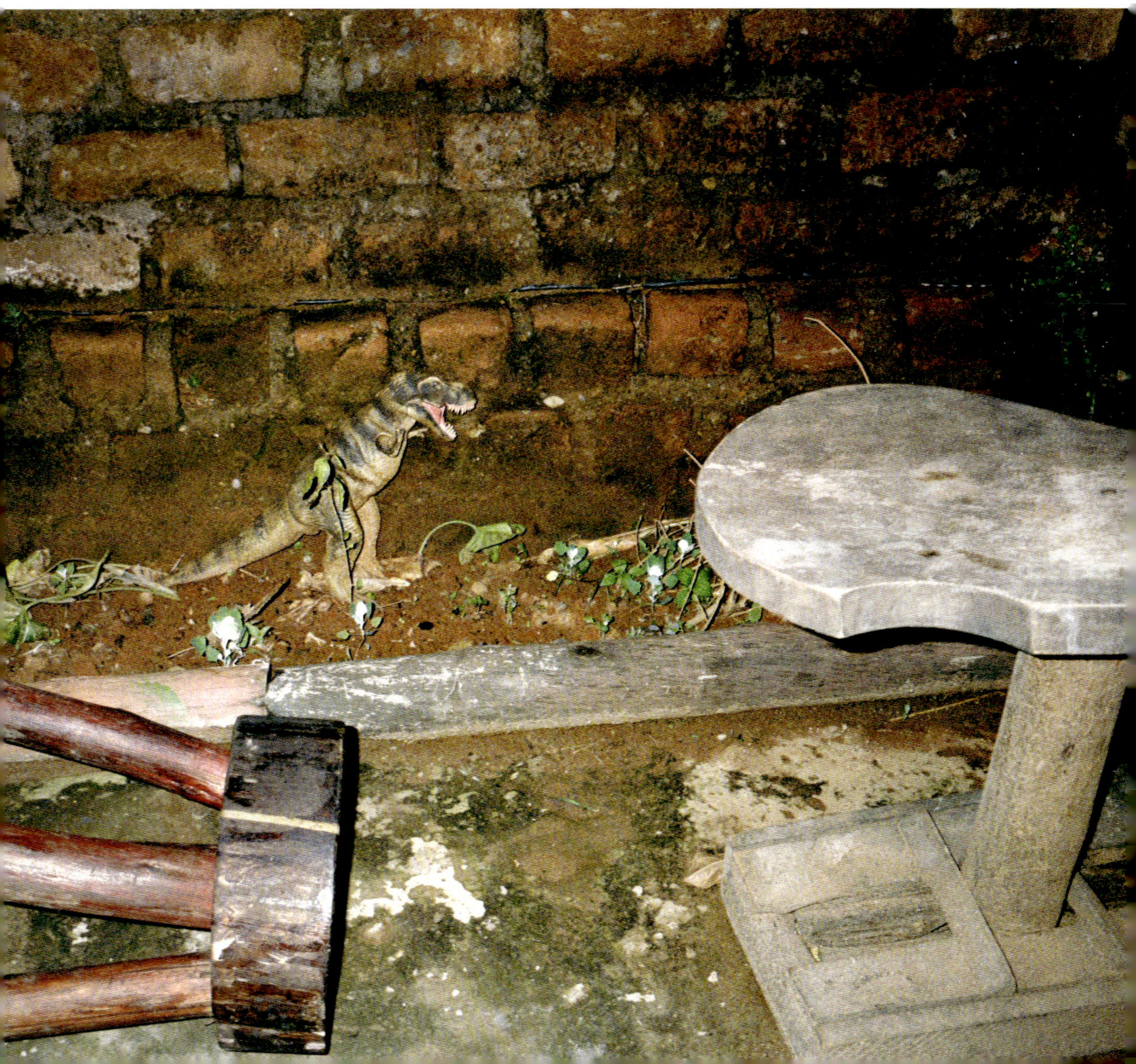

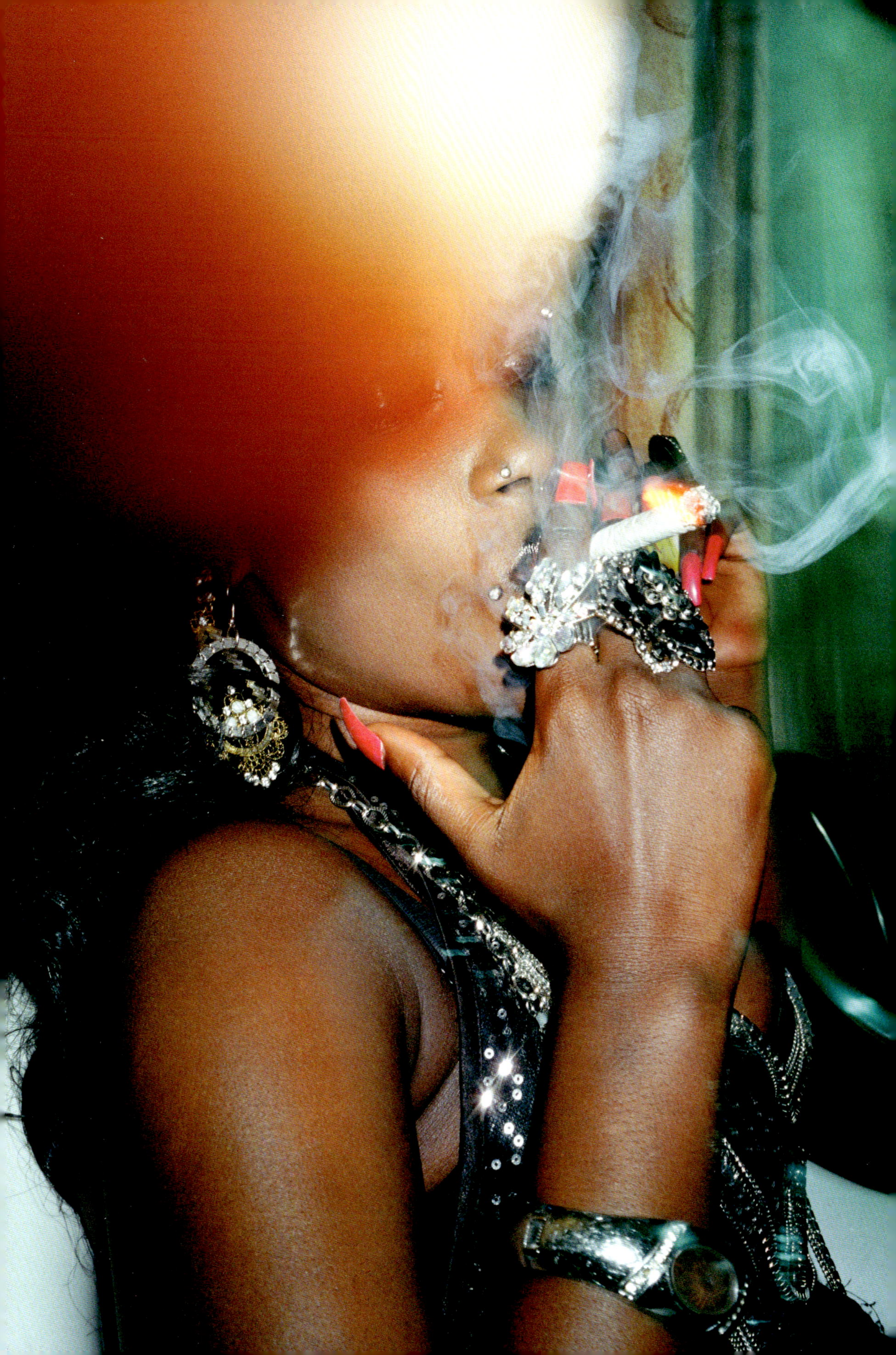

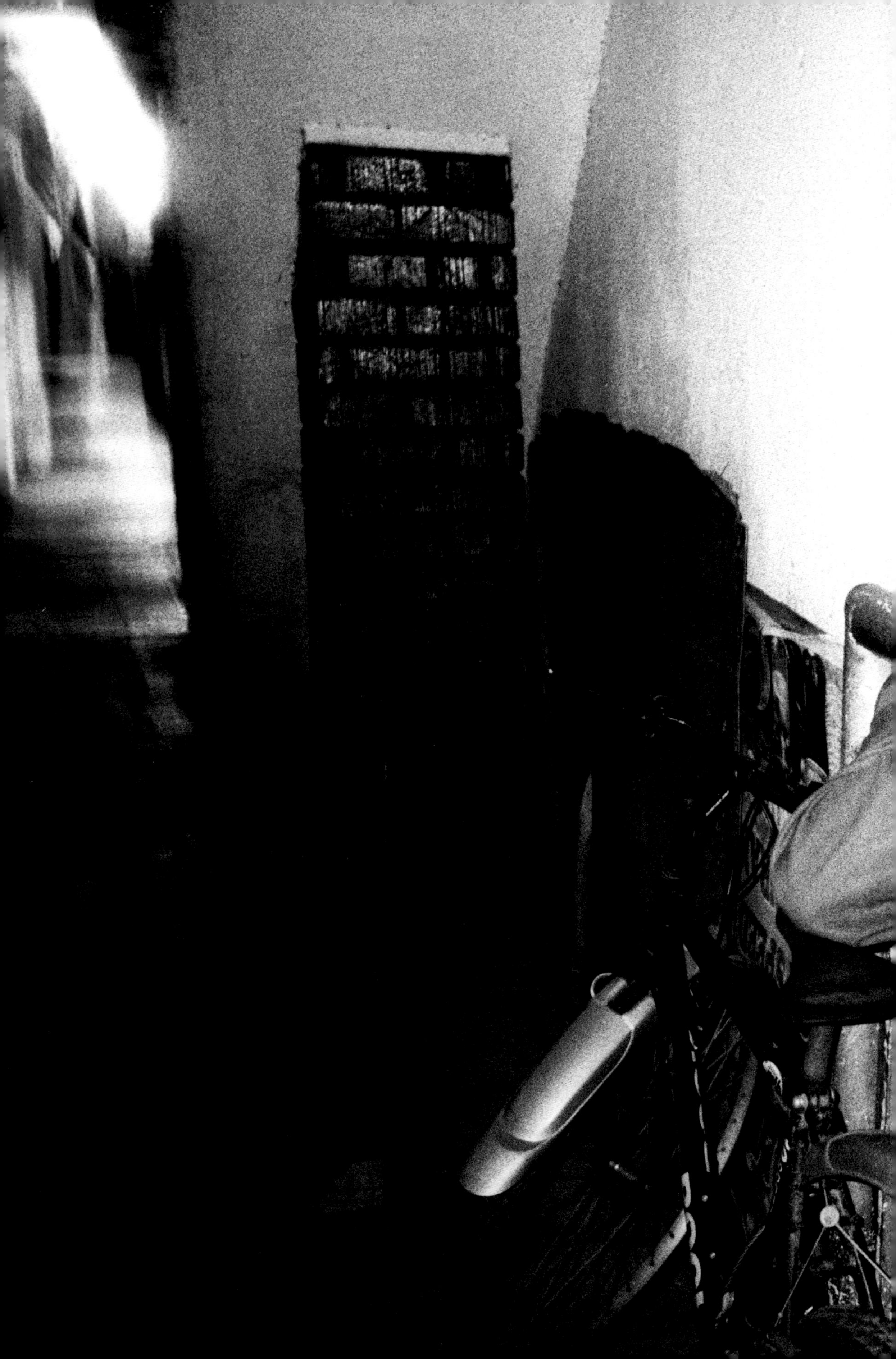

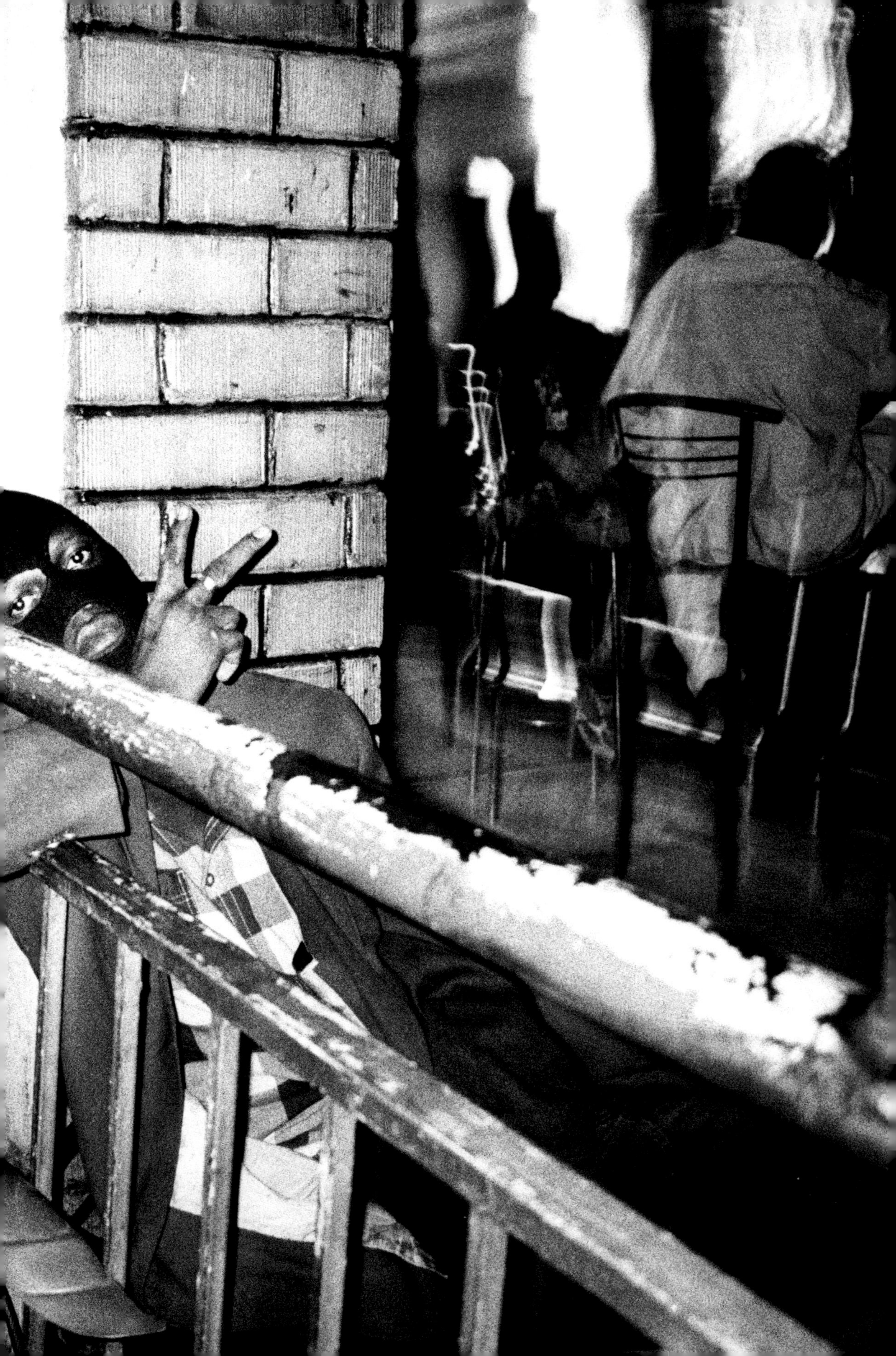

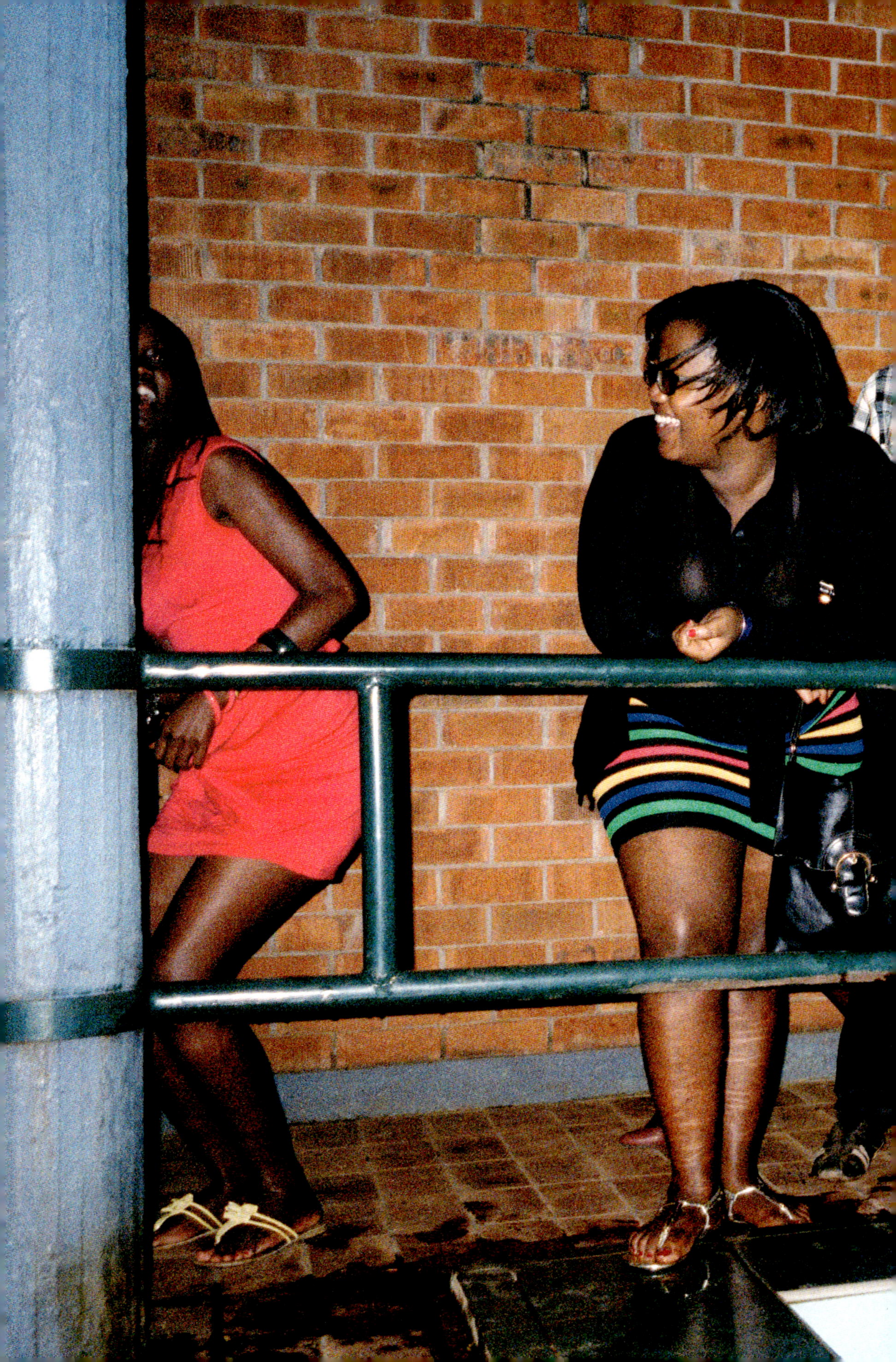

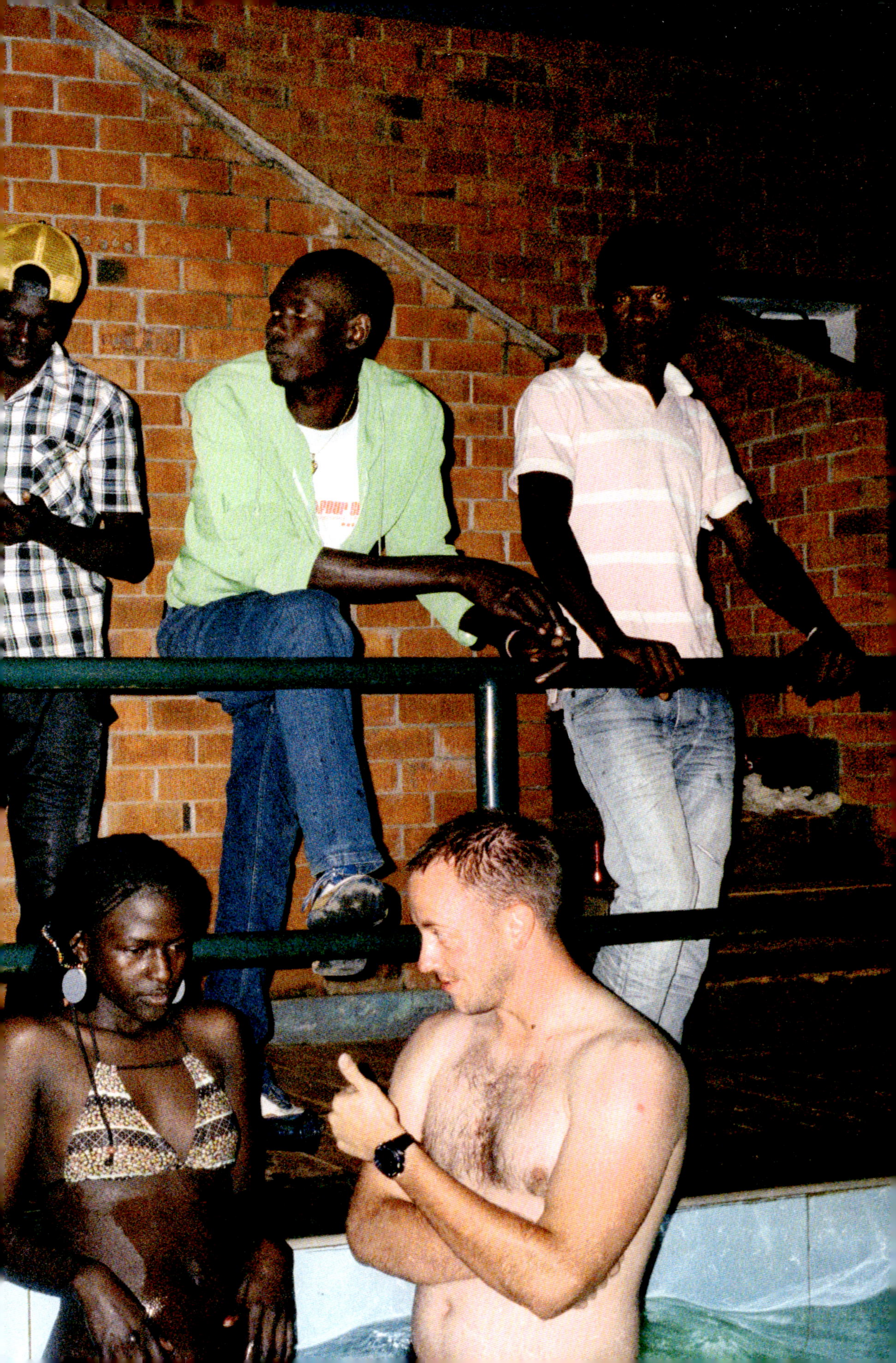

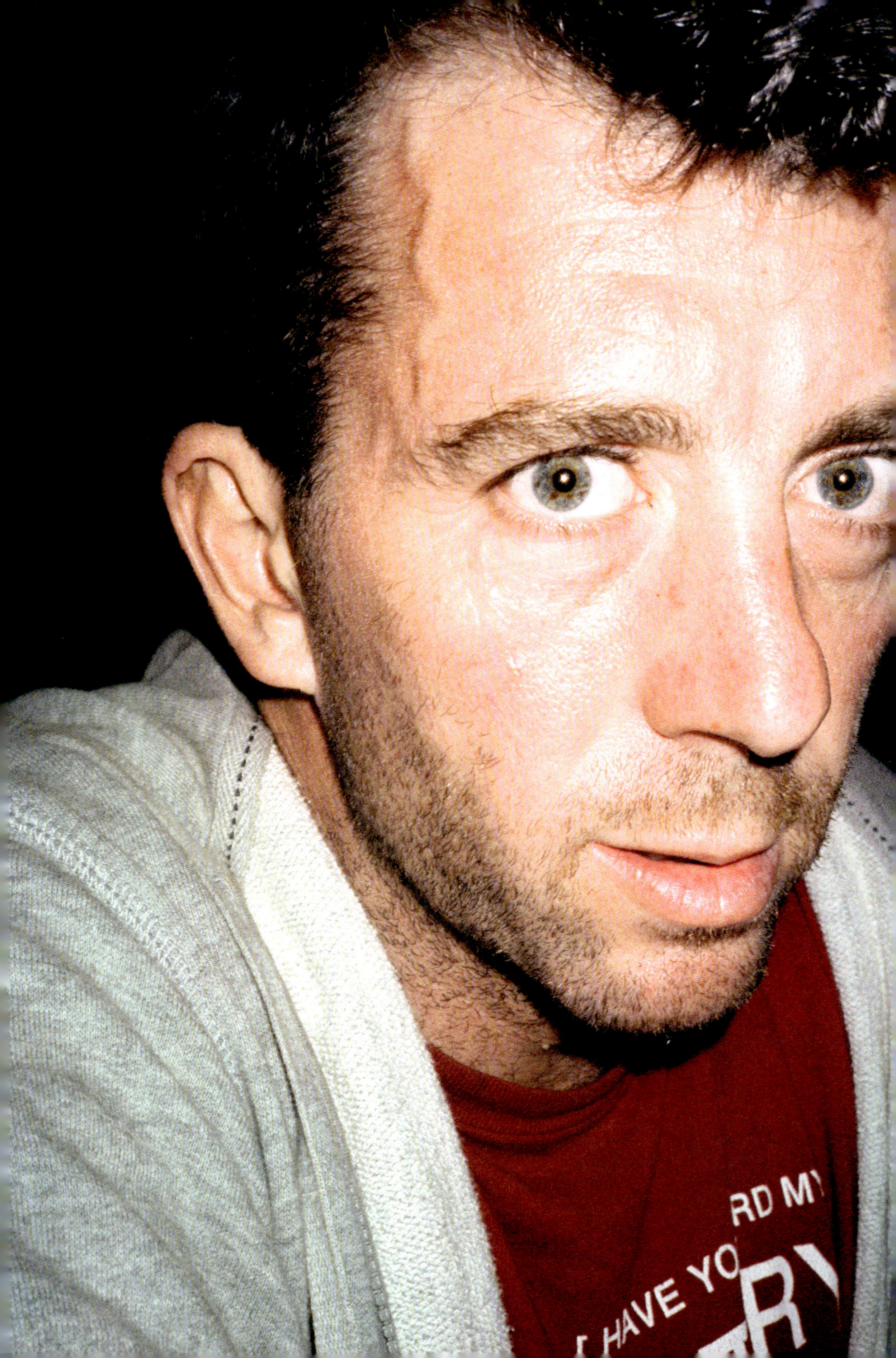
RD MY
HAVE YO

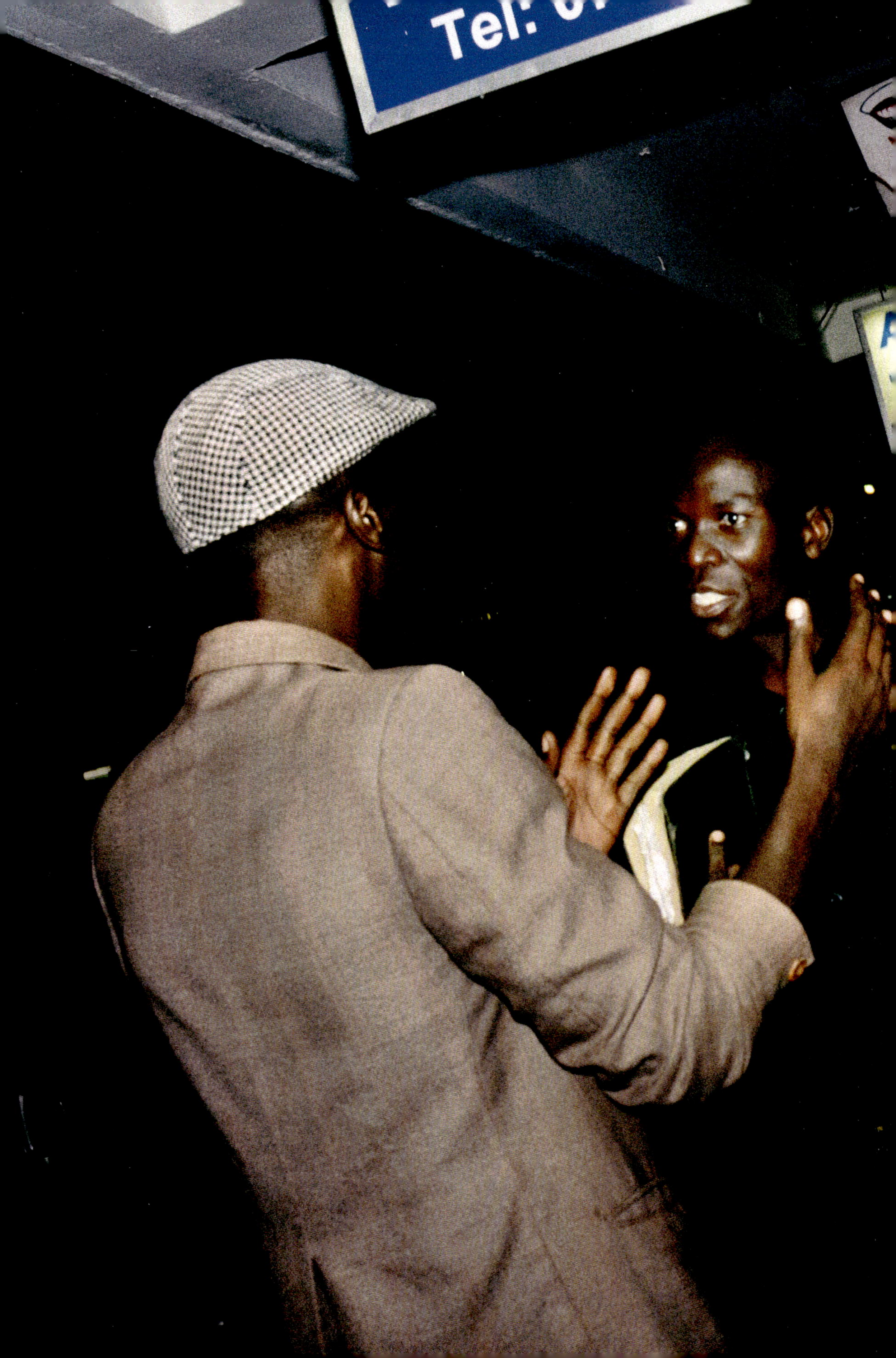
Tel:

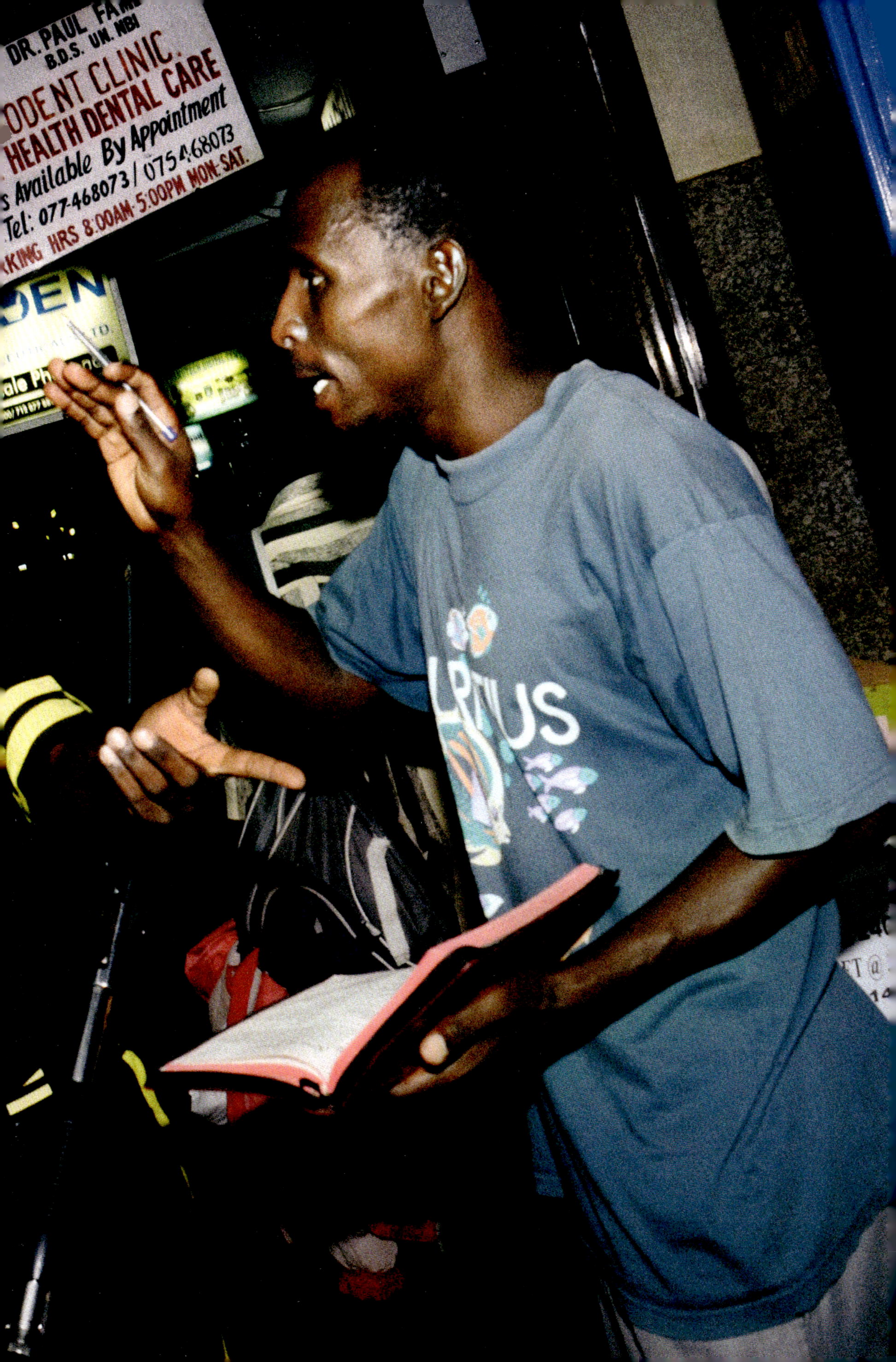
DR. PAUL
B.D.S. UN. NBI
CLINIC
HEALTH DENTAL CARE
Available By Appointment
Tel: 077-468073/ 075468073
HRS 8:00AM-5:00PM MON-SAT

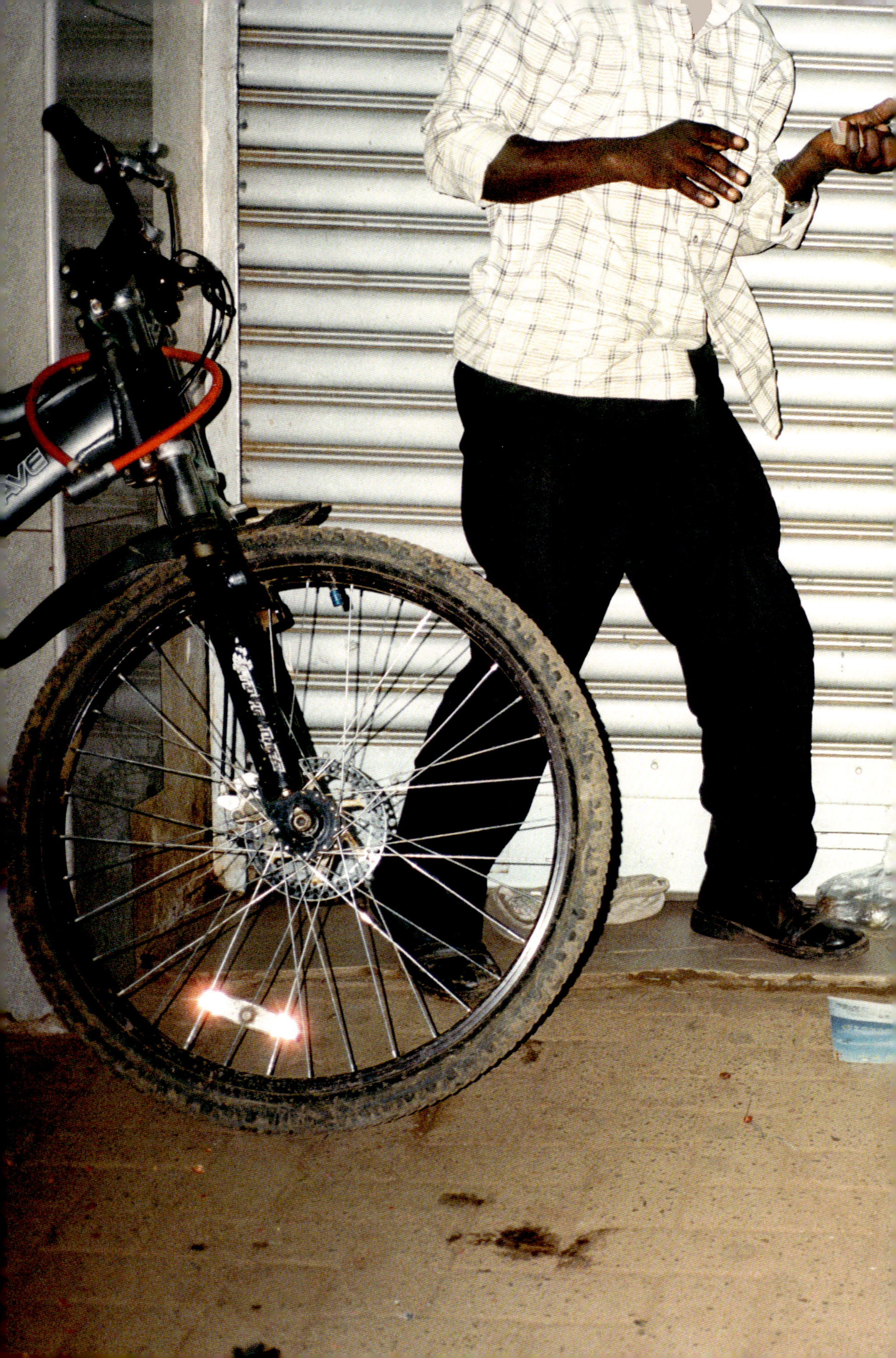

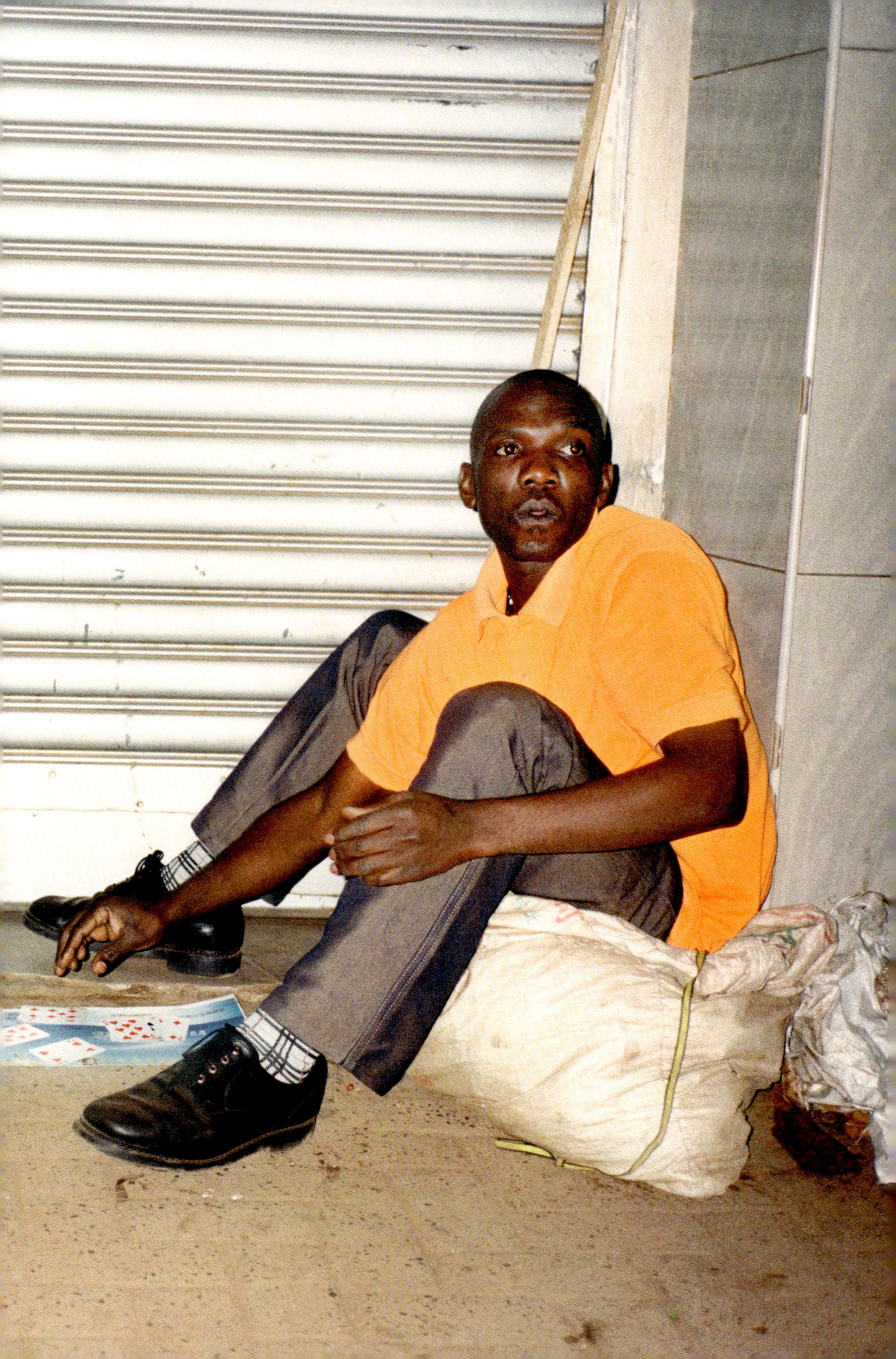

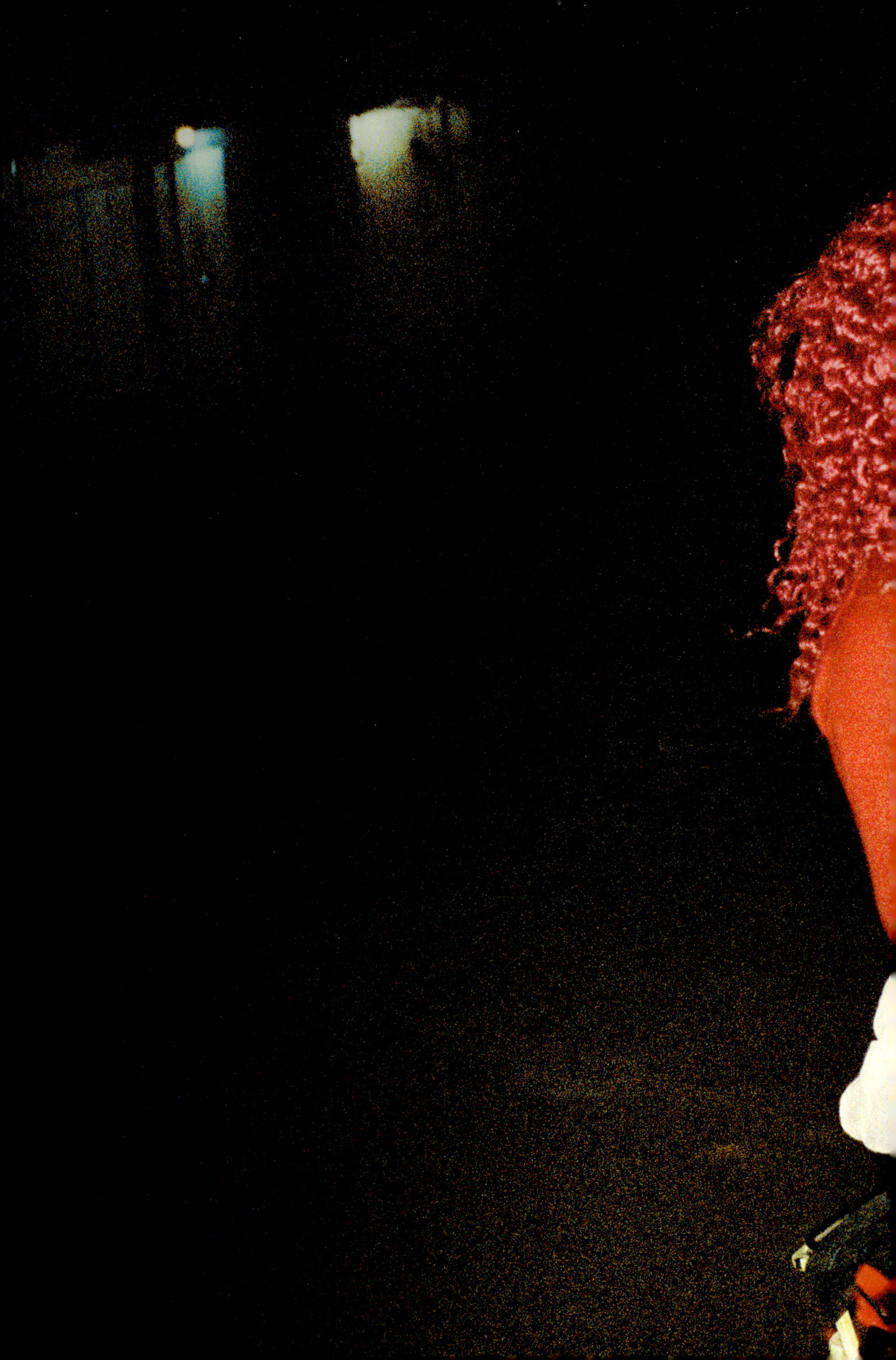

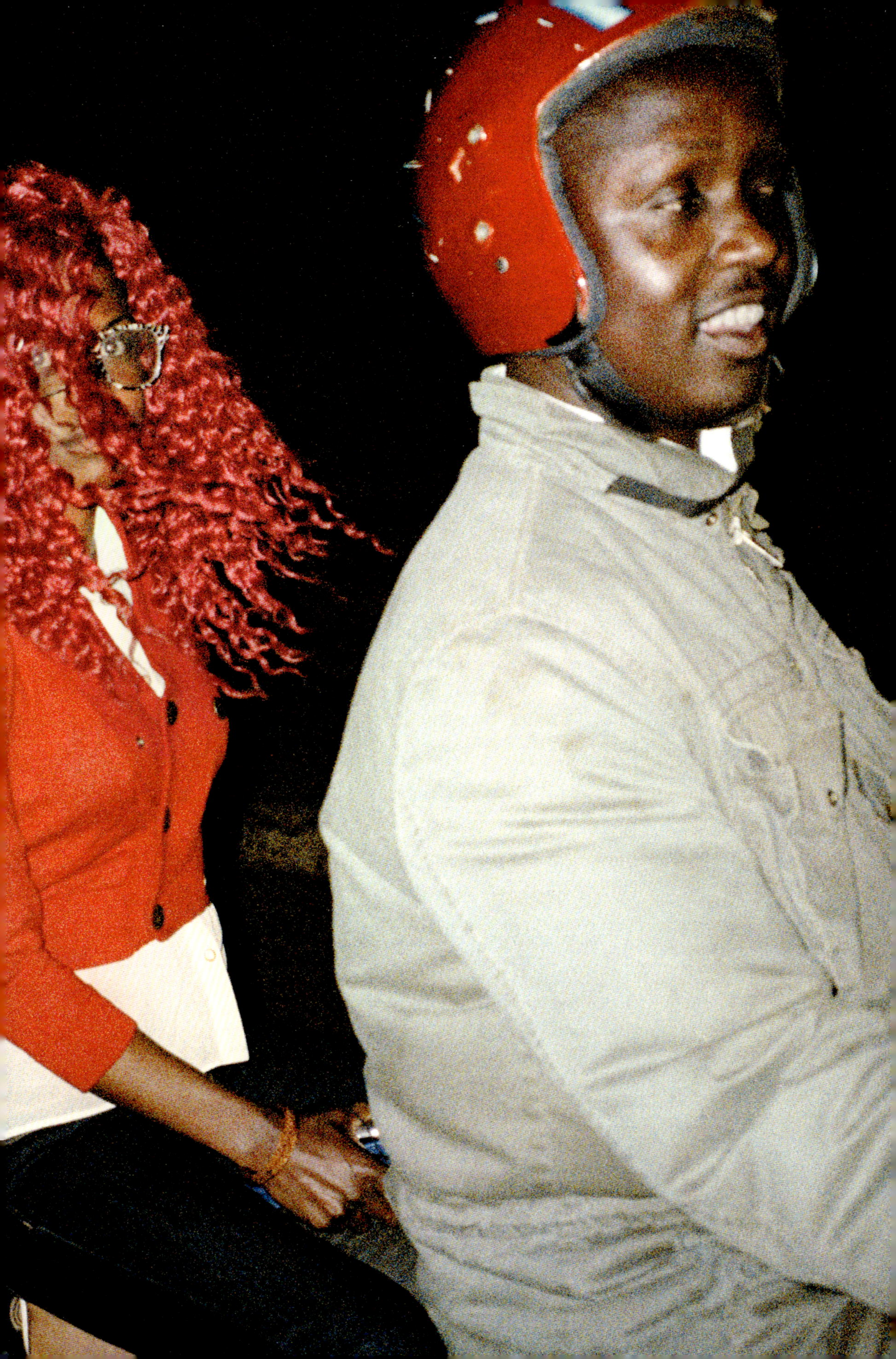

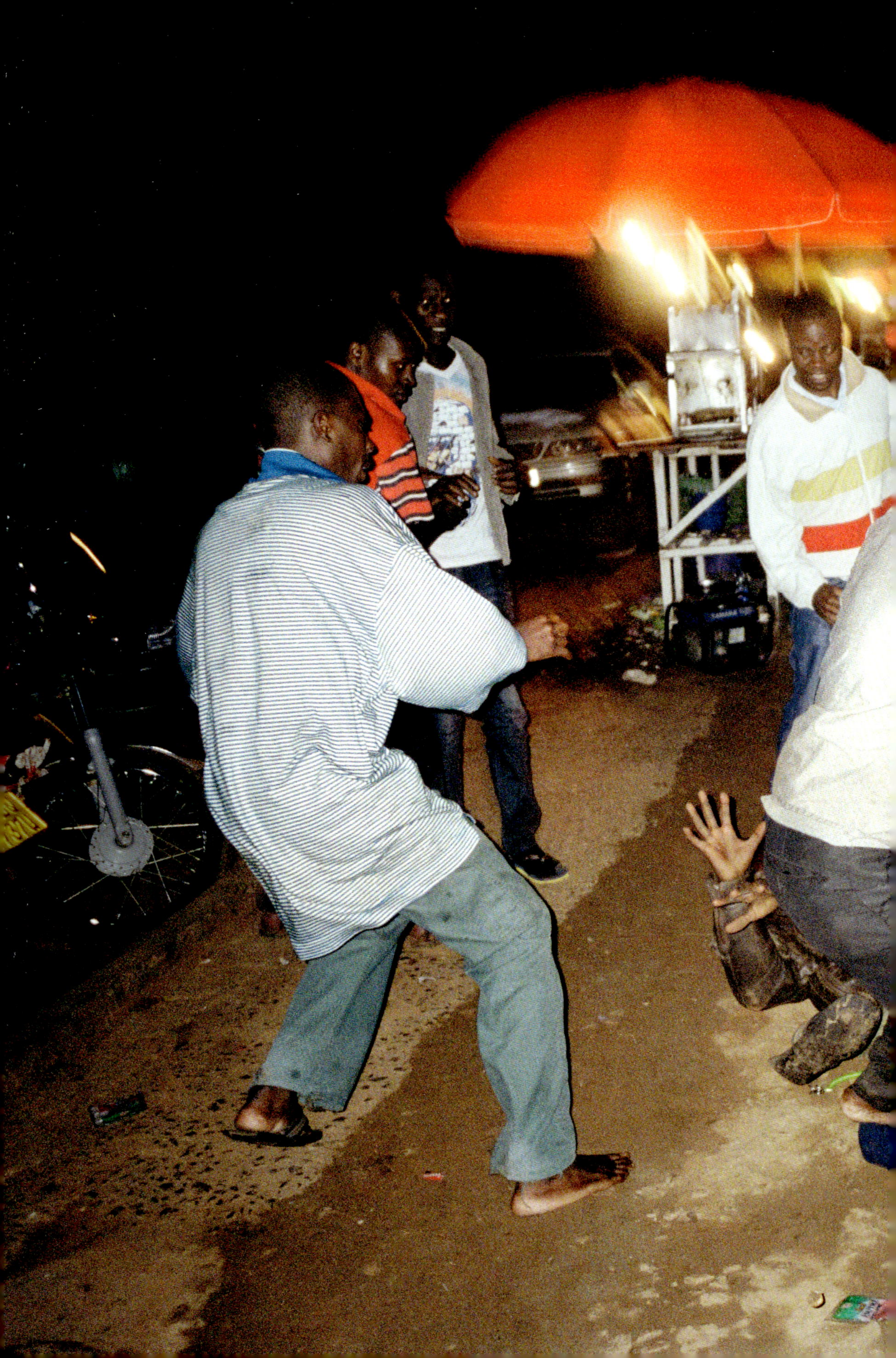

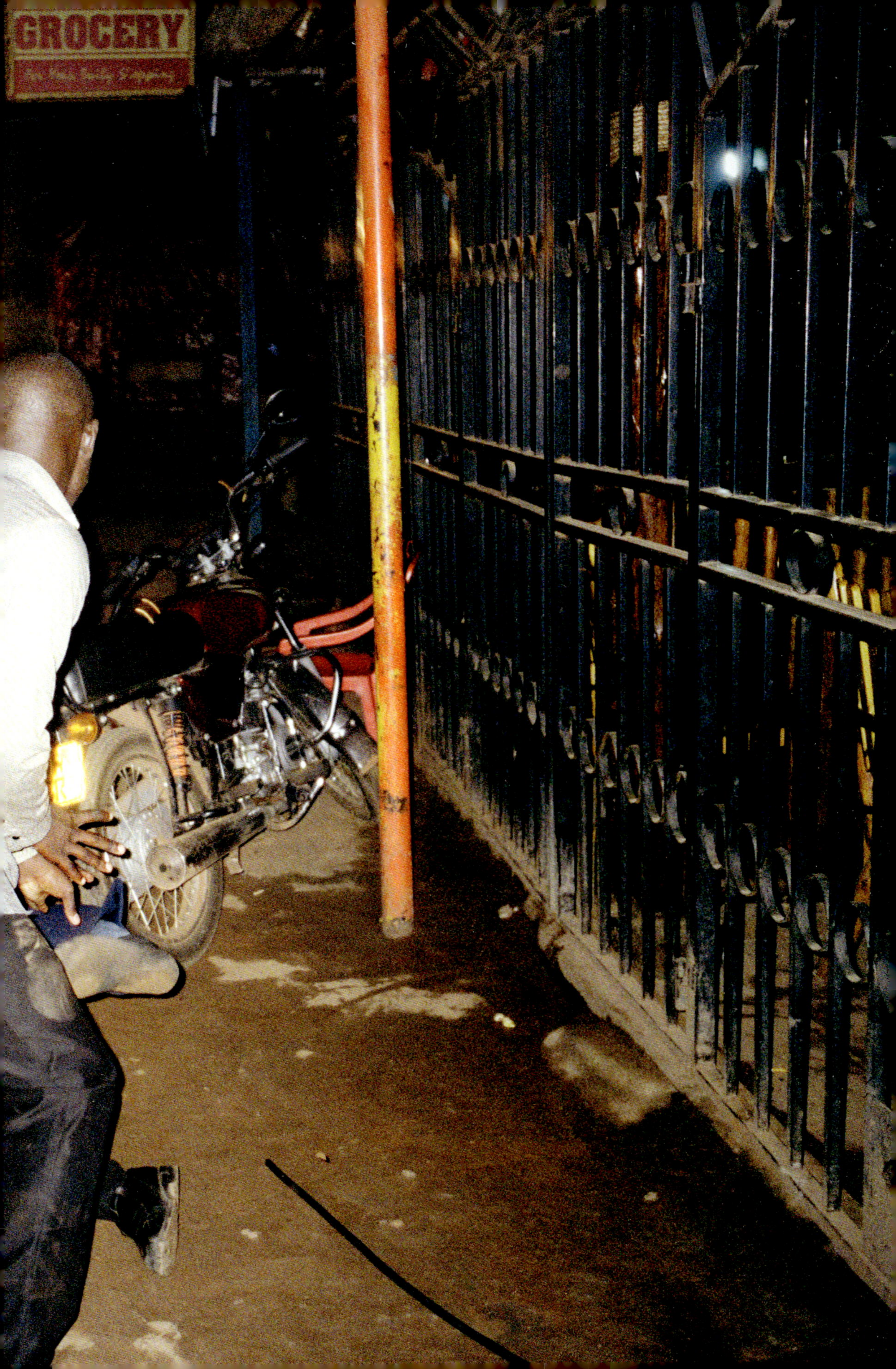
GROCERY

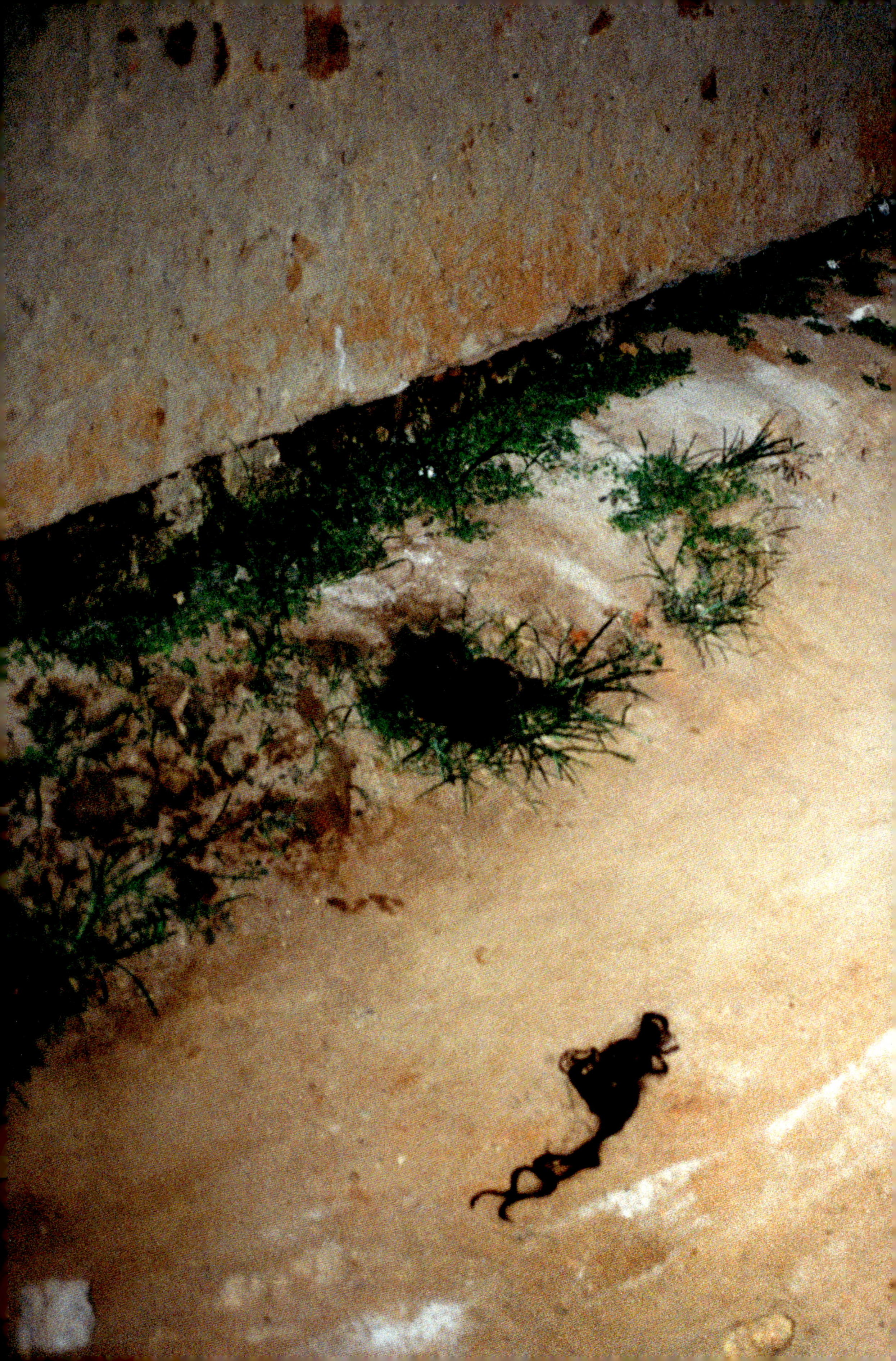

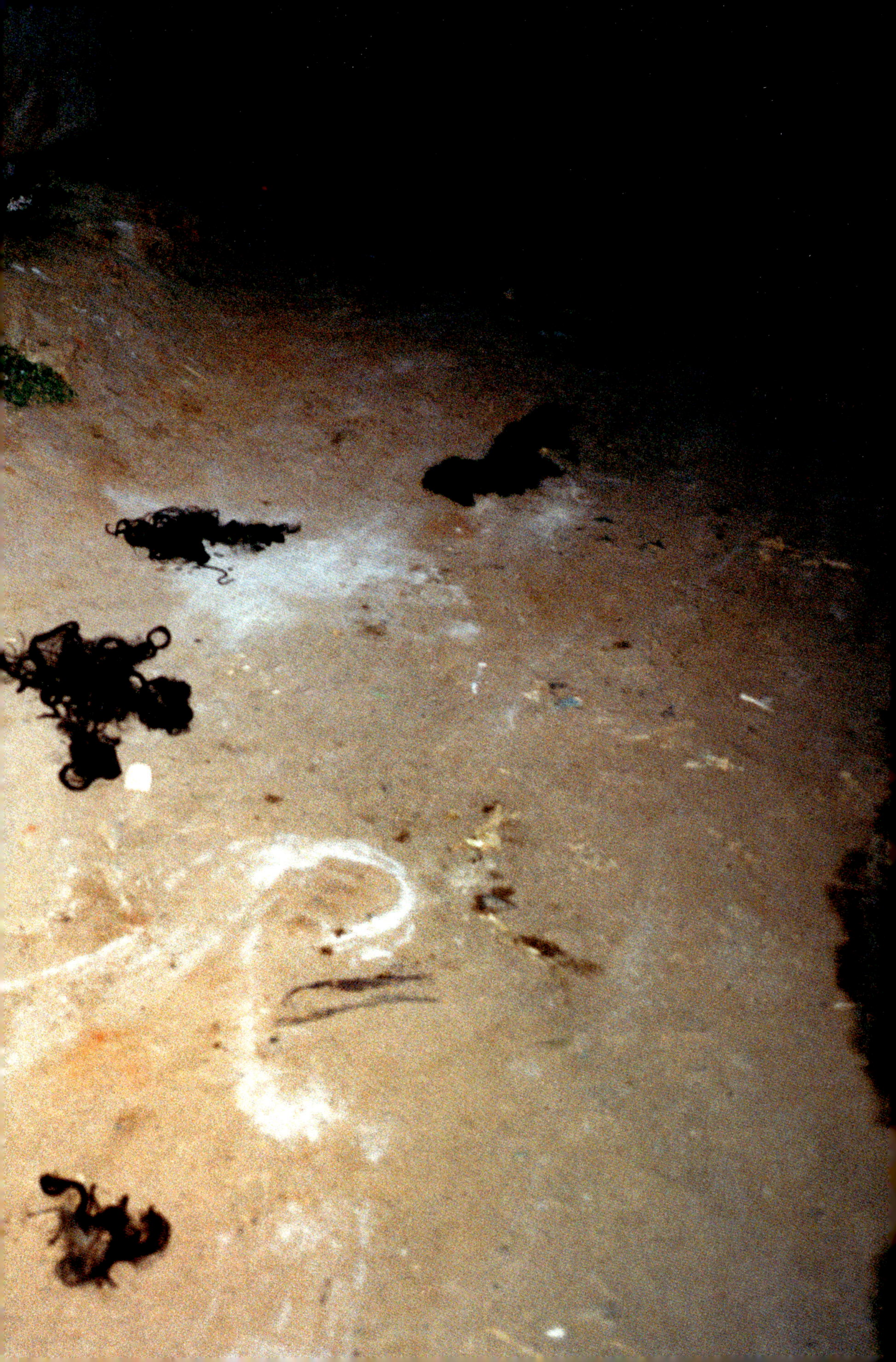

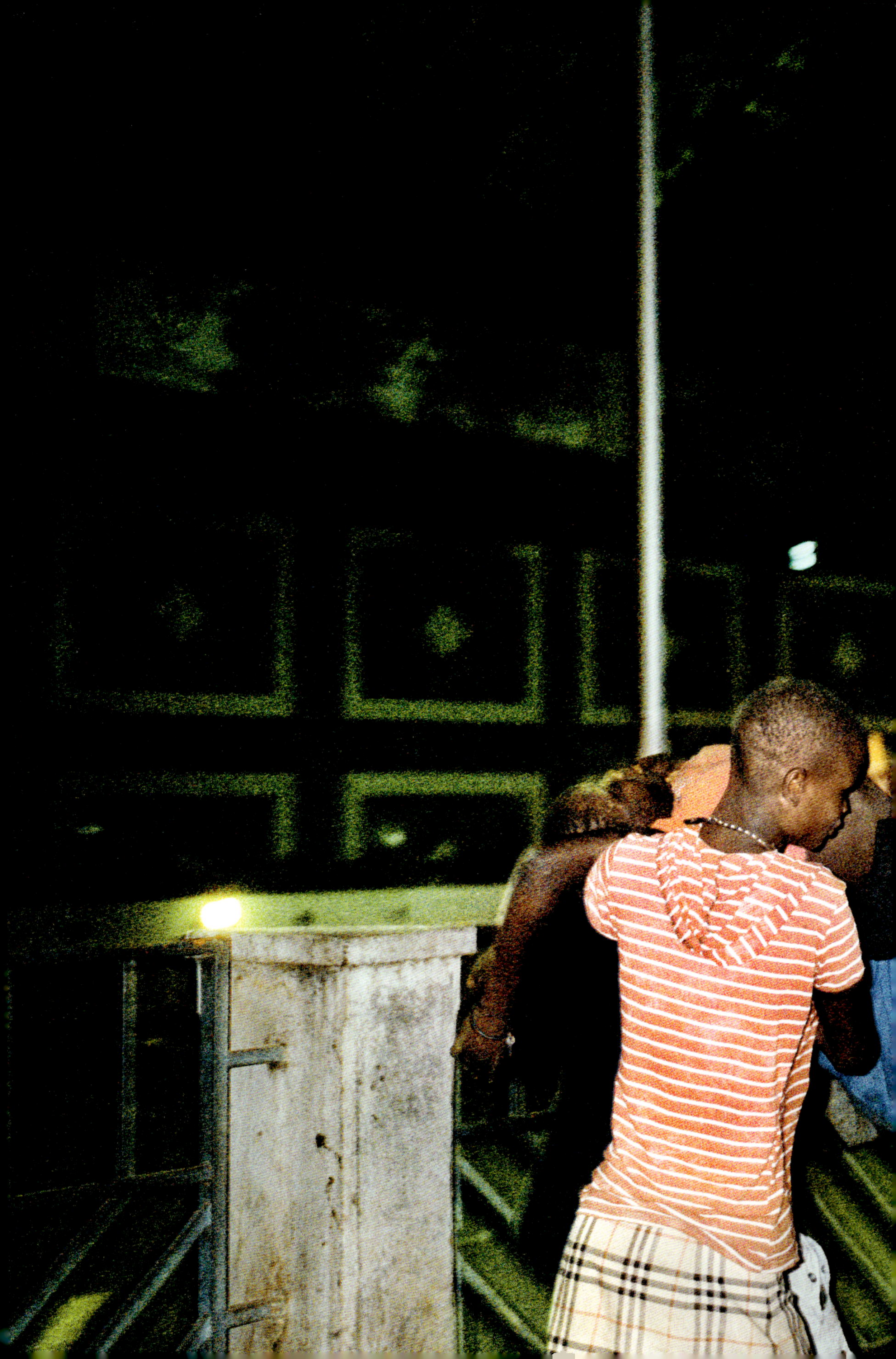

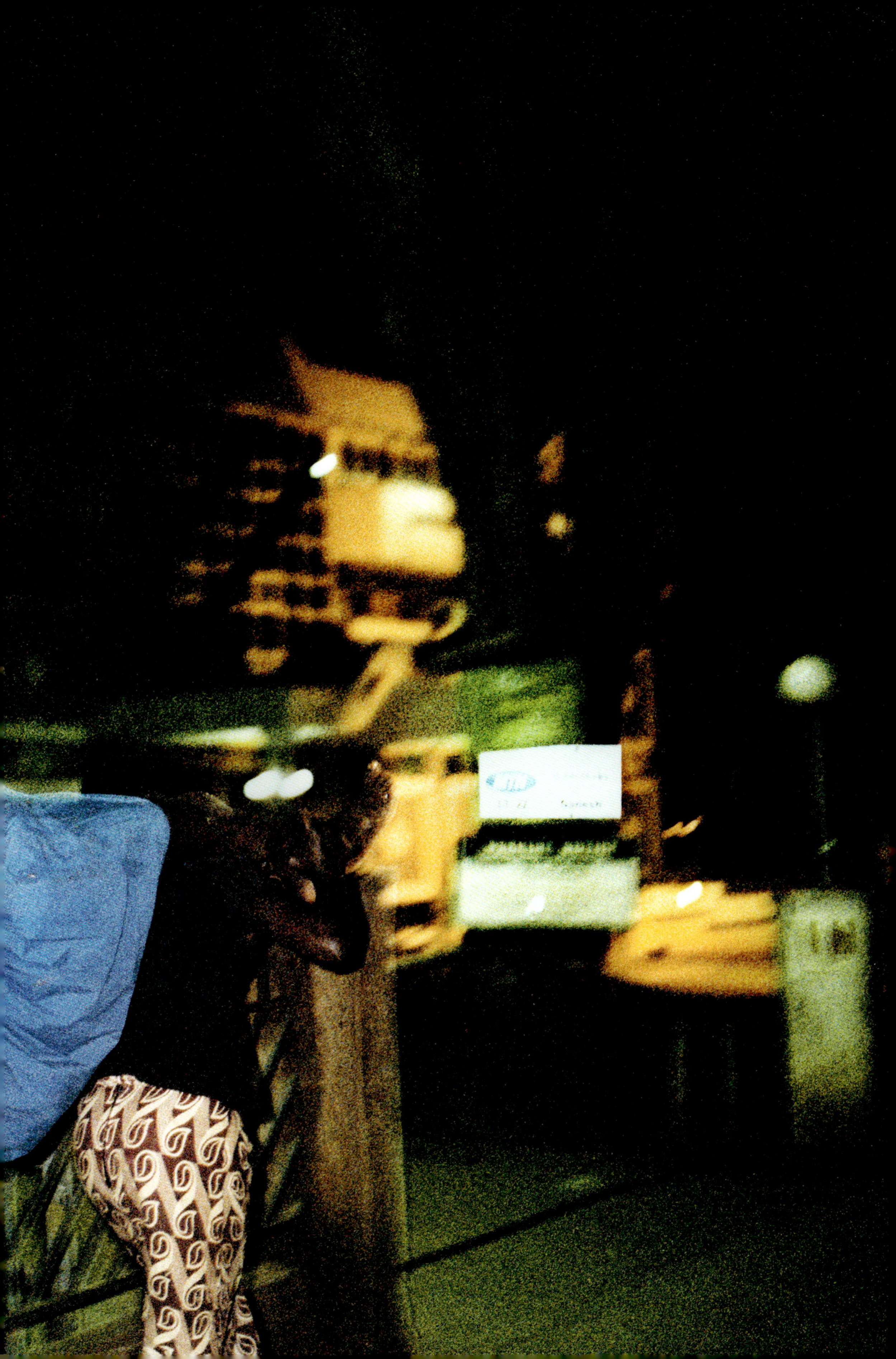

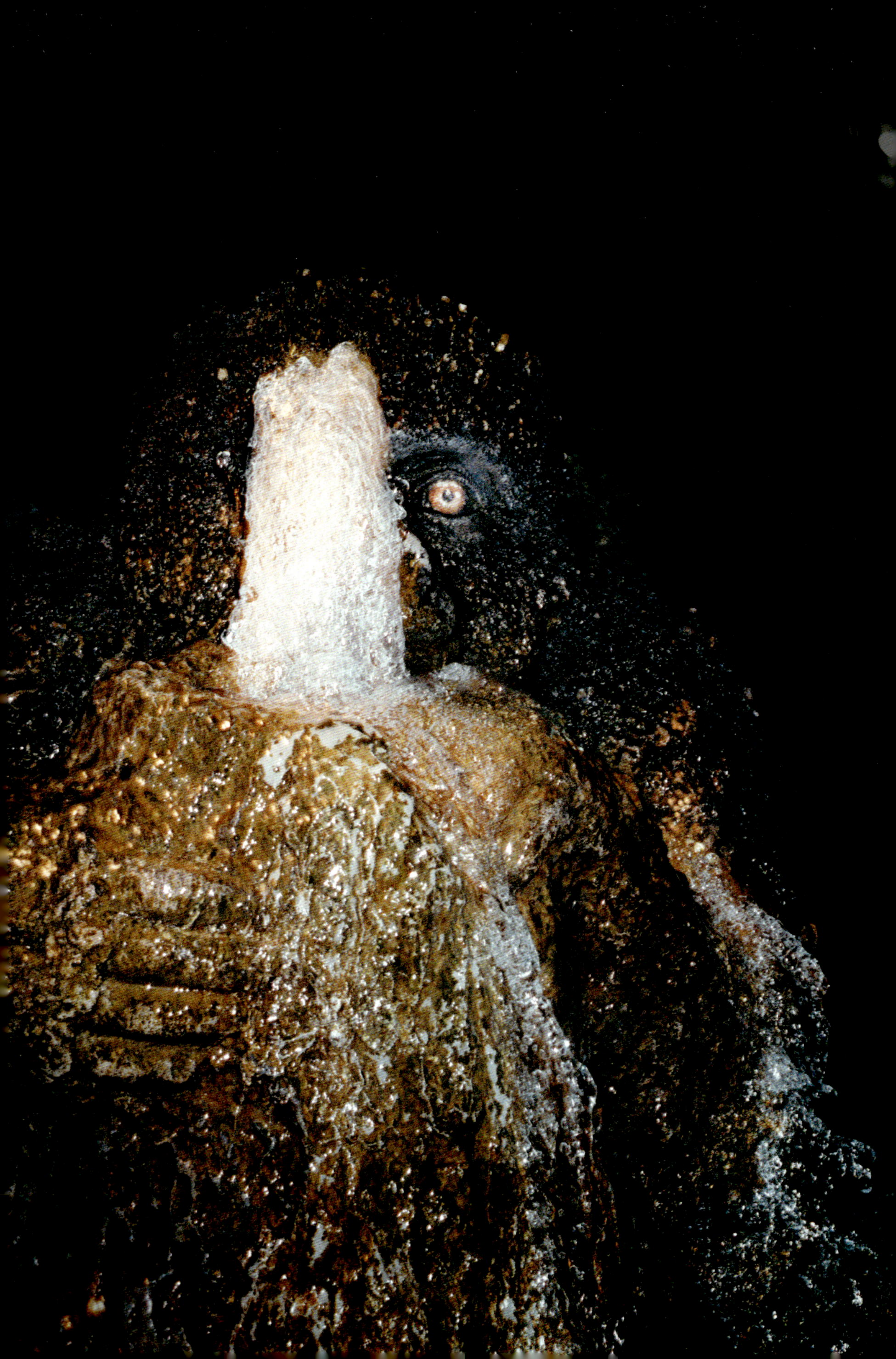

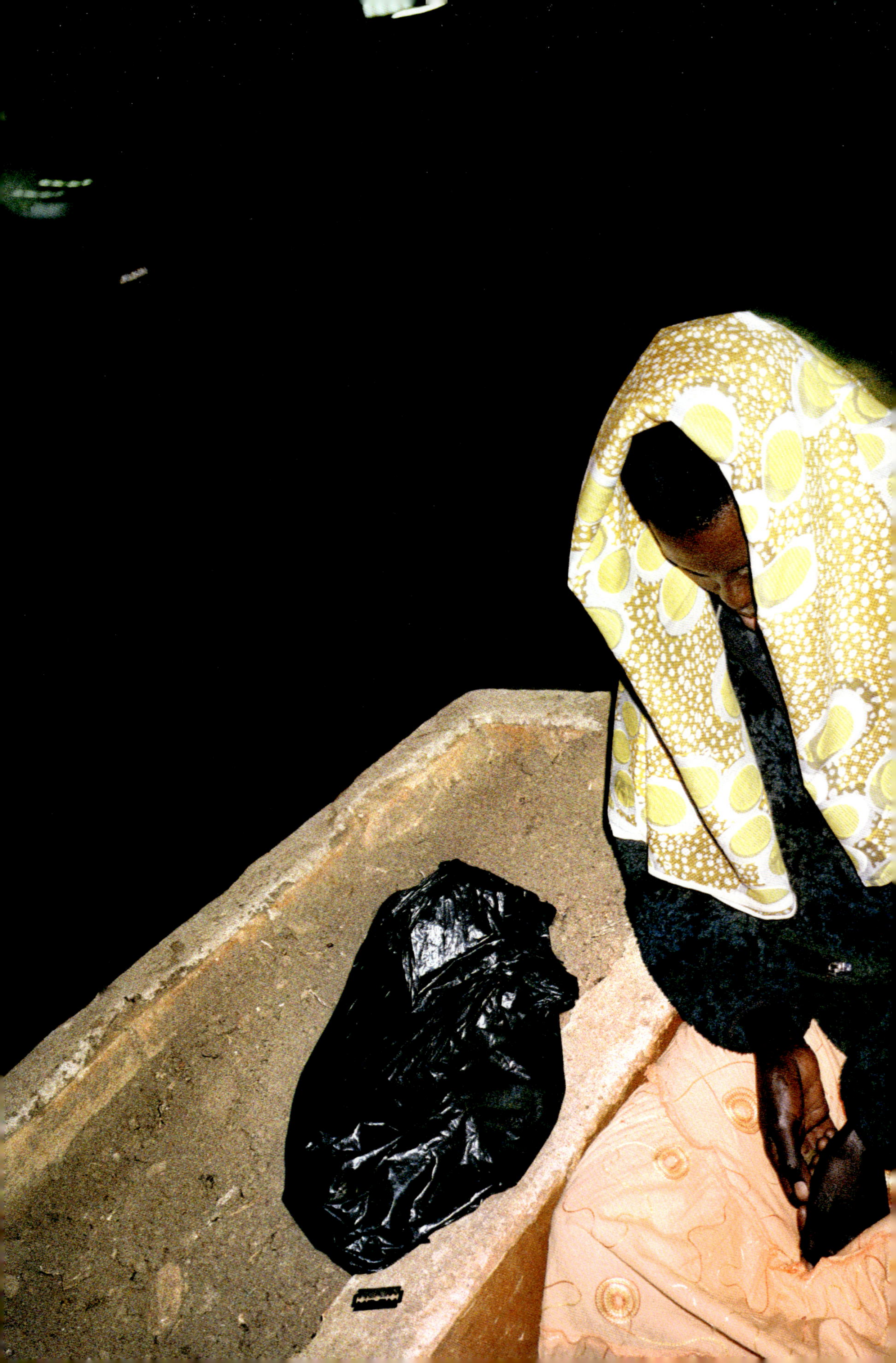

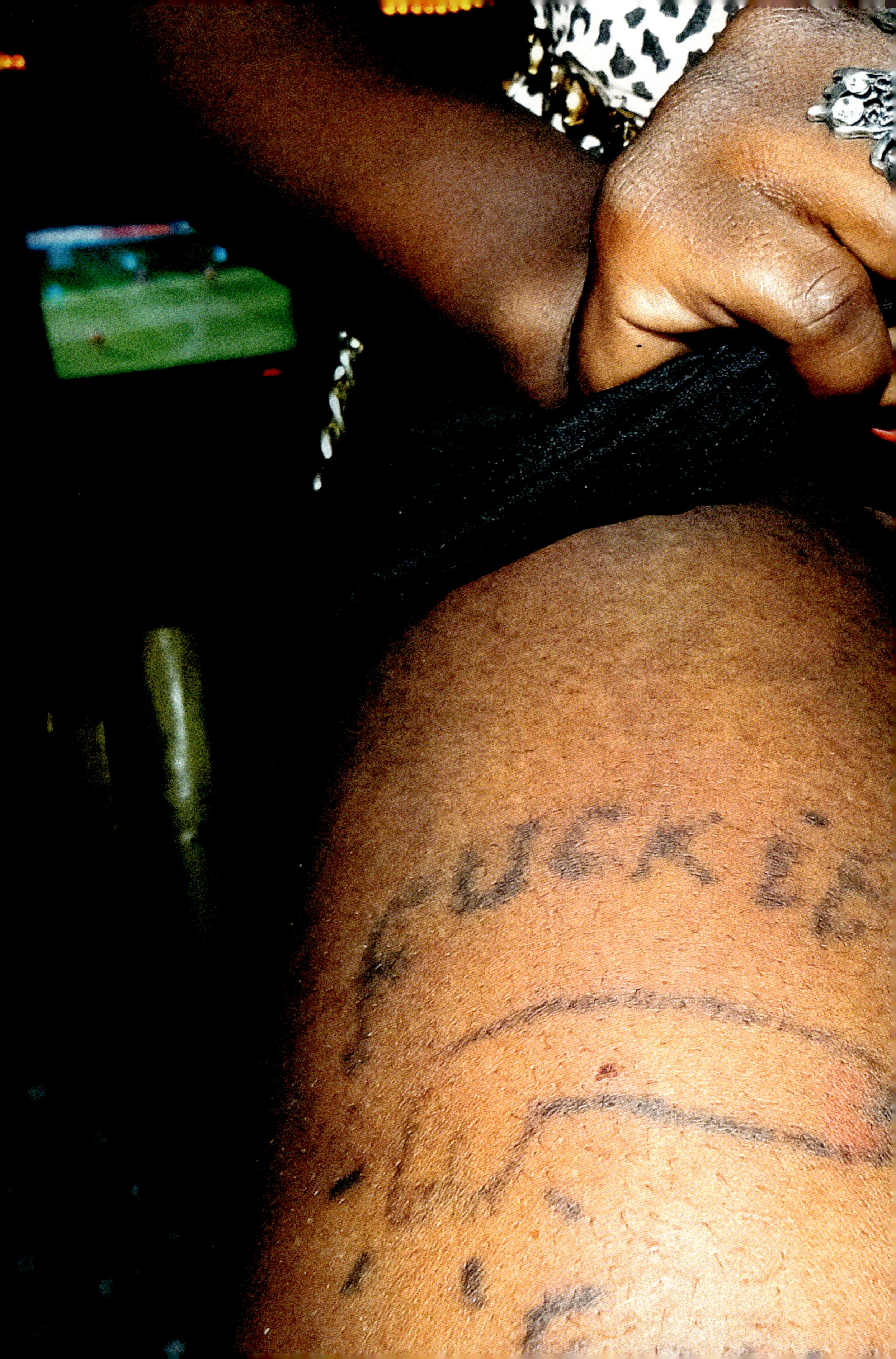

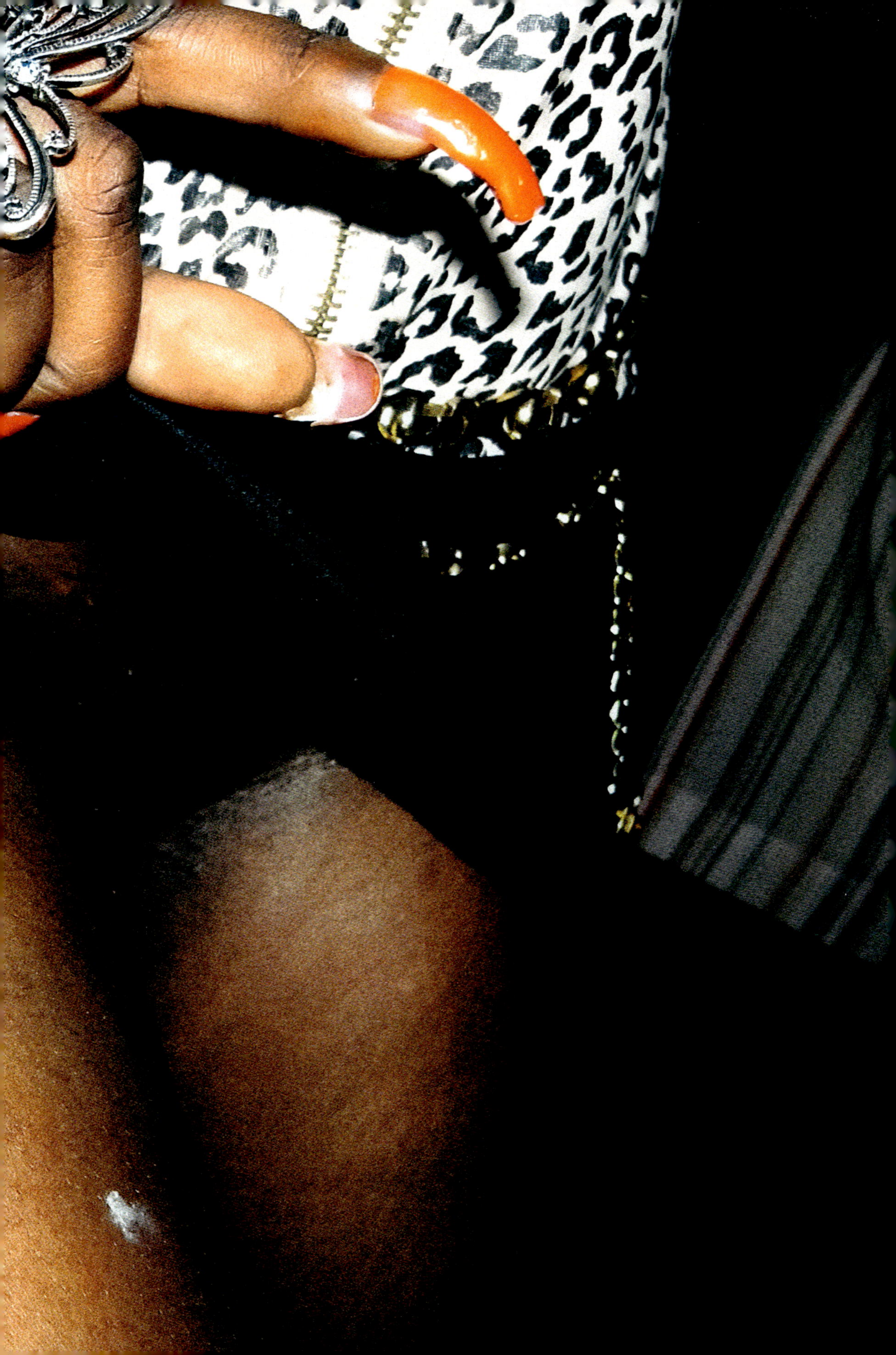

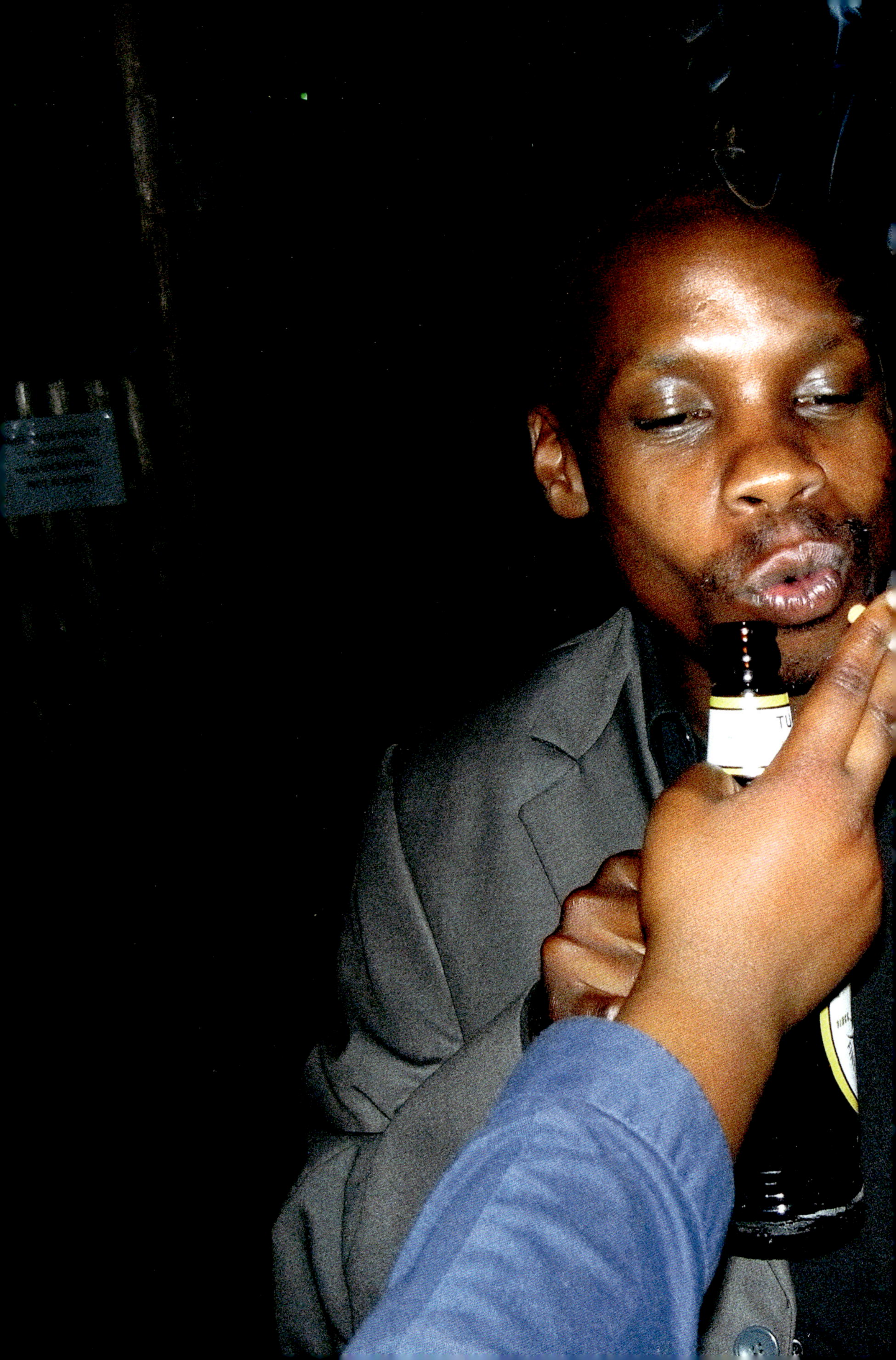

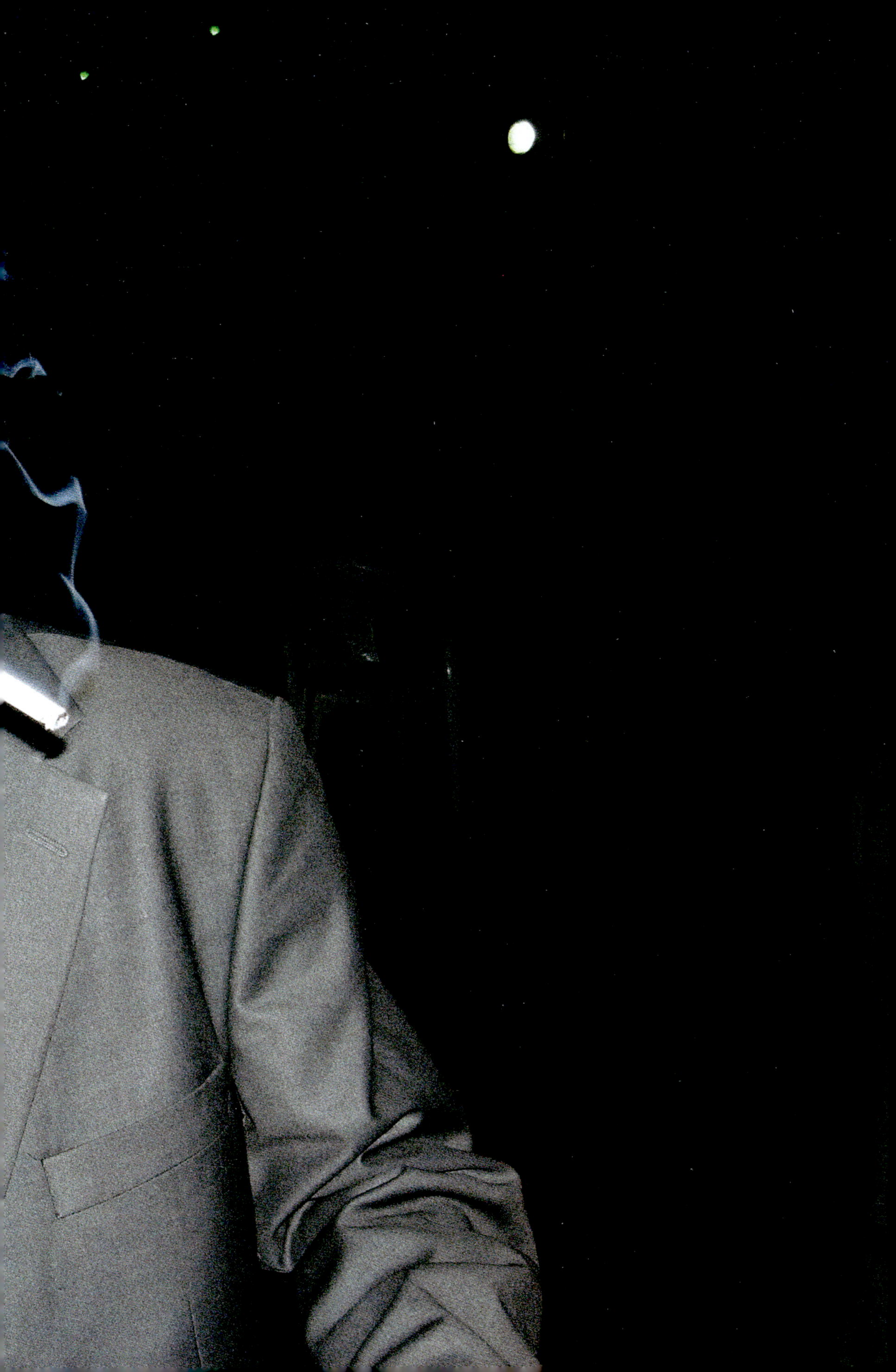

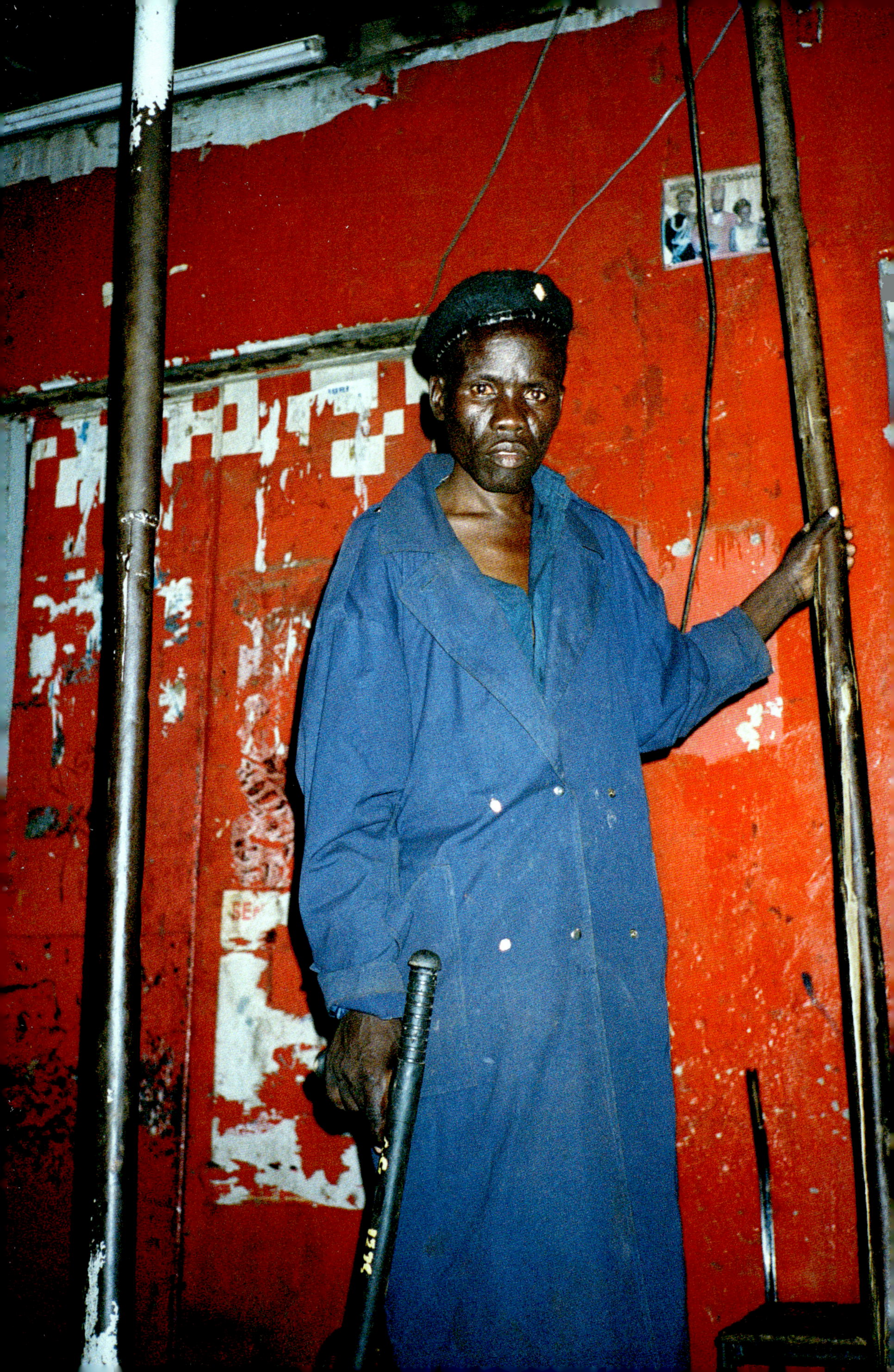

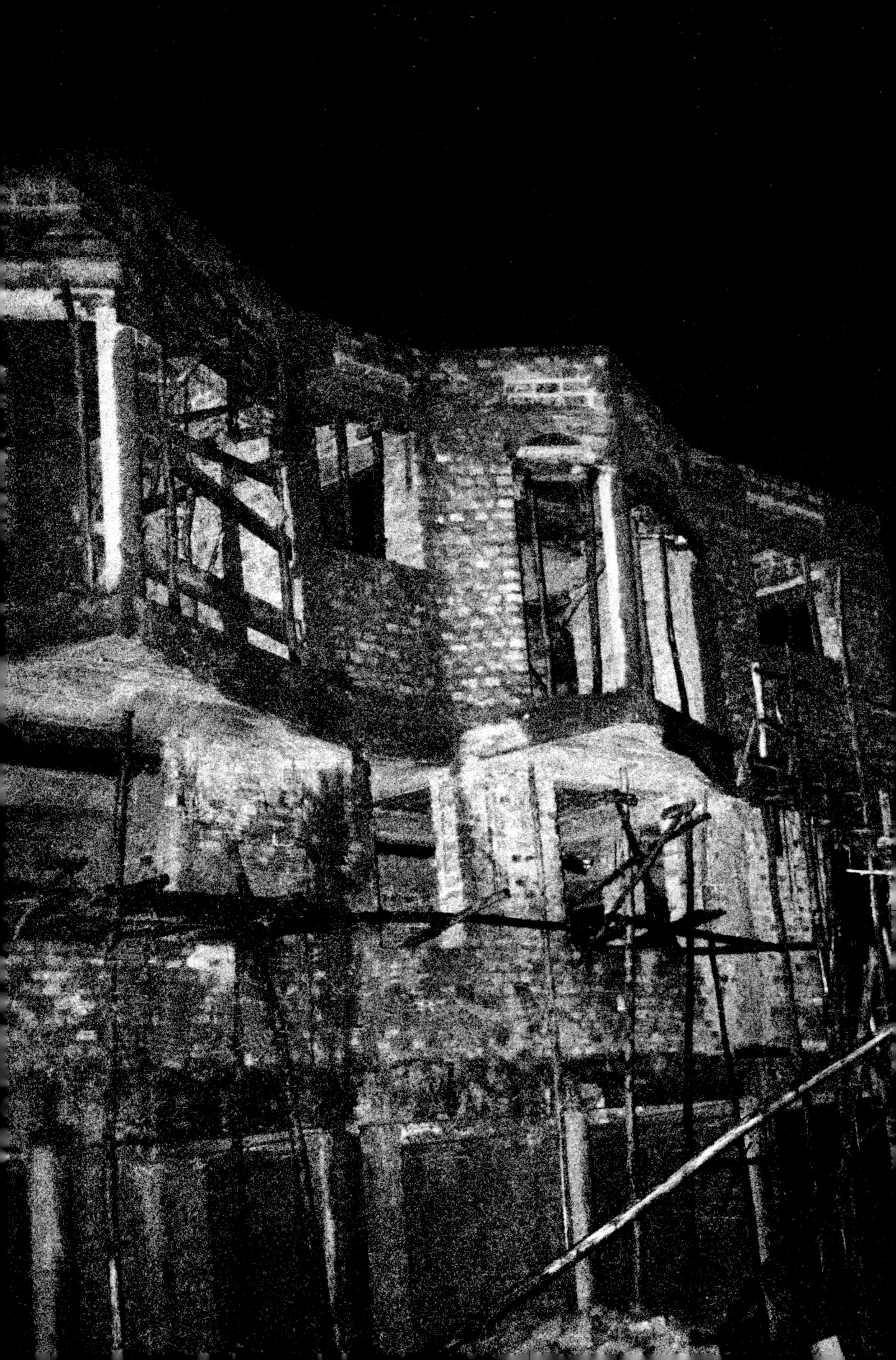

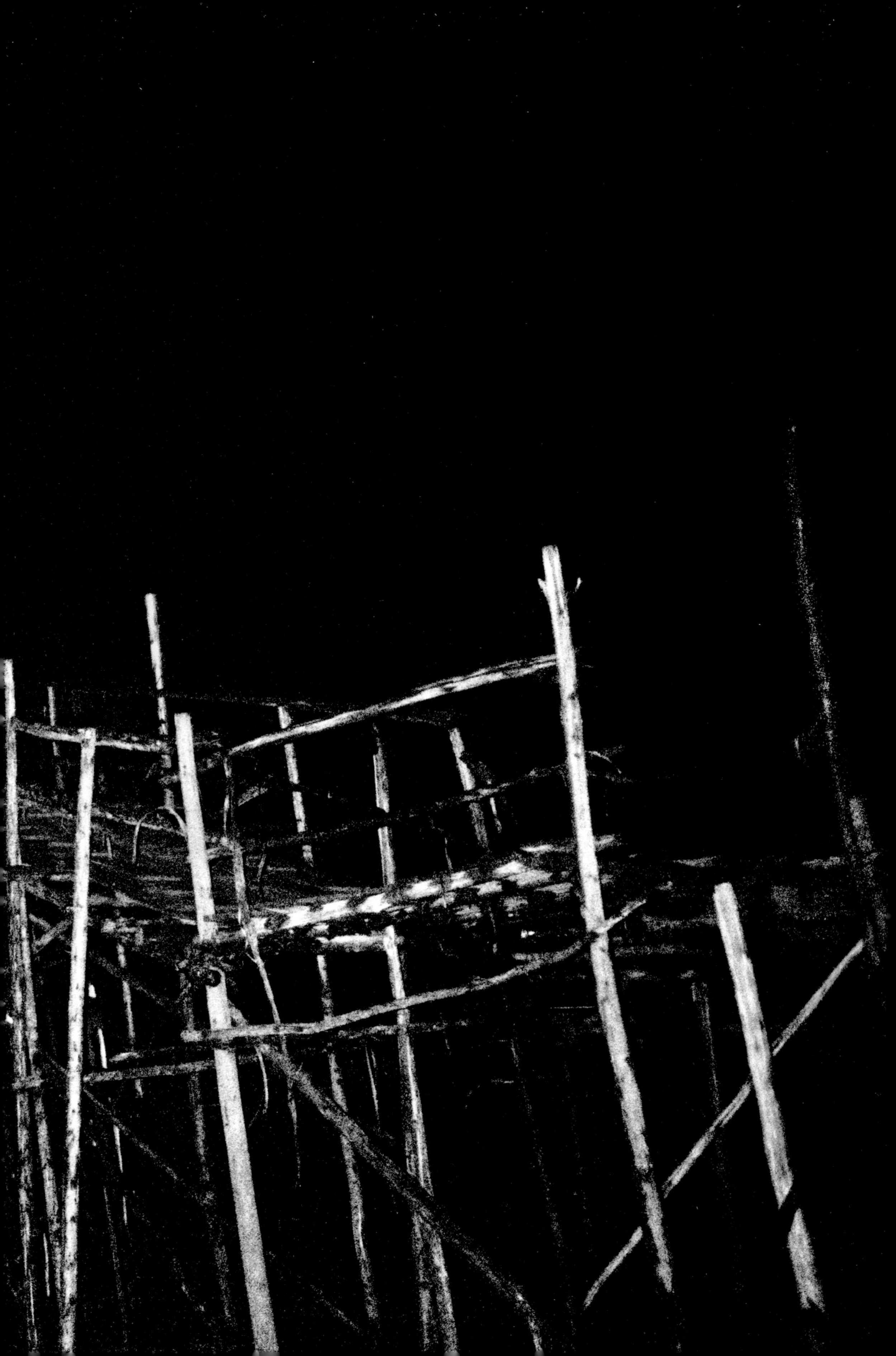

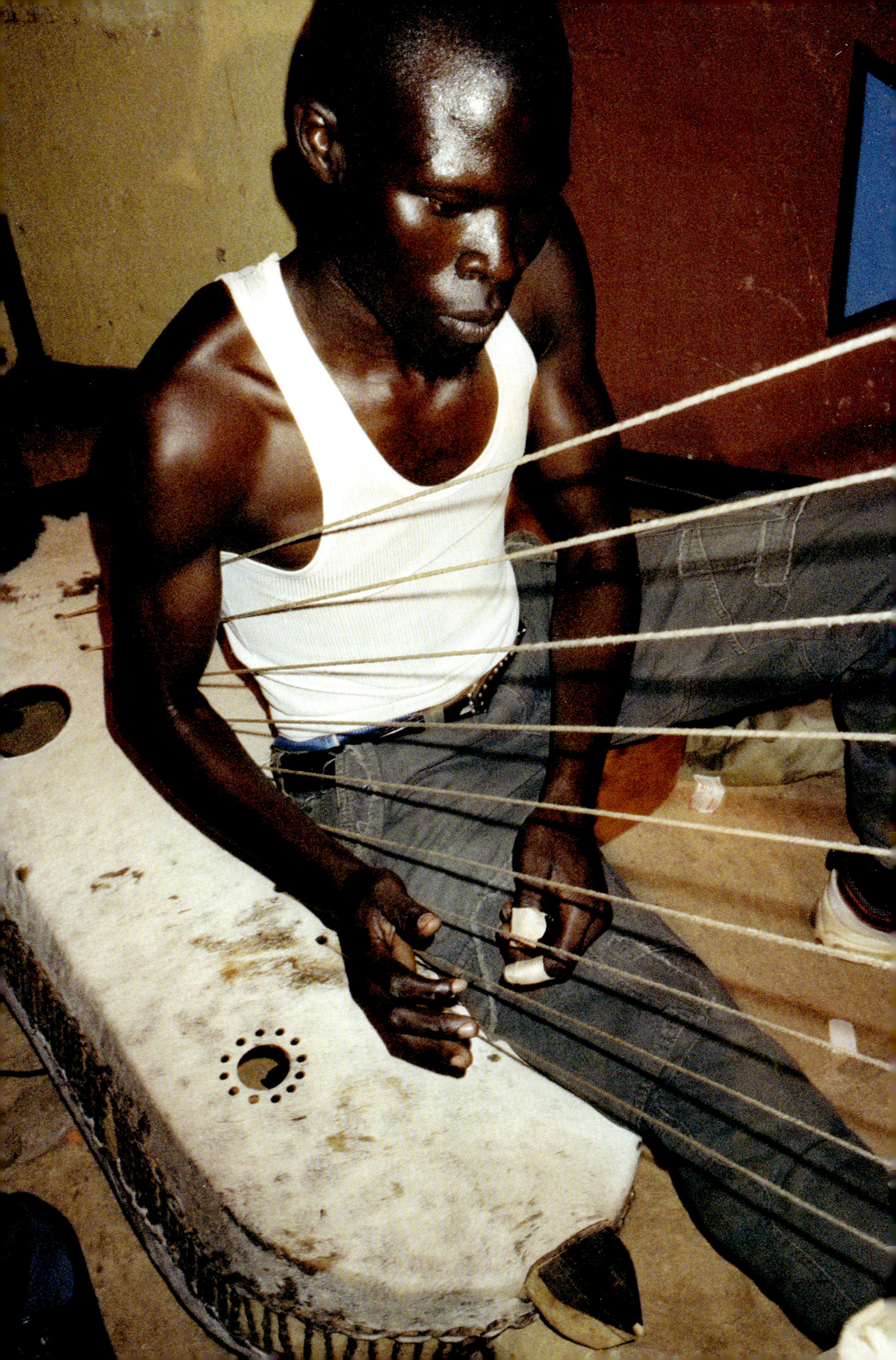

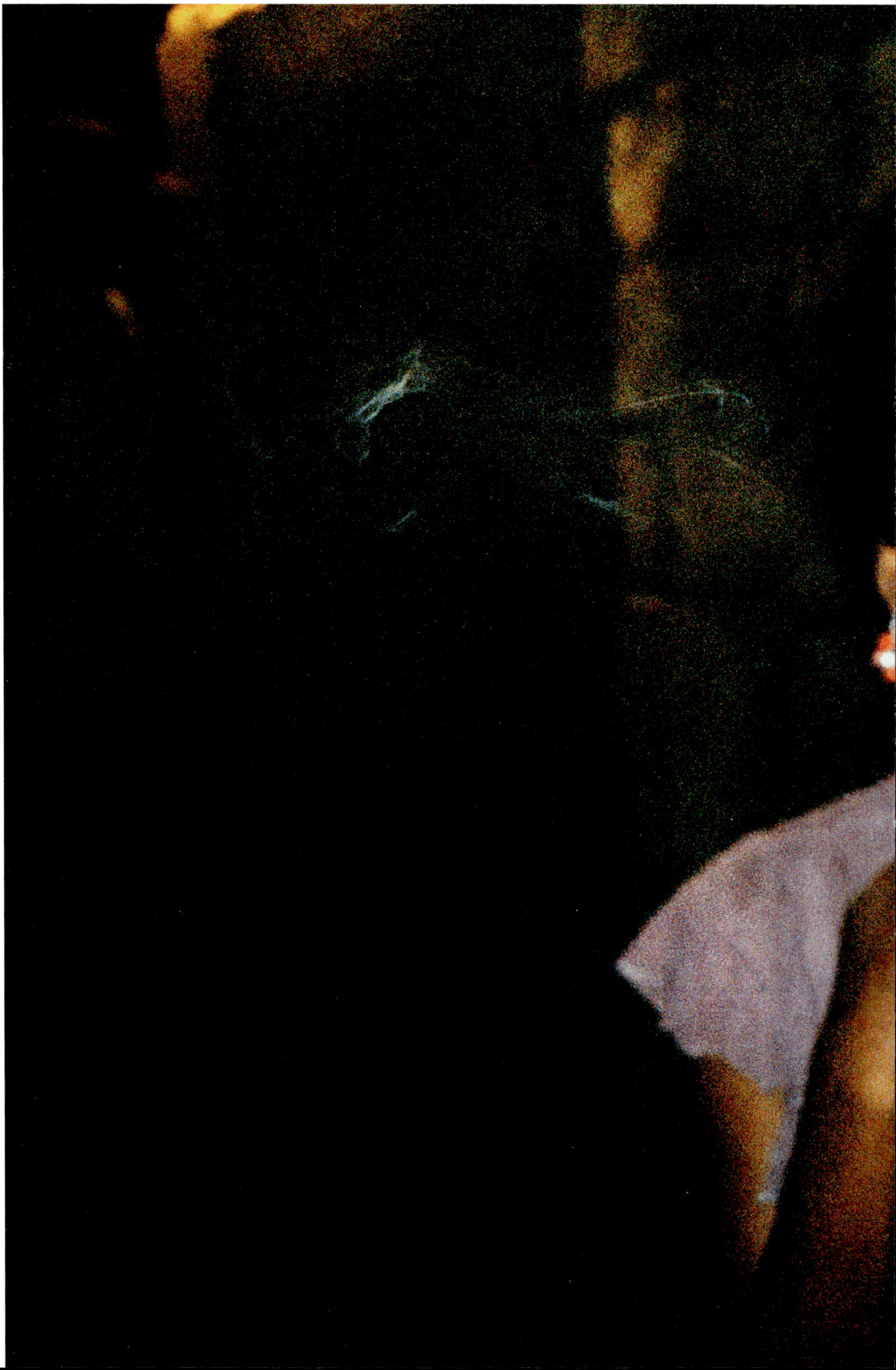

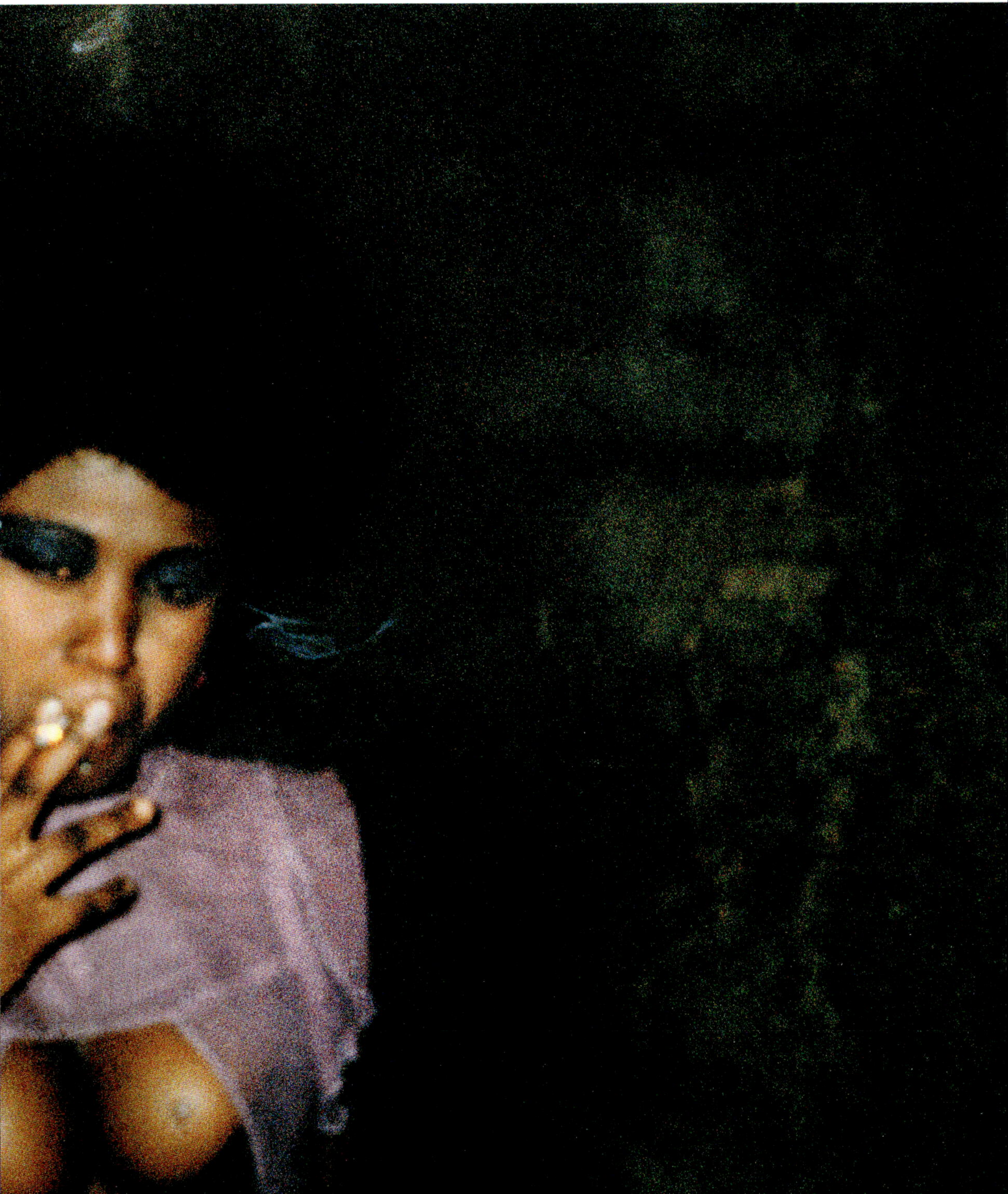

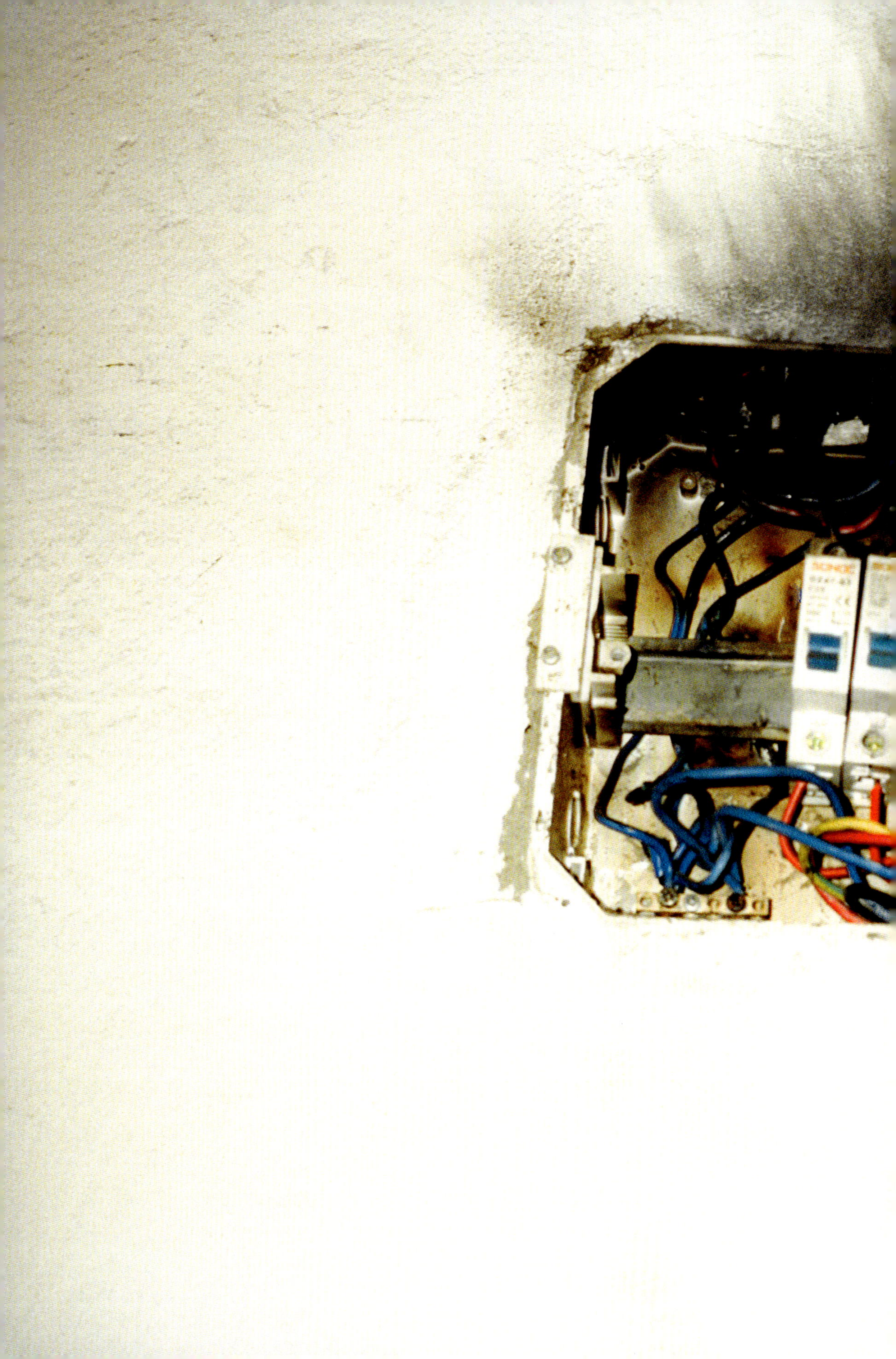

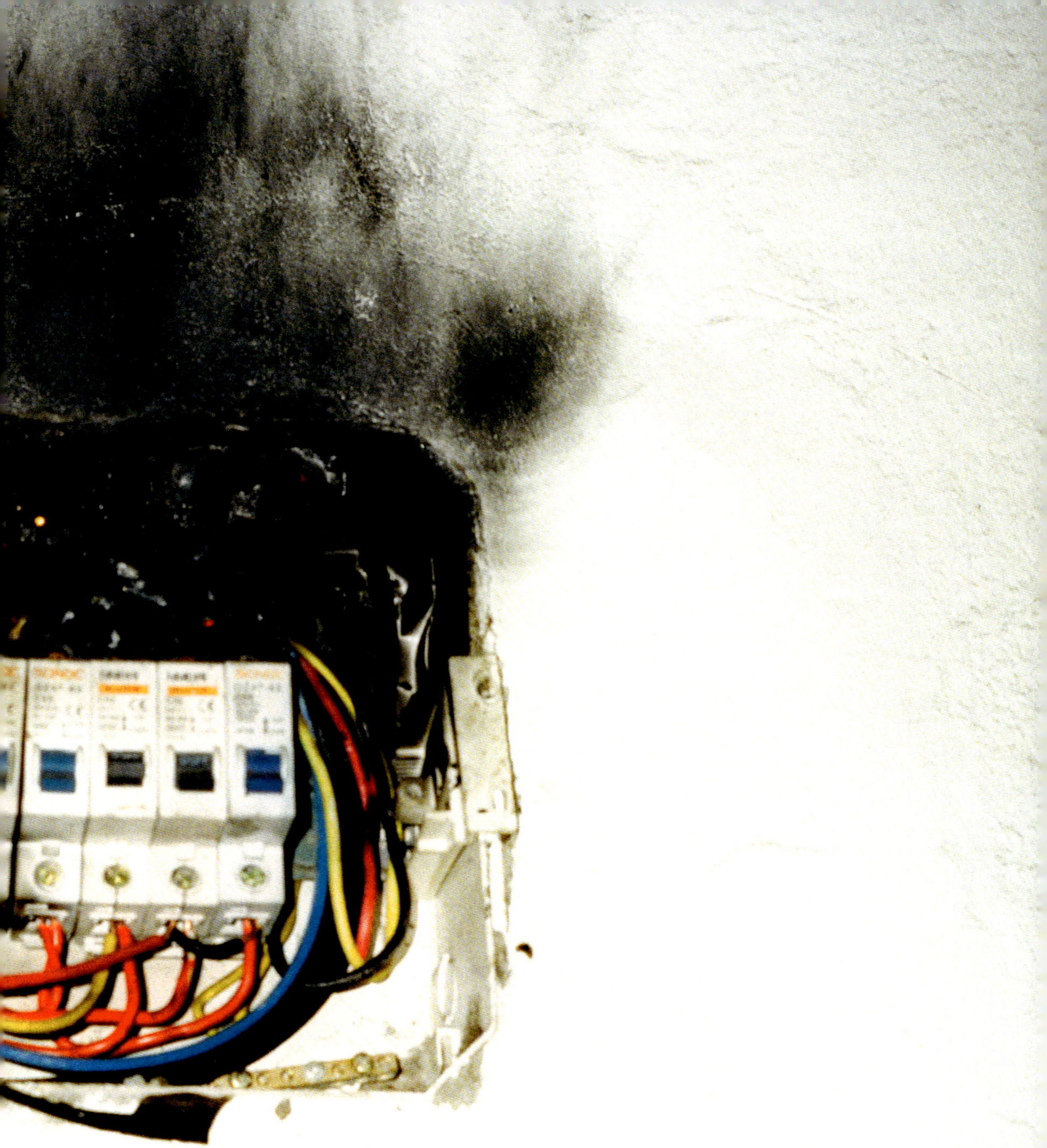

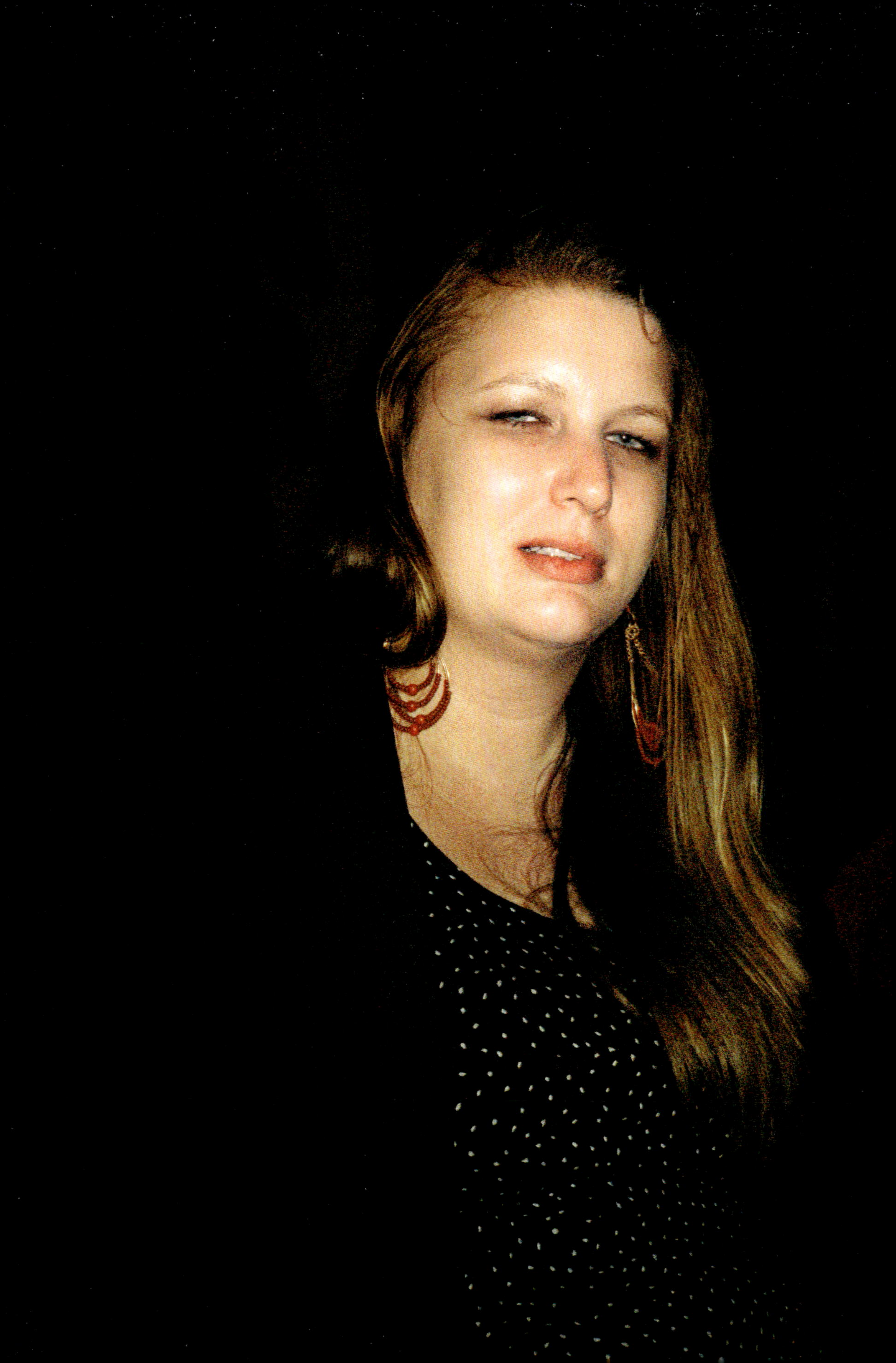

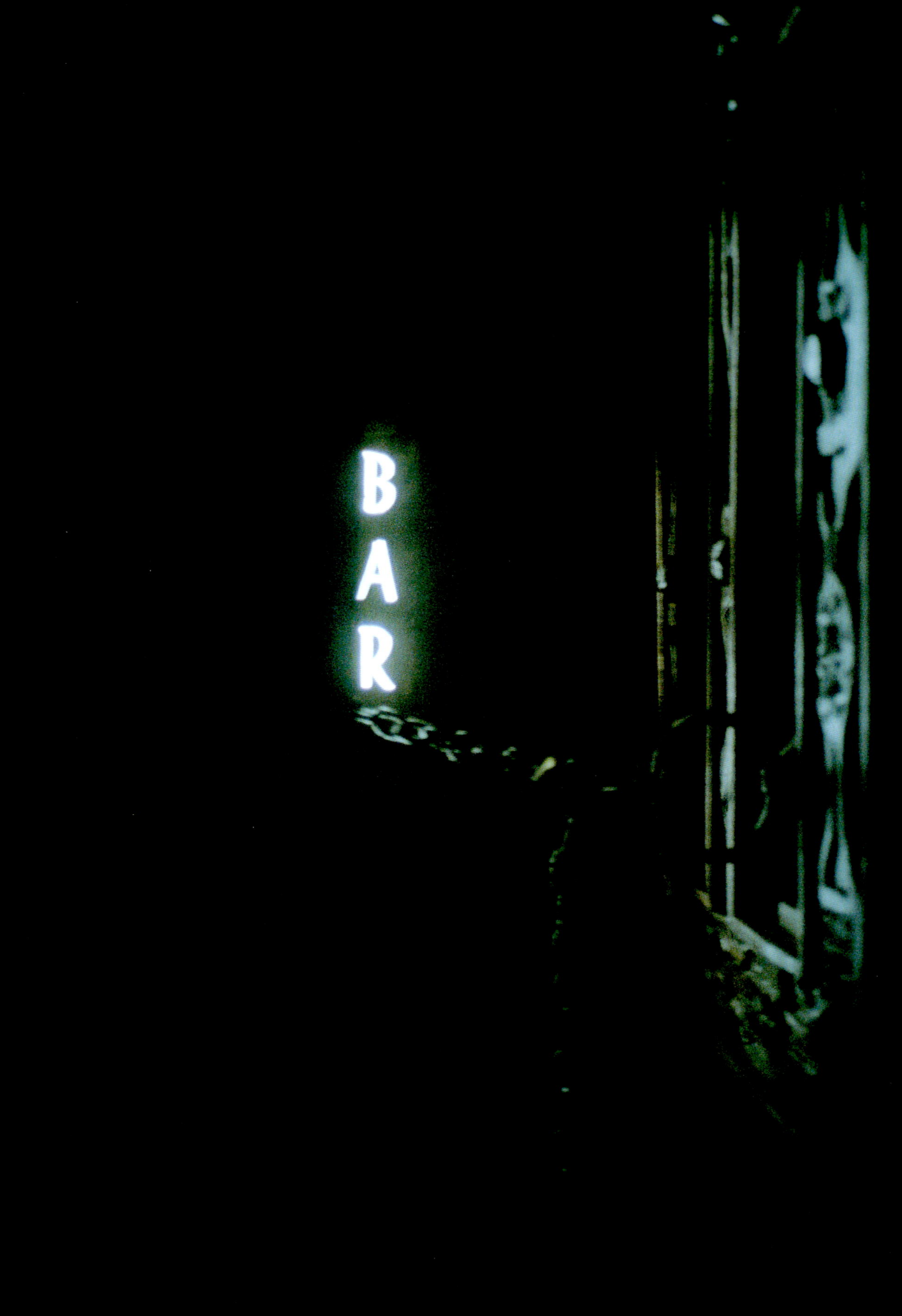
BAR

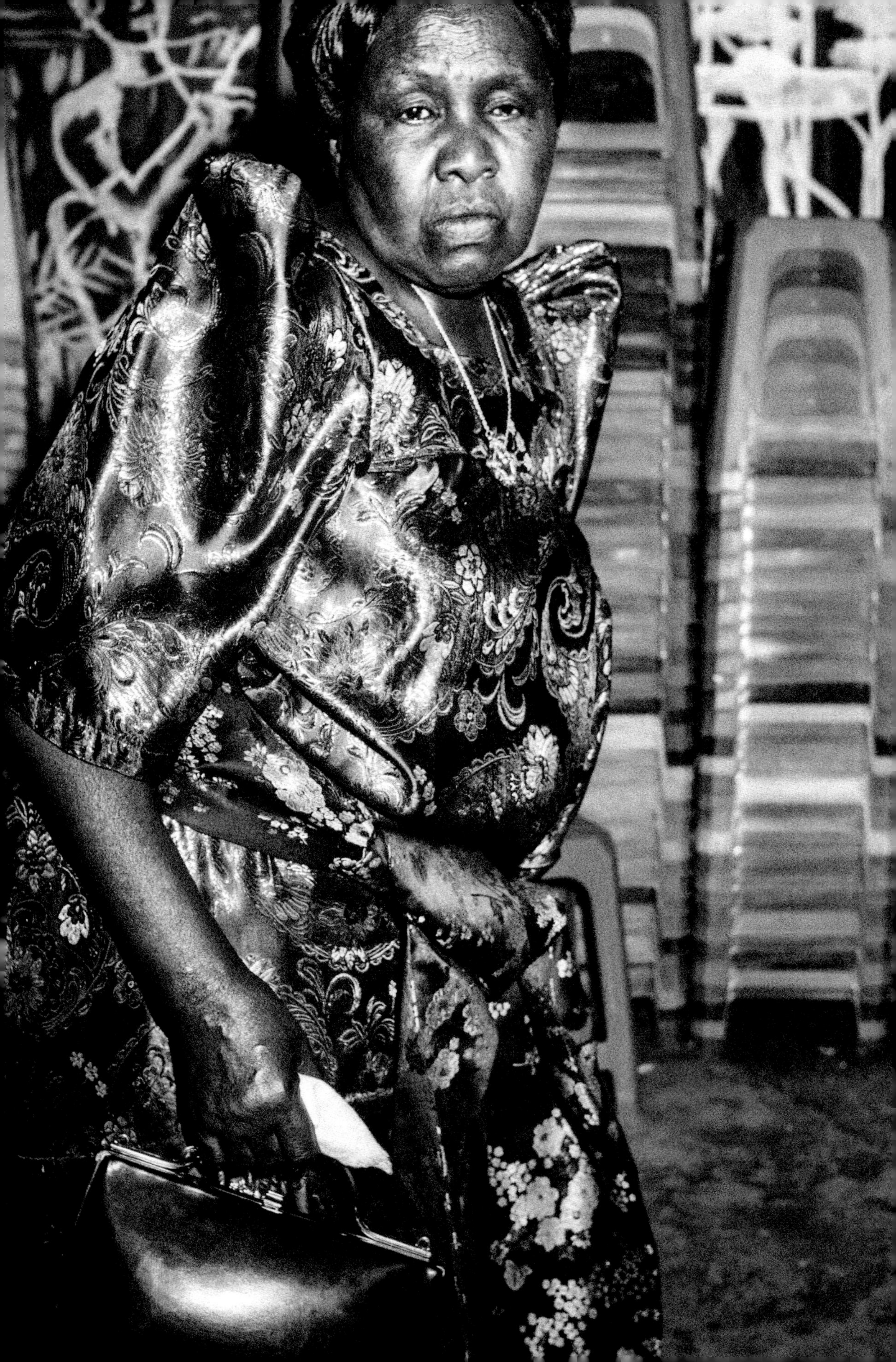

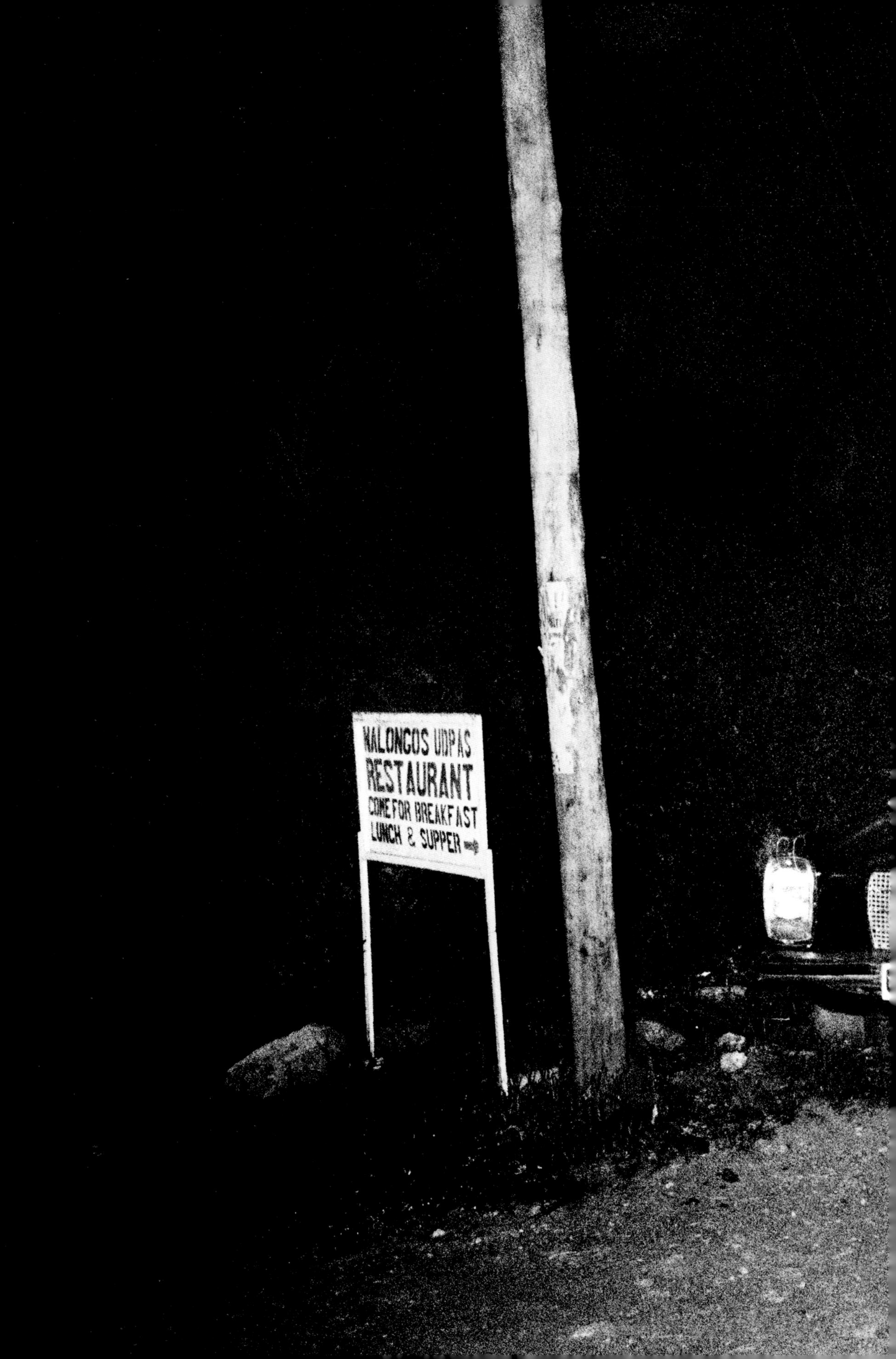
MALONGOS UDPAS
RESTAURANT
COME FOR BREAKFAST
LUNCH & SUPPER

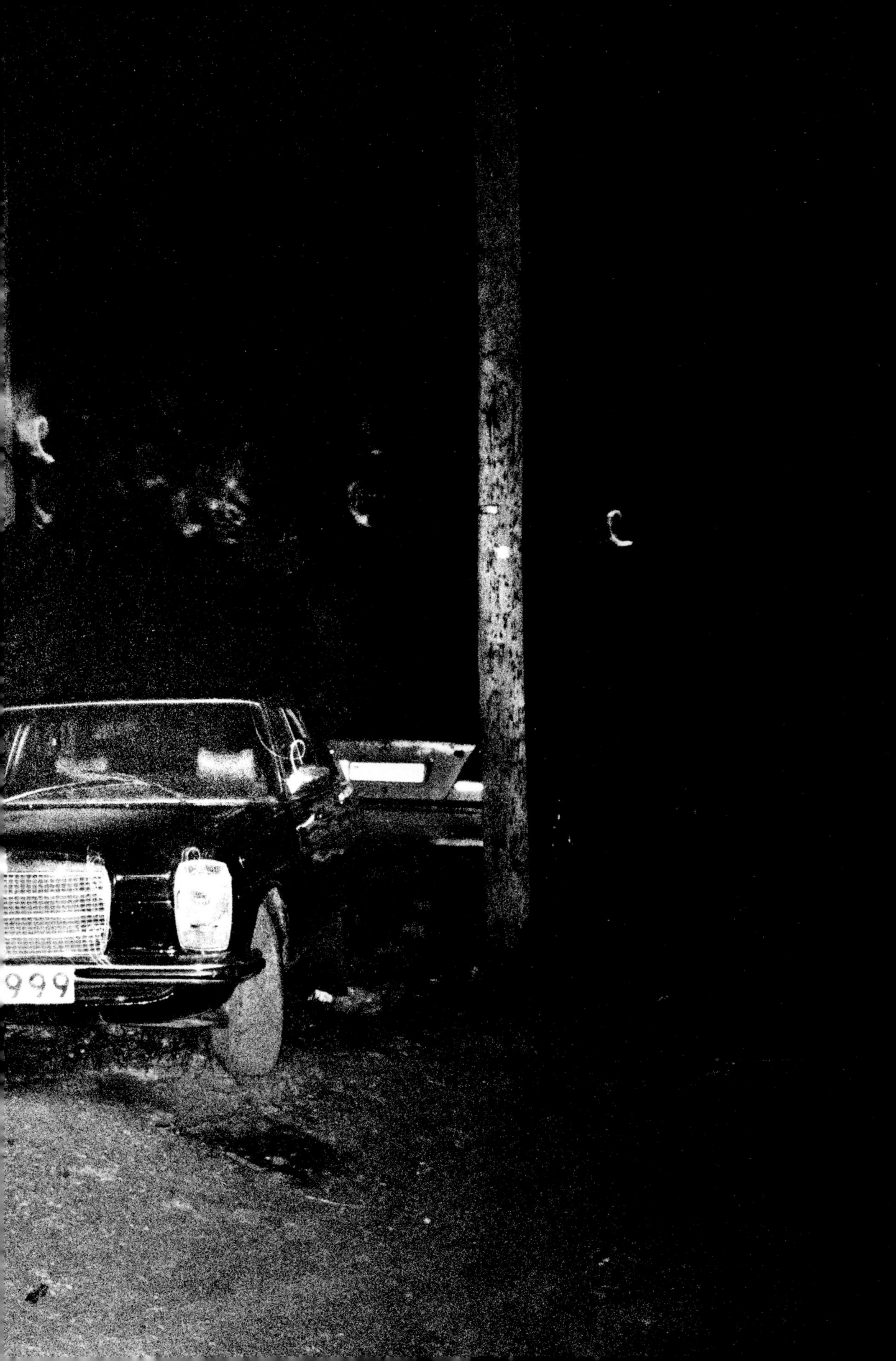
999

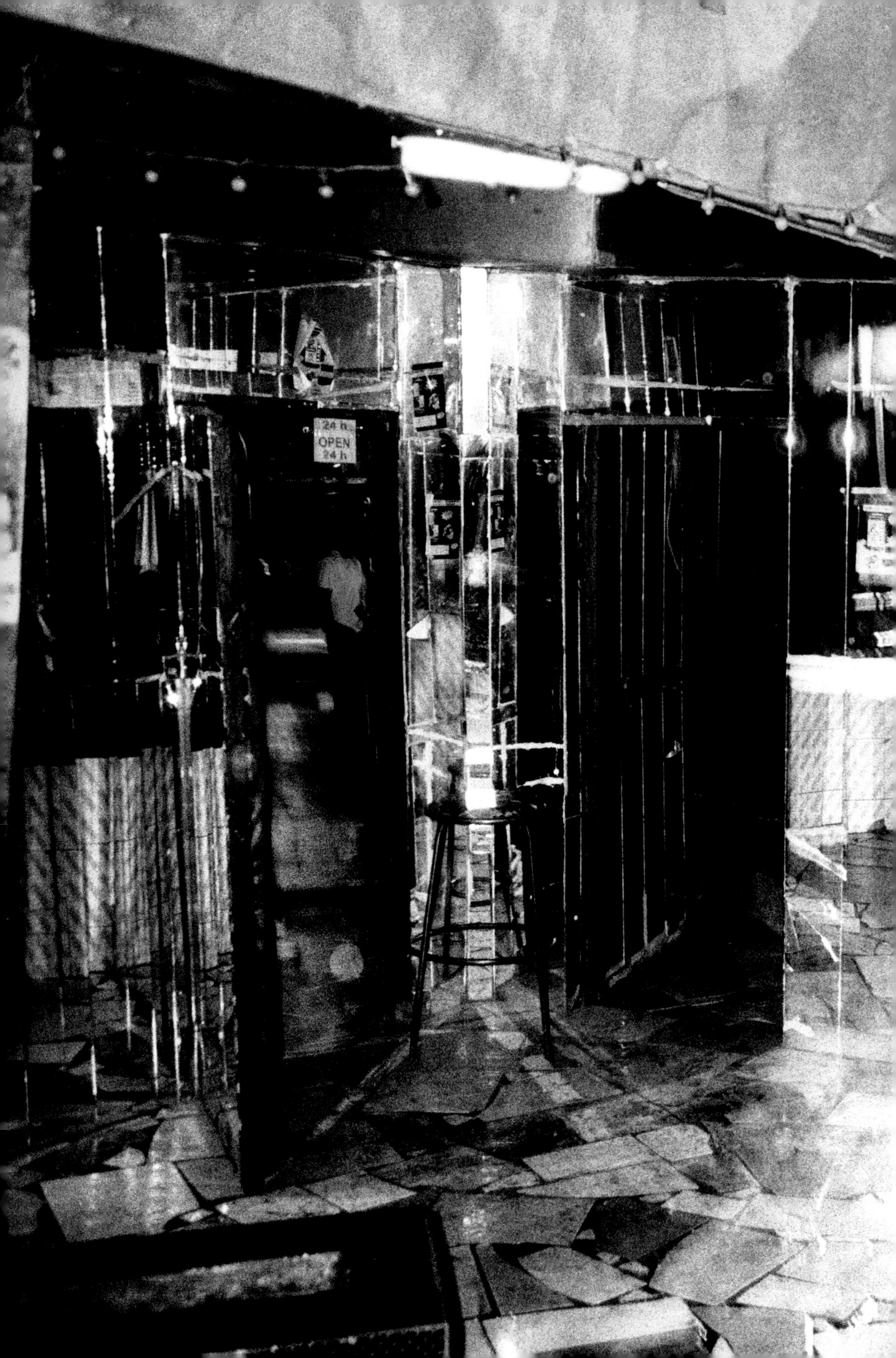
24 h
OPEN
24 h

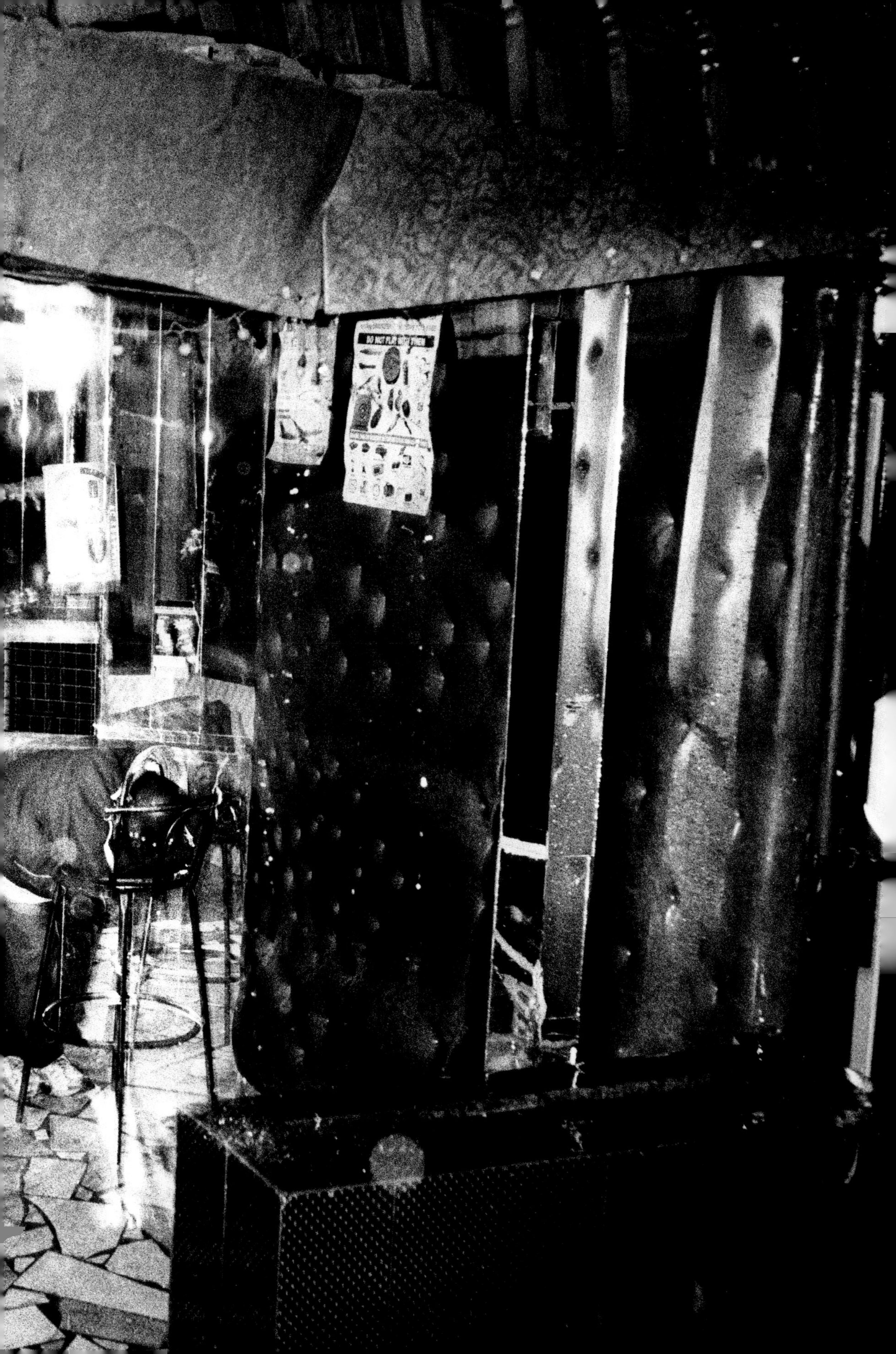

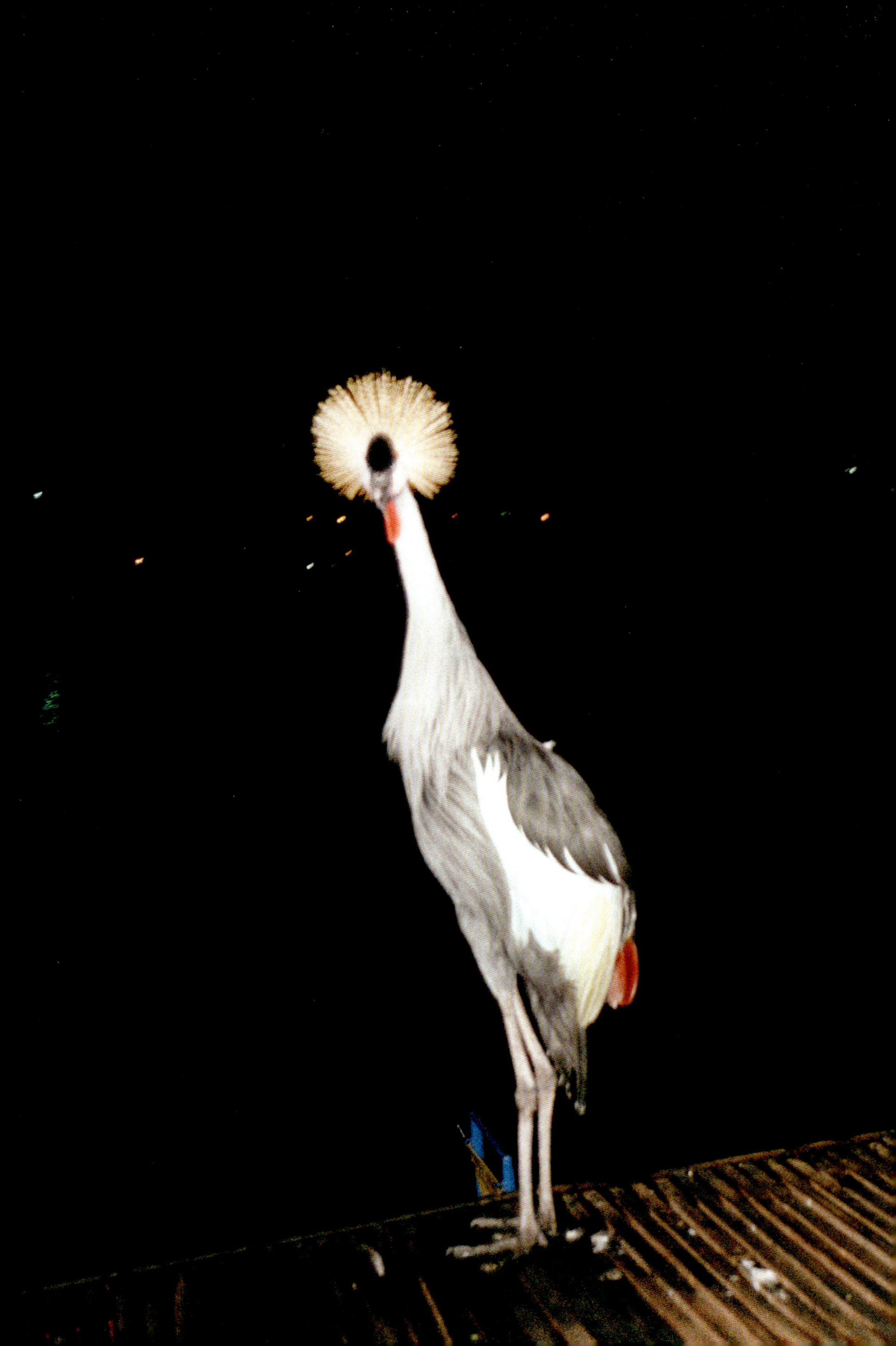

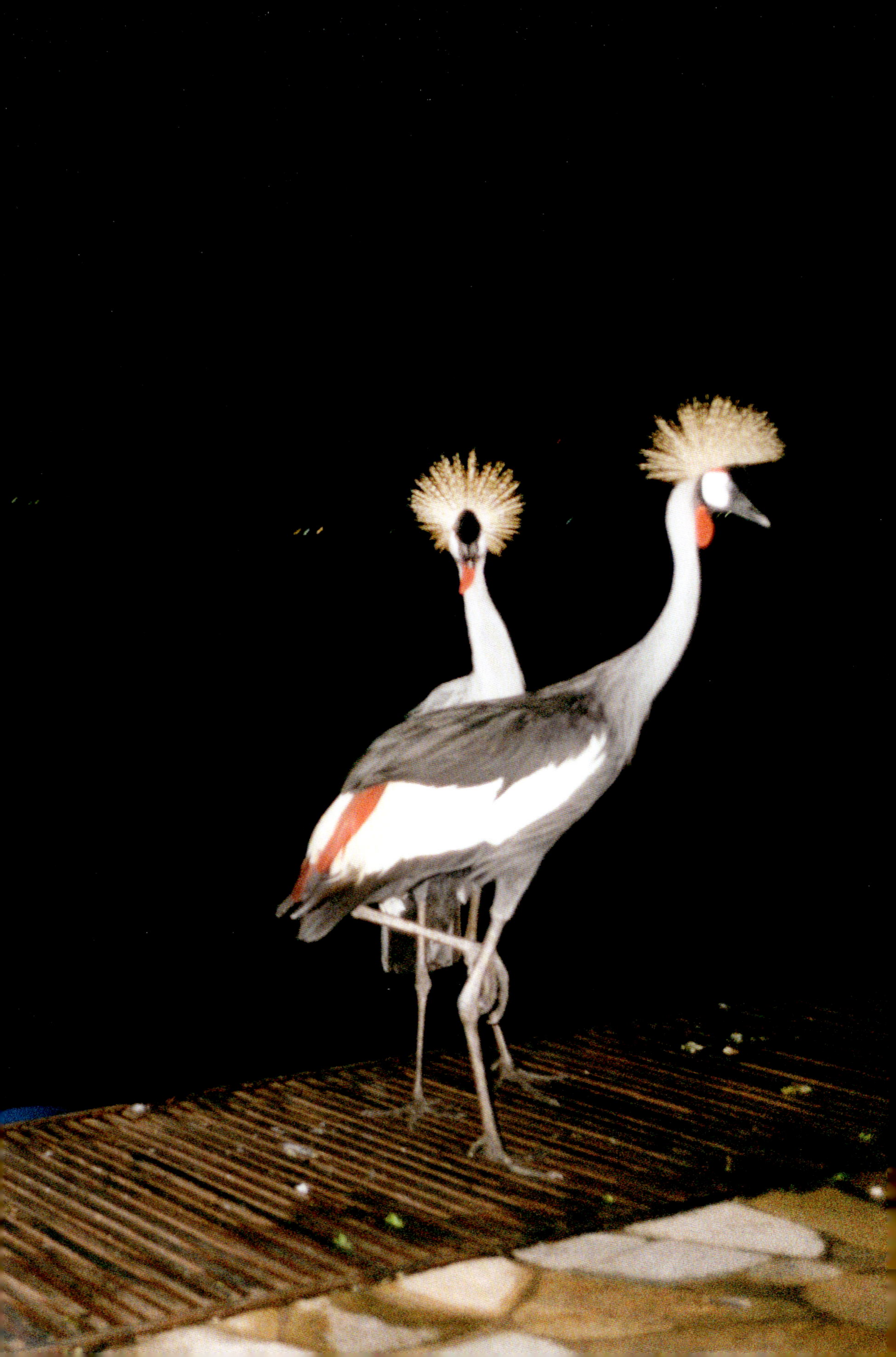

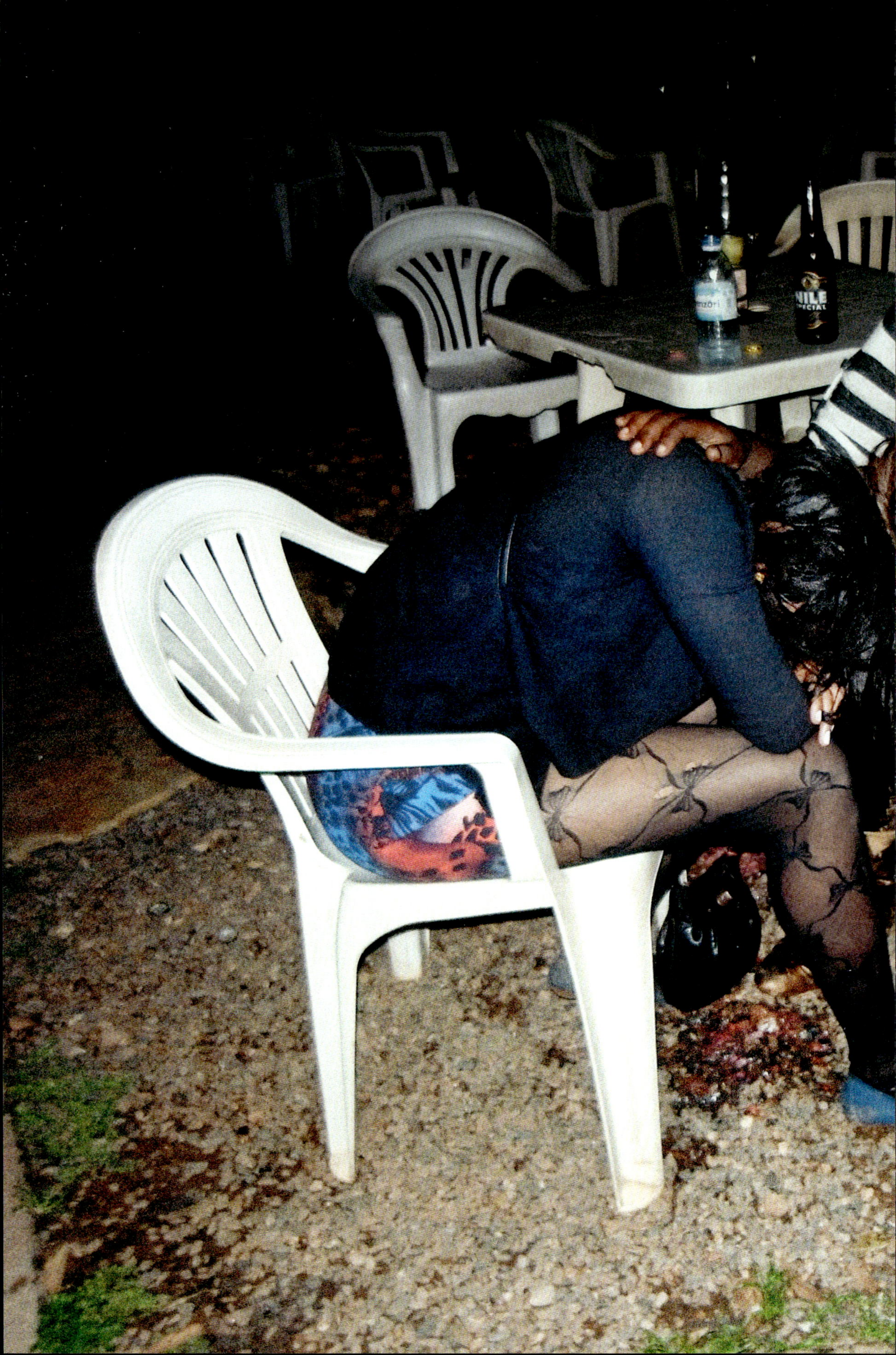
NILE

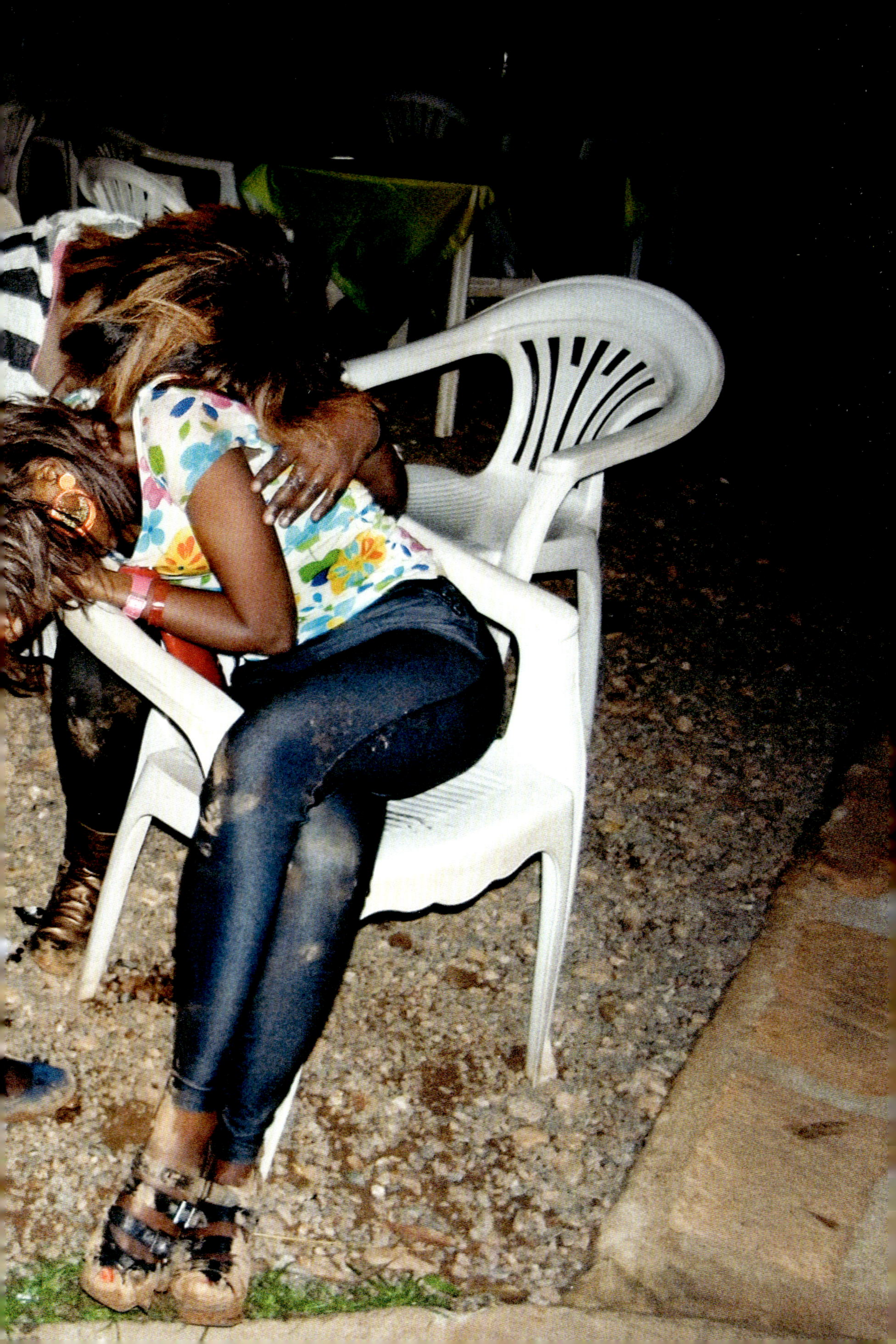

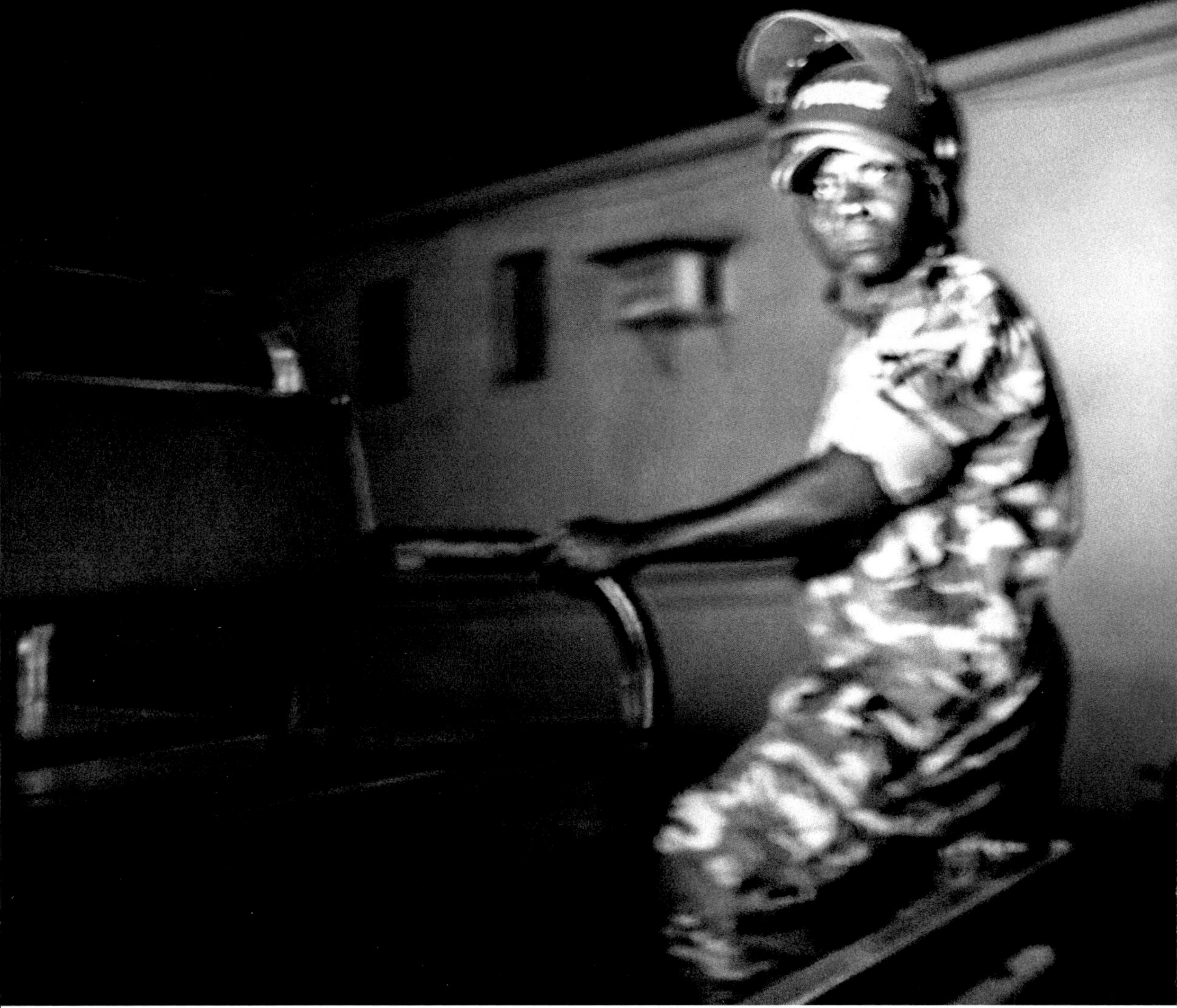

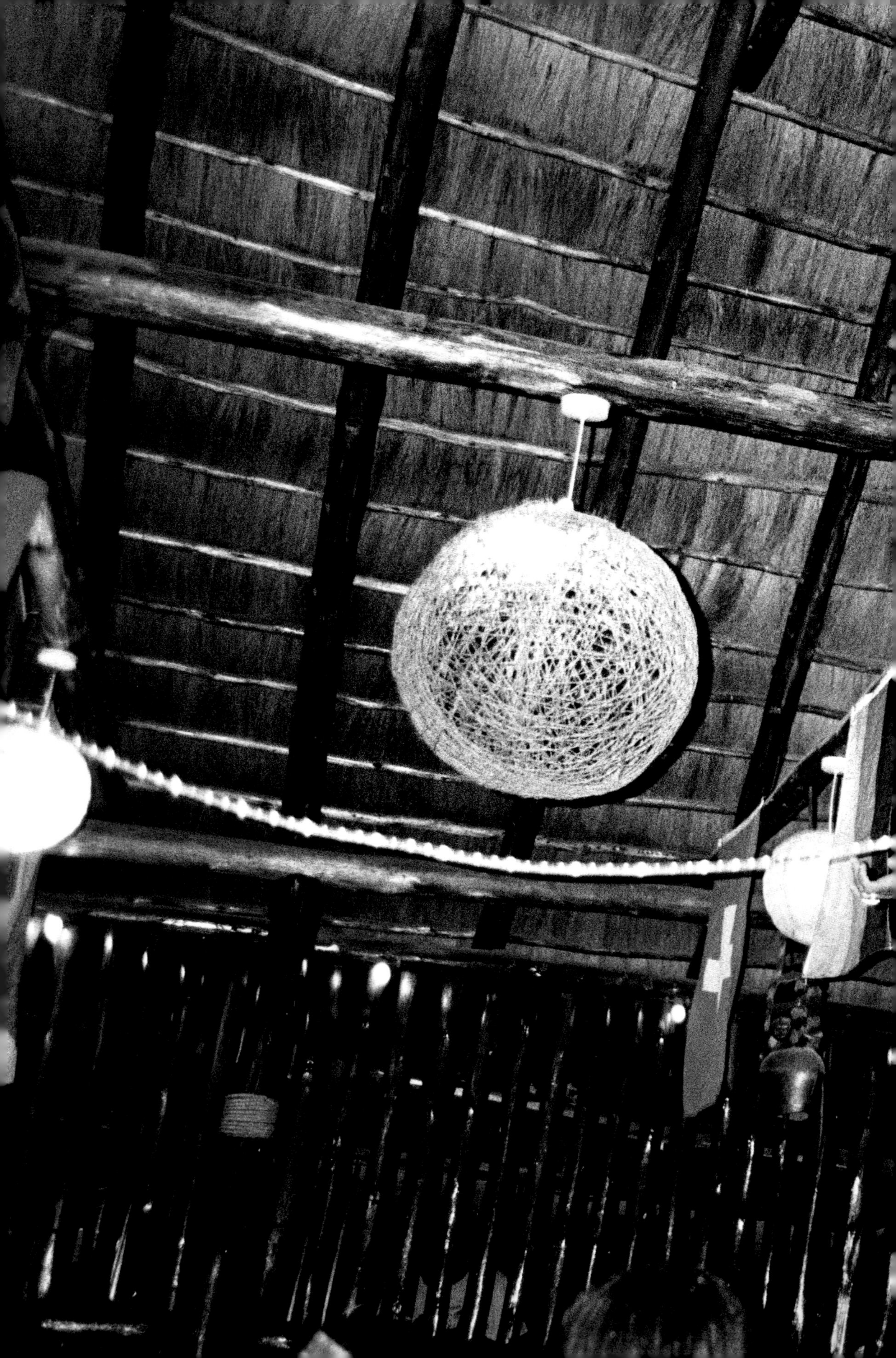

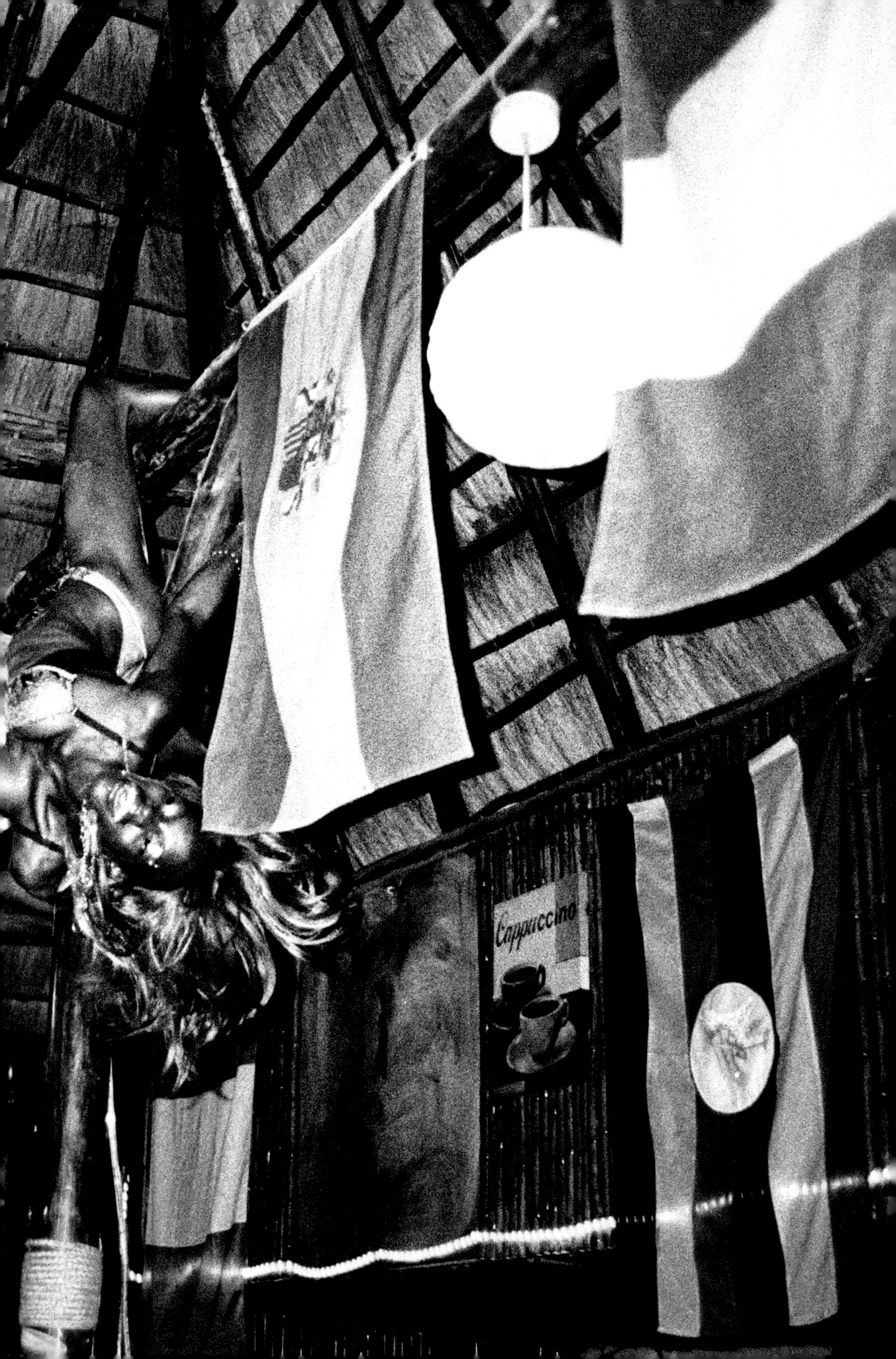
Cappuccino

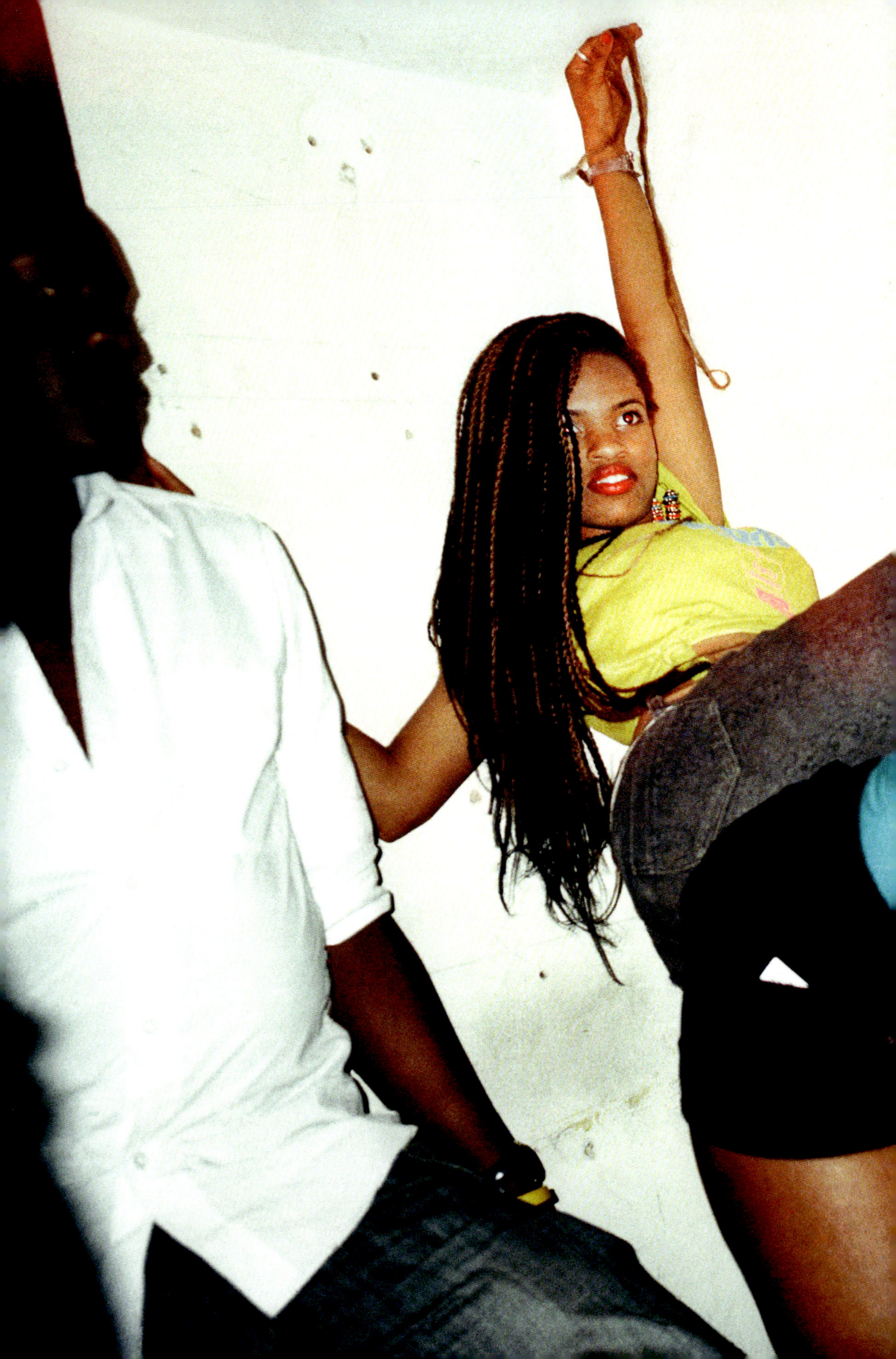

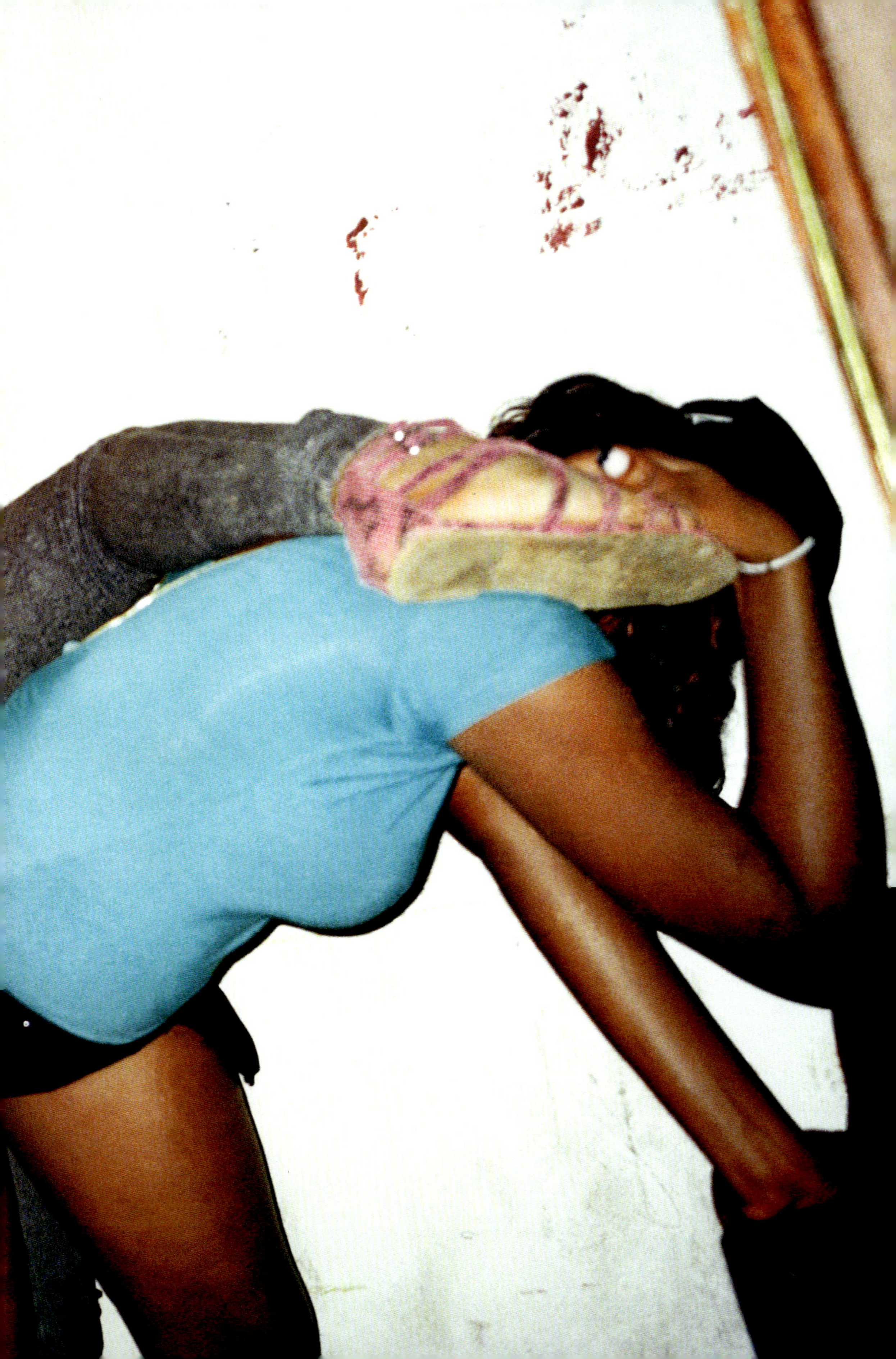

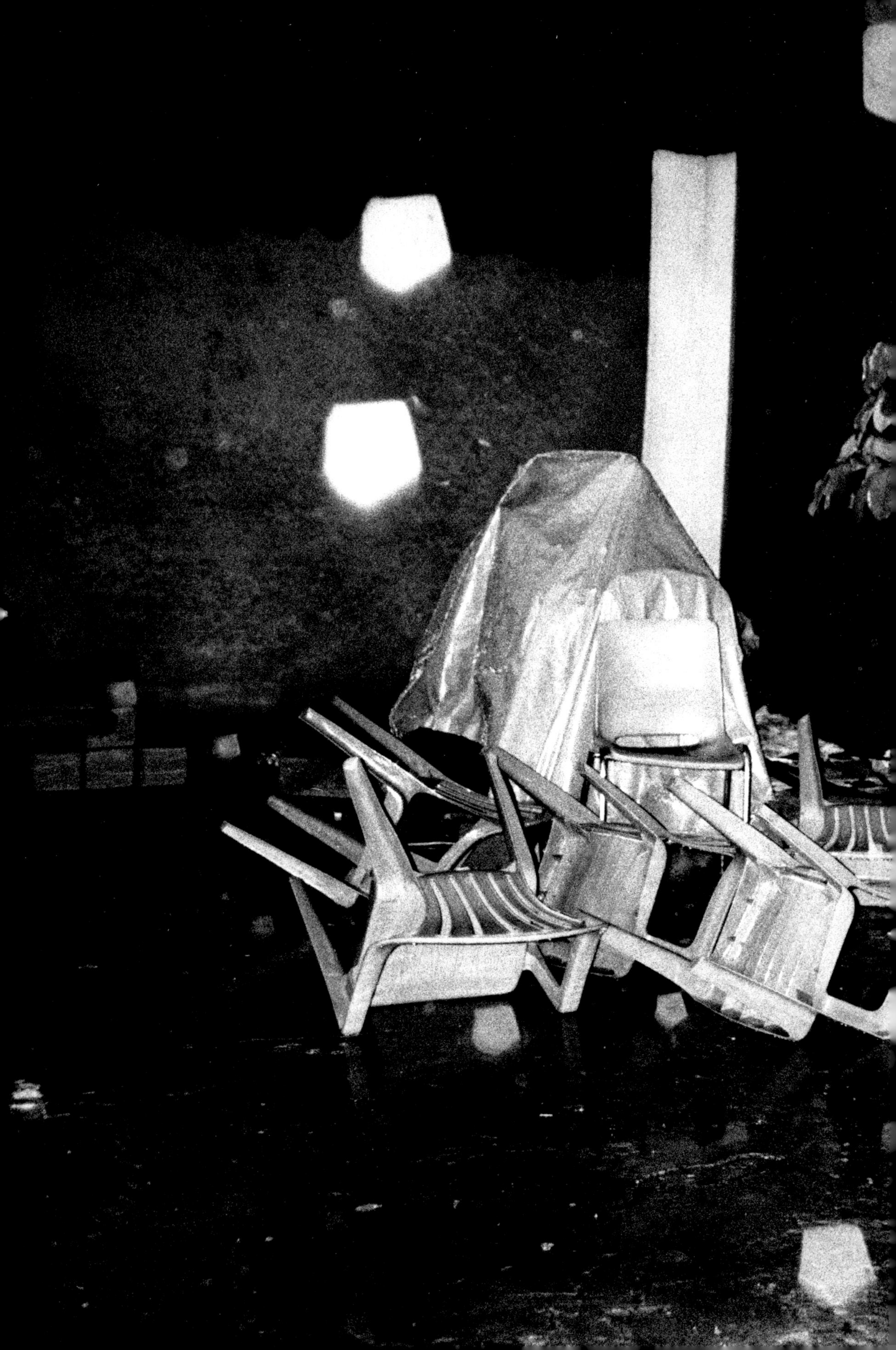

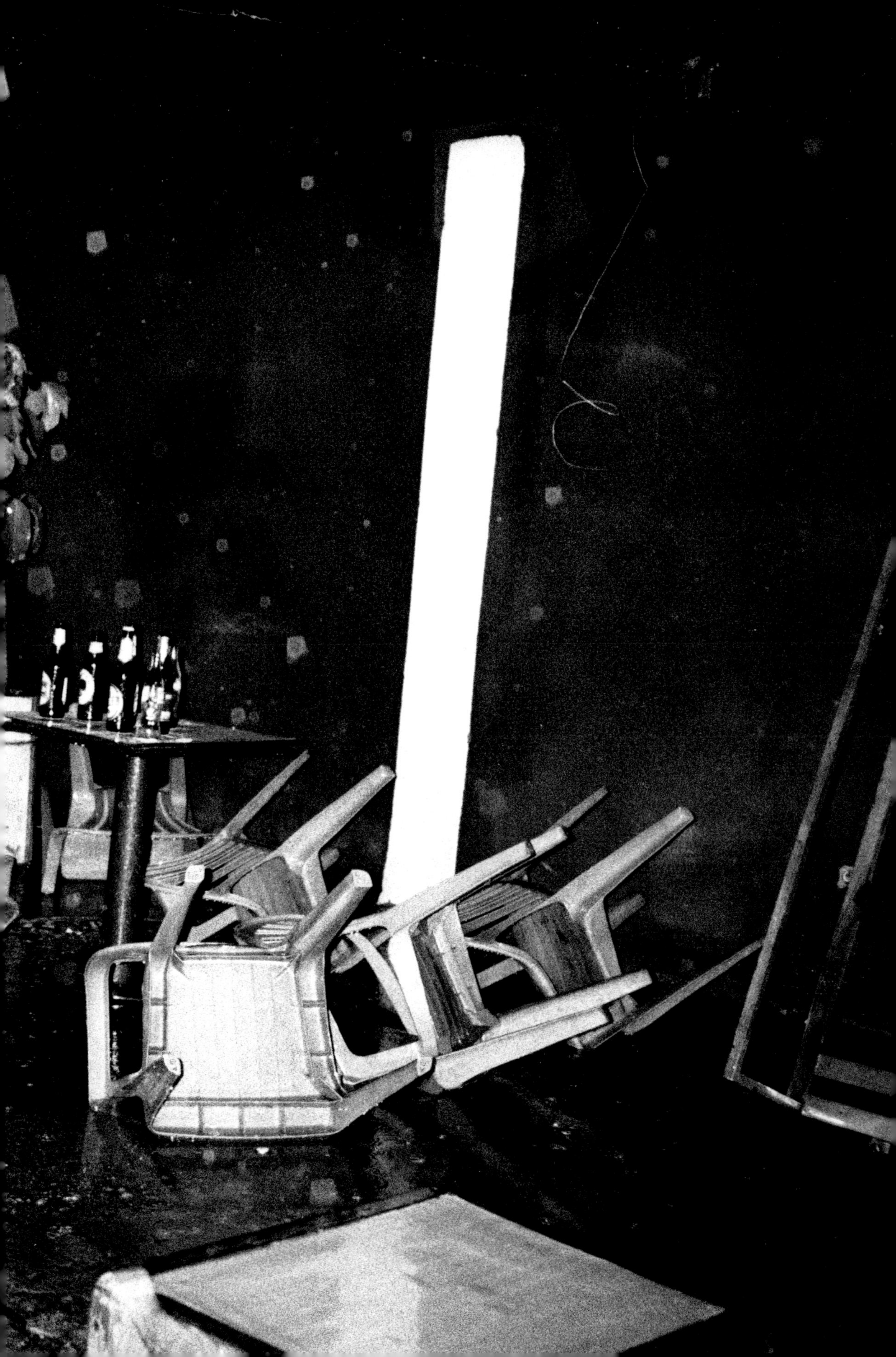

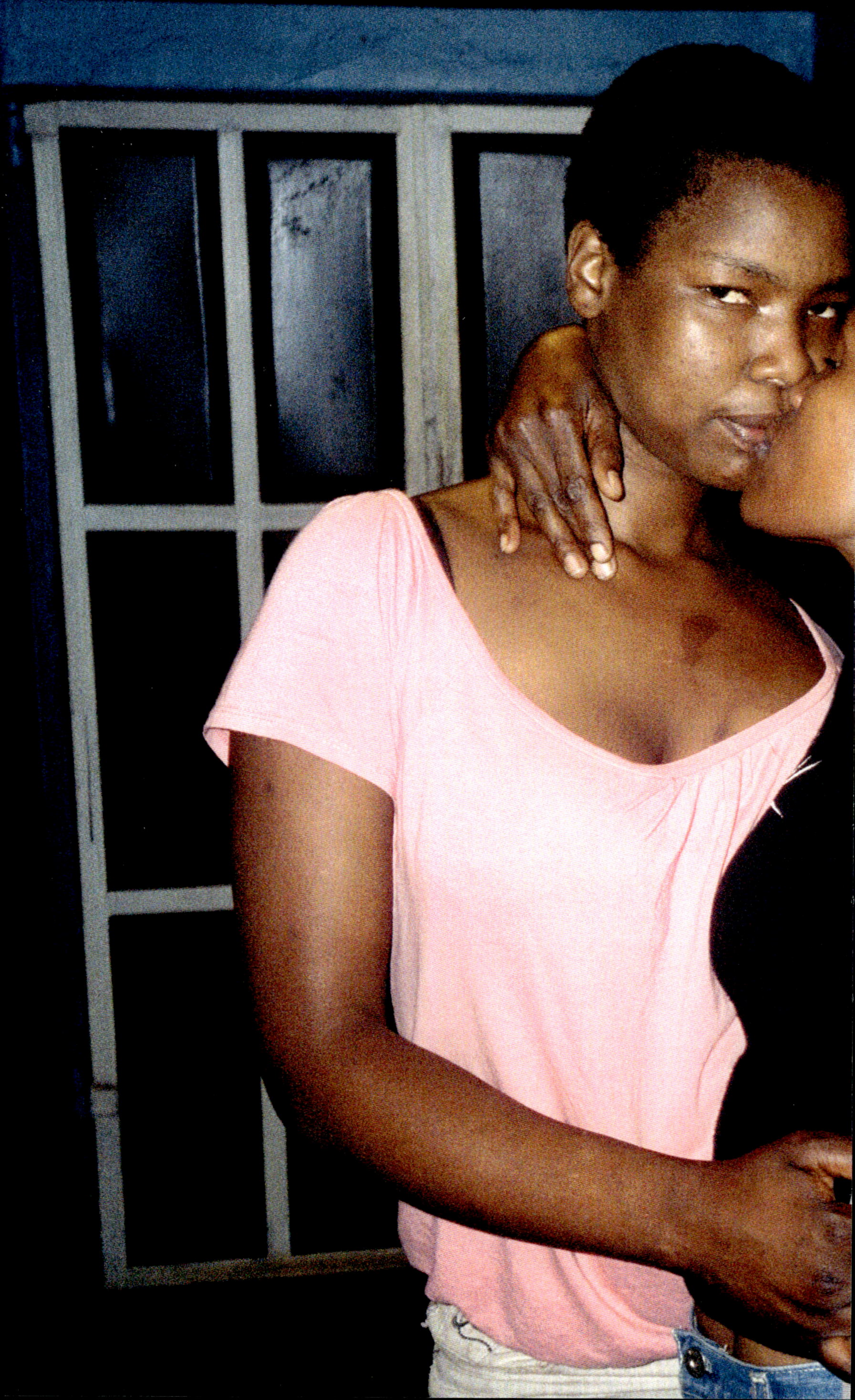

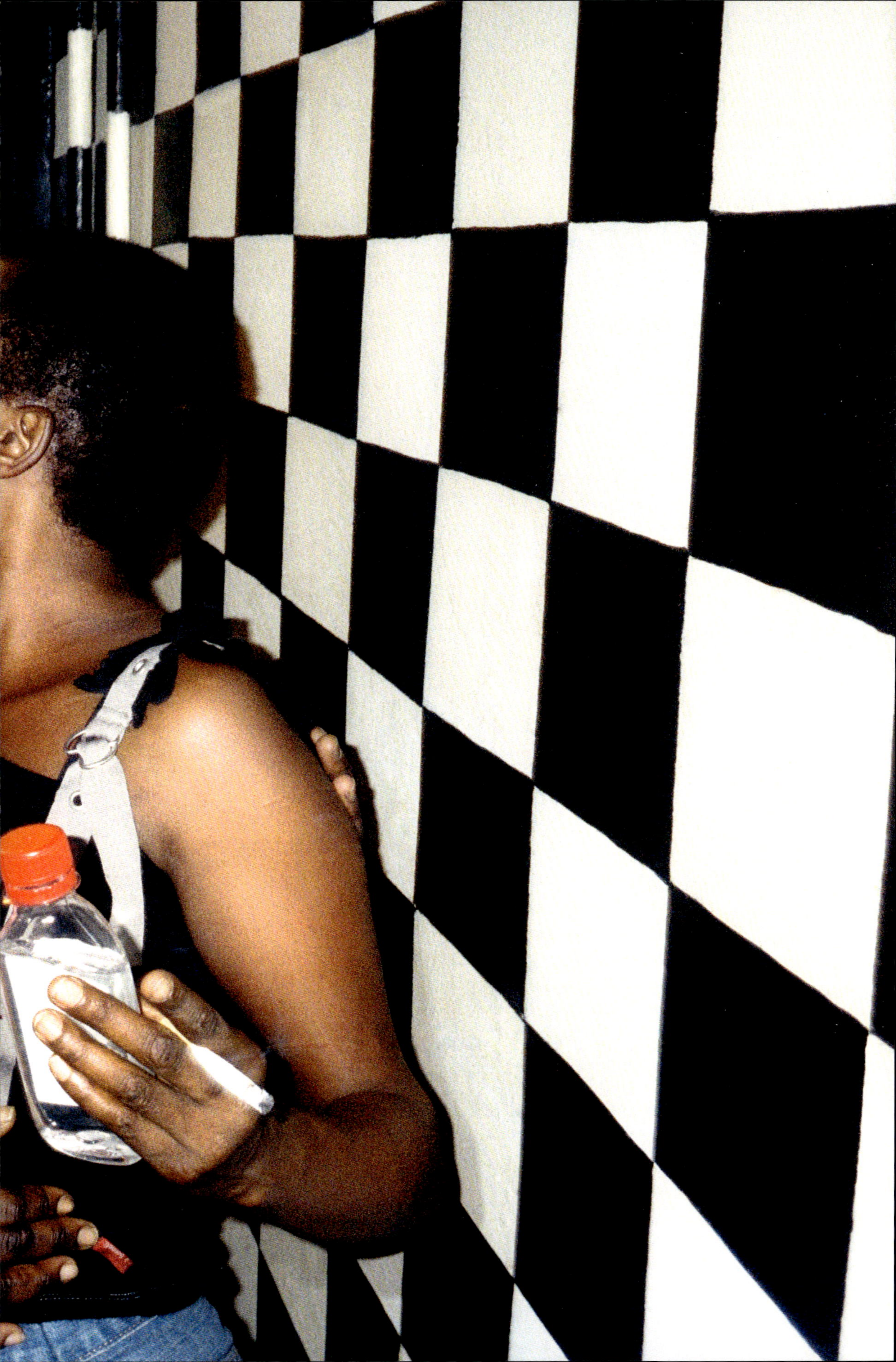

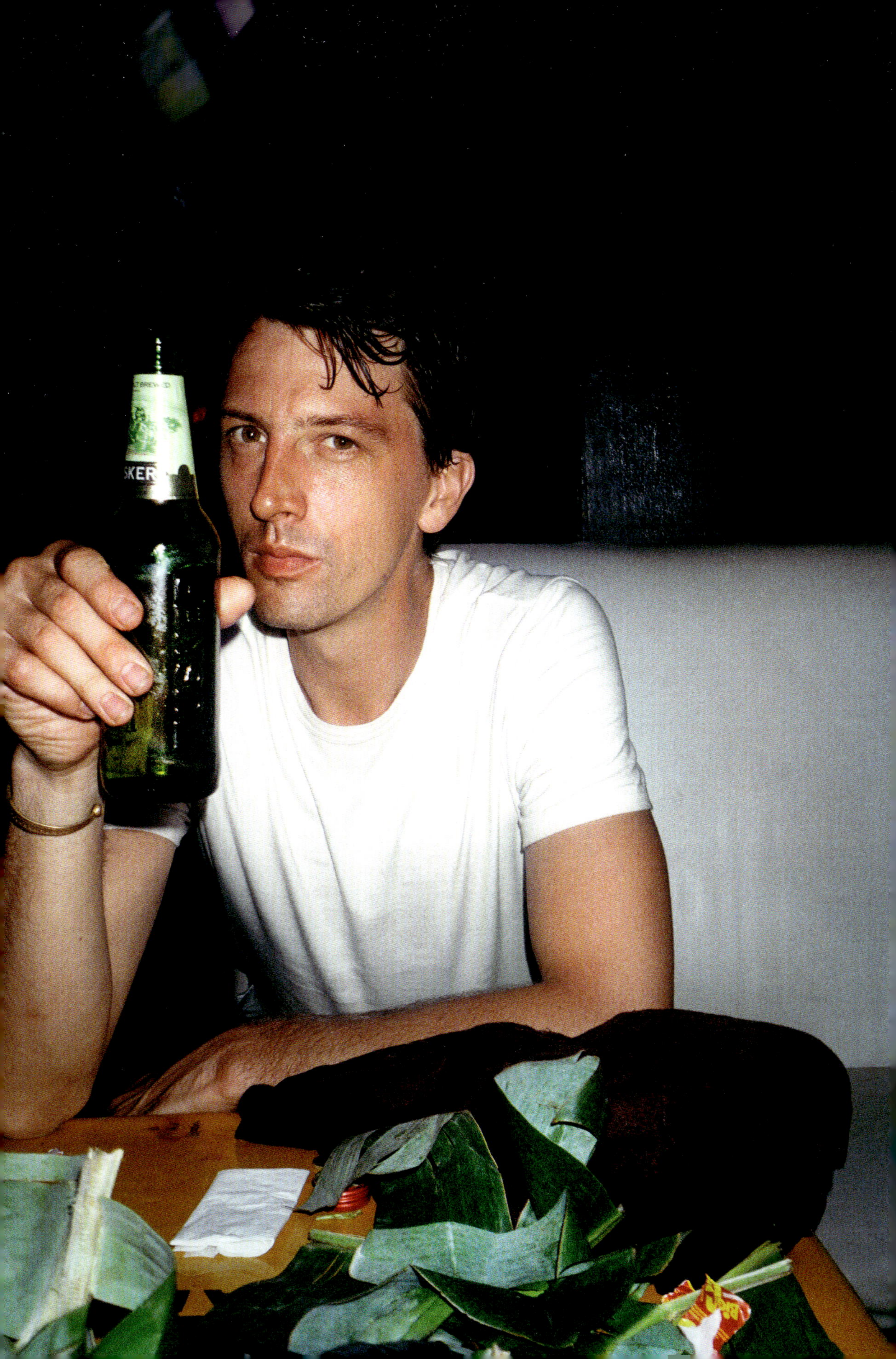

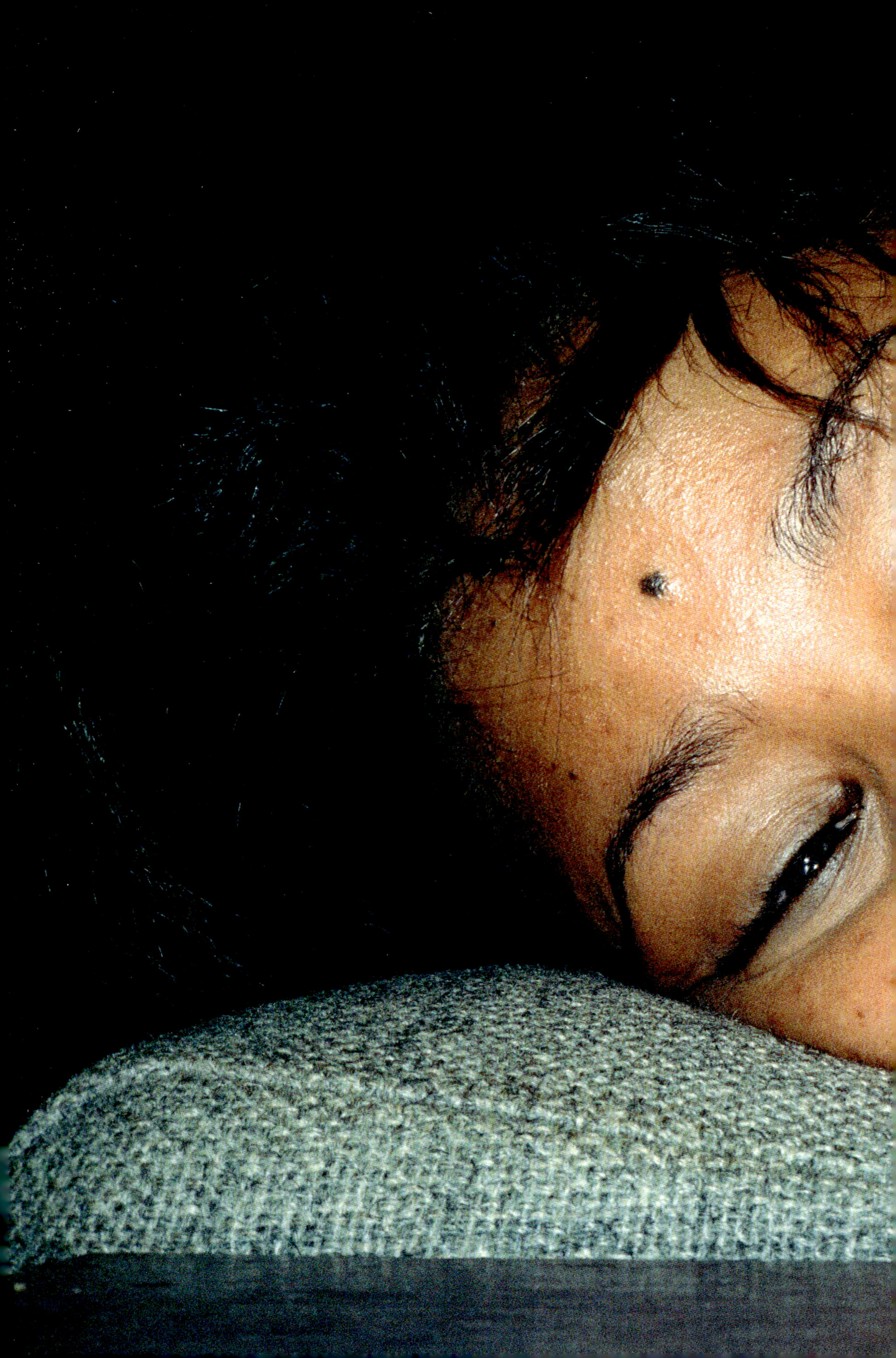

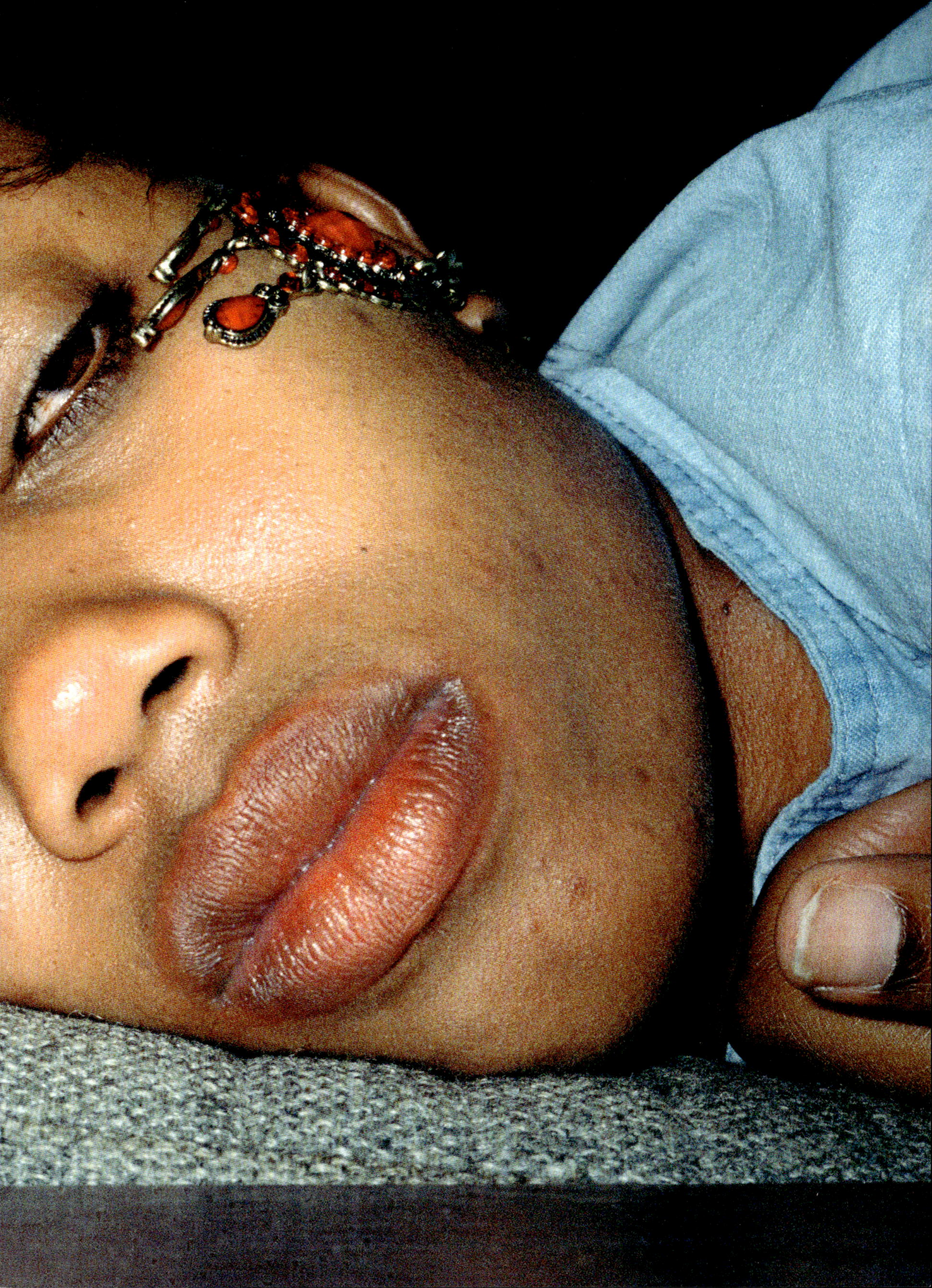

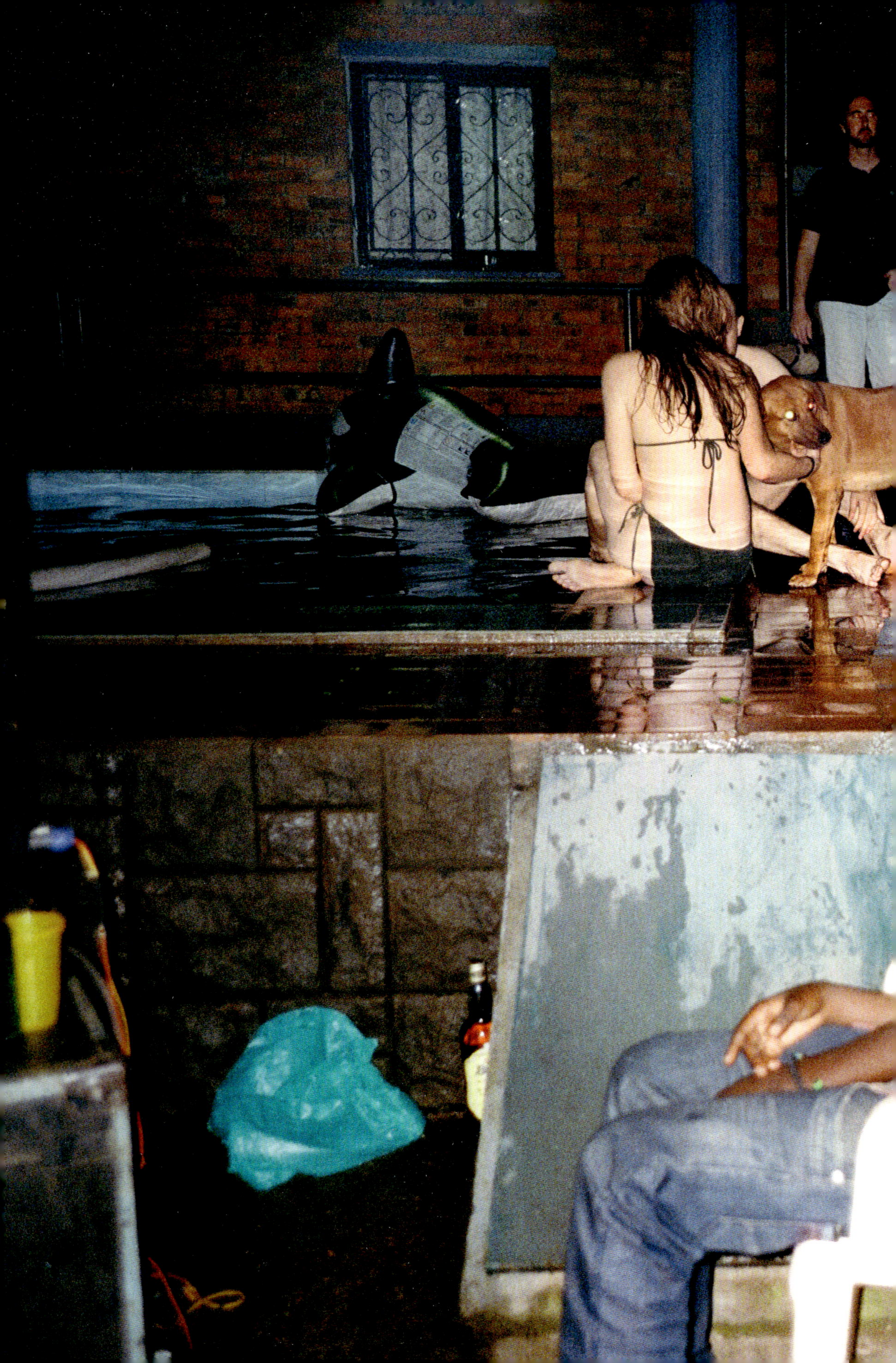

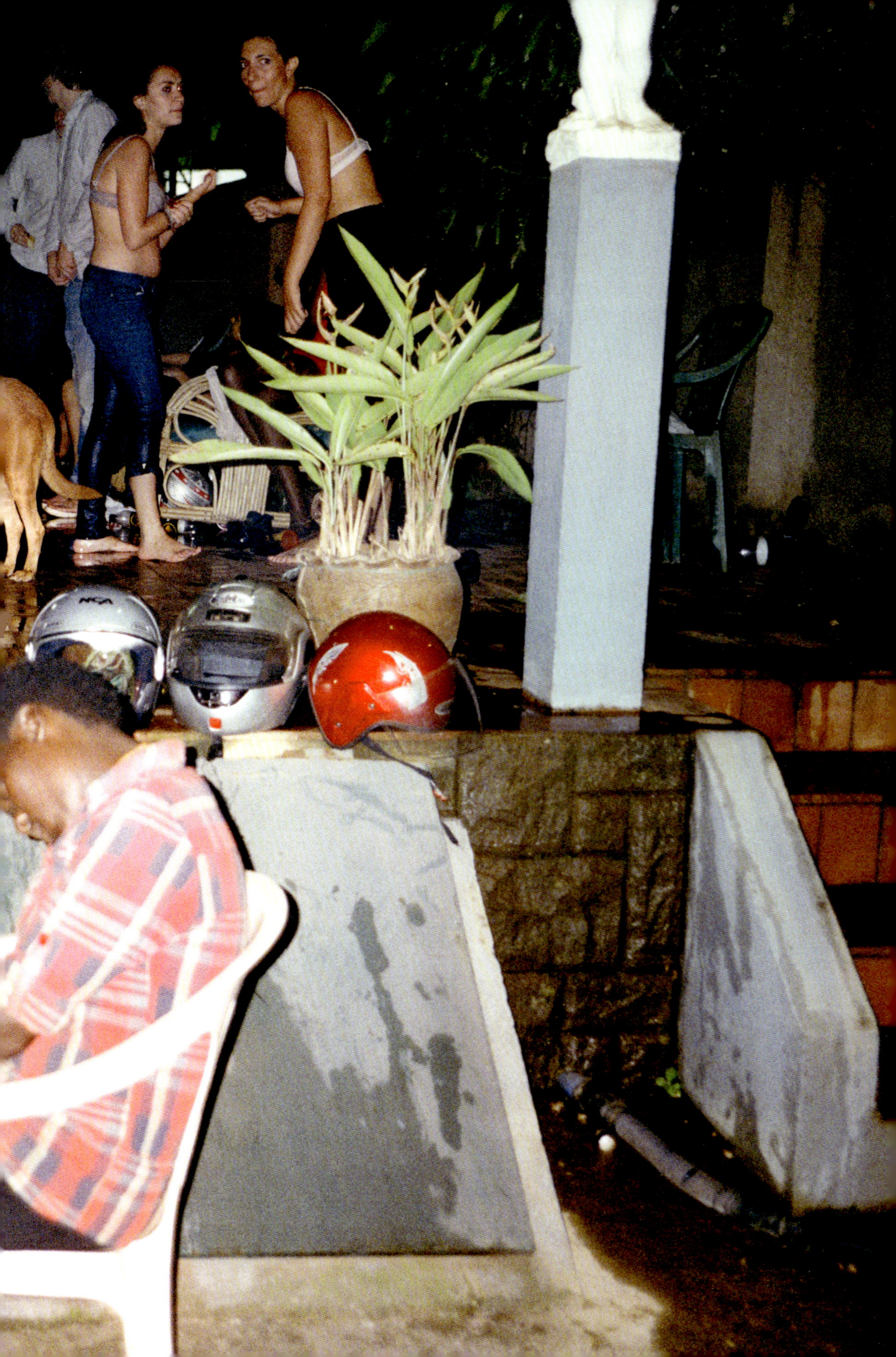

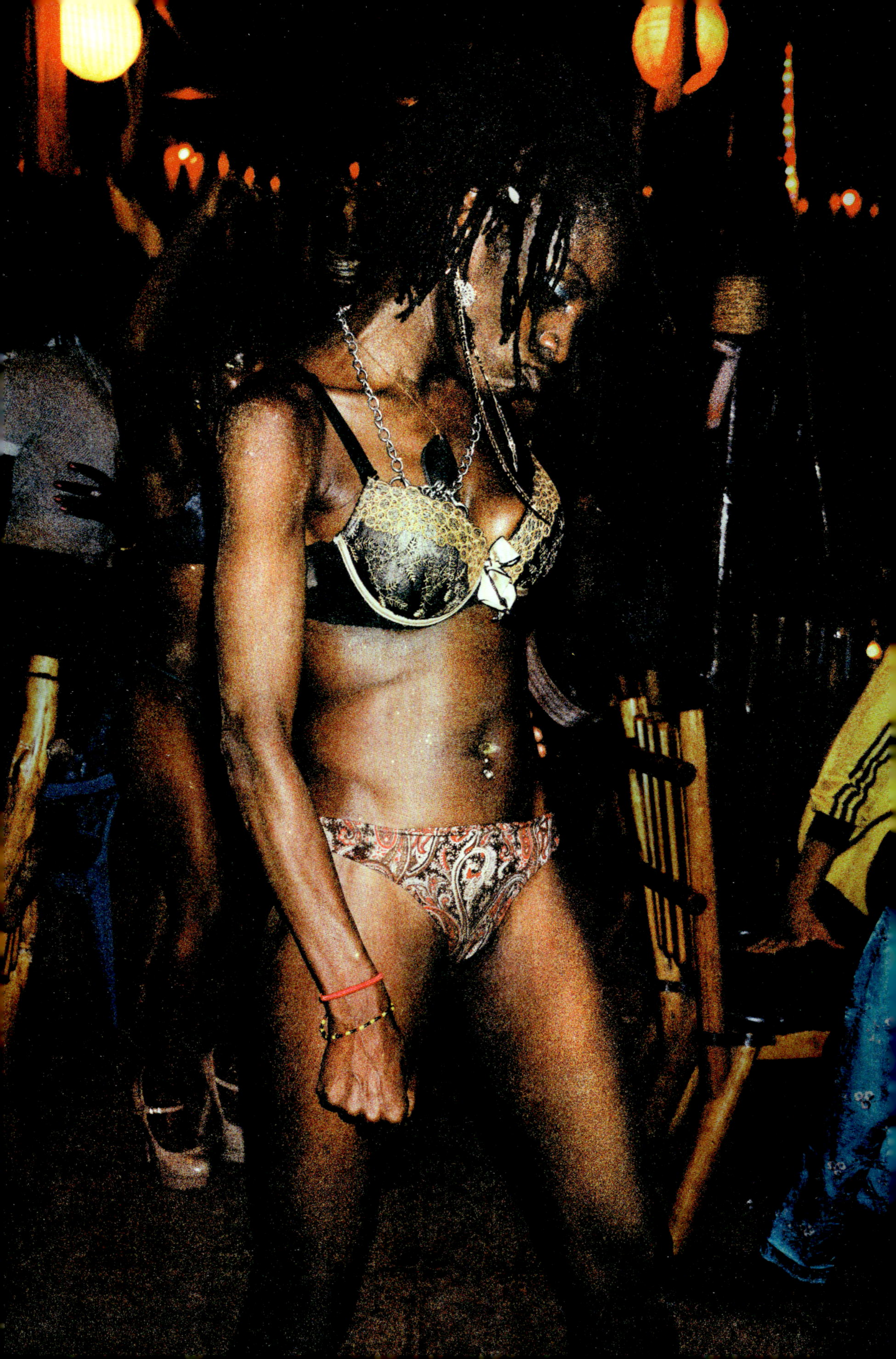

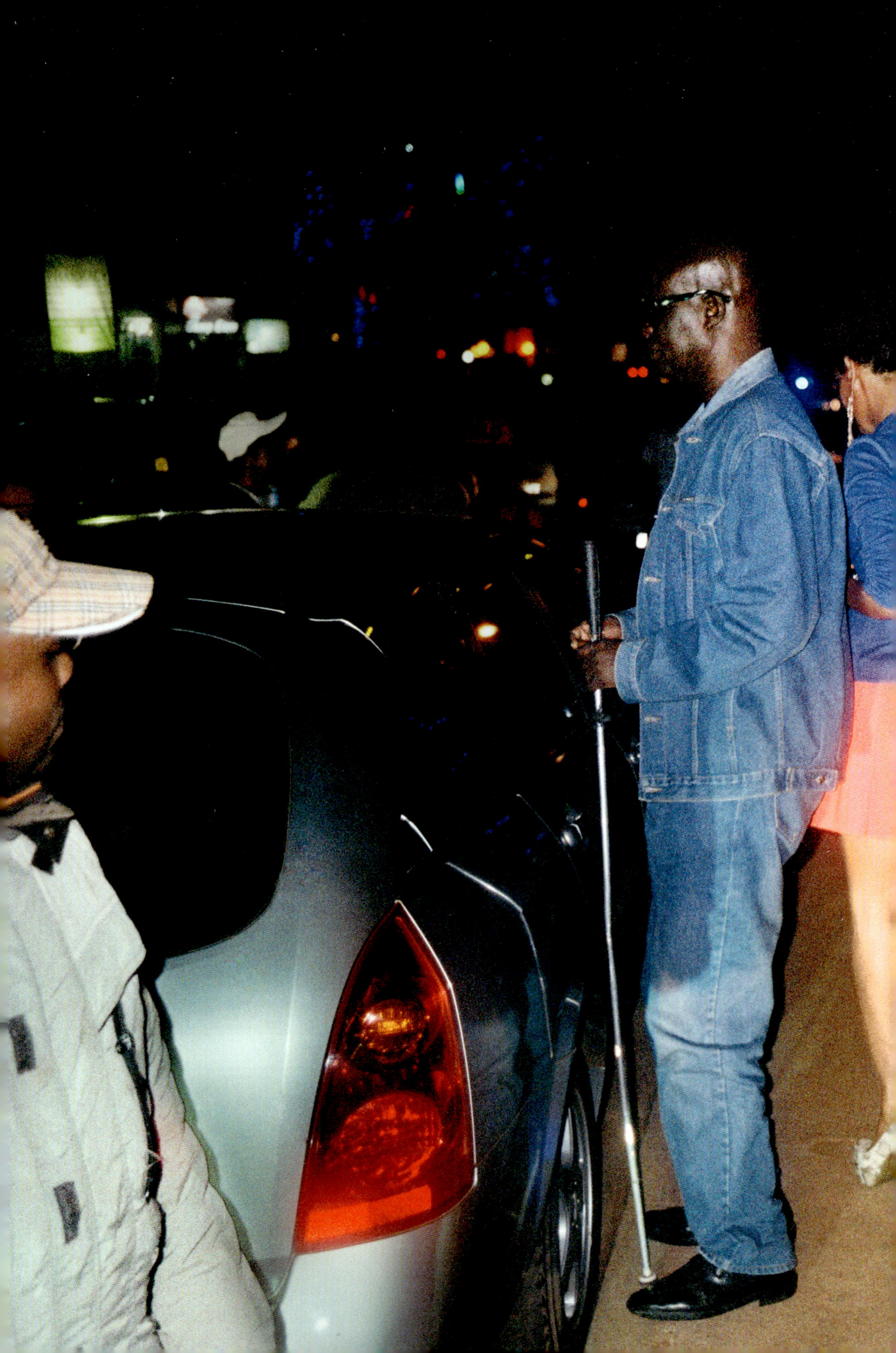

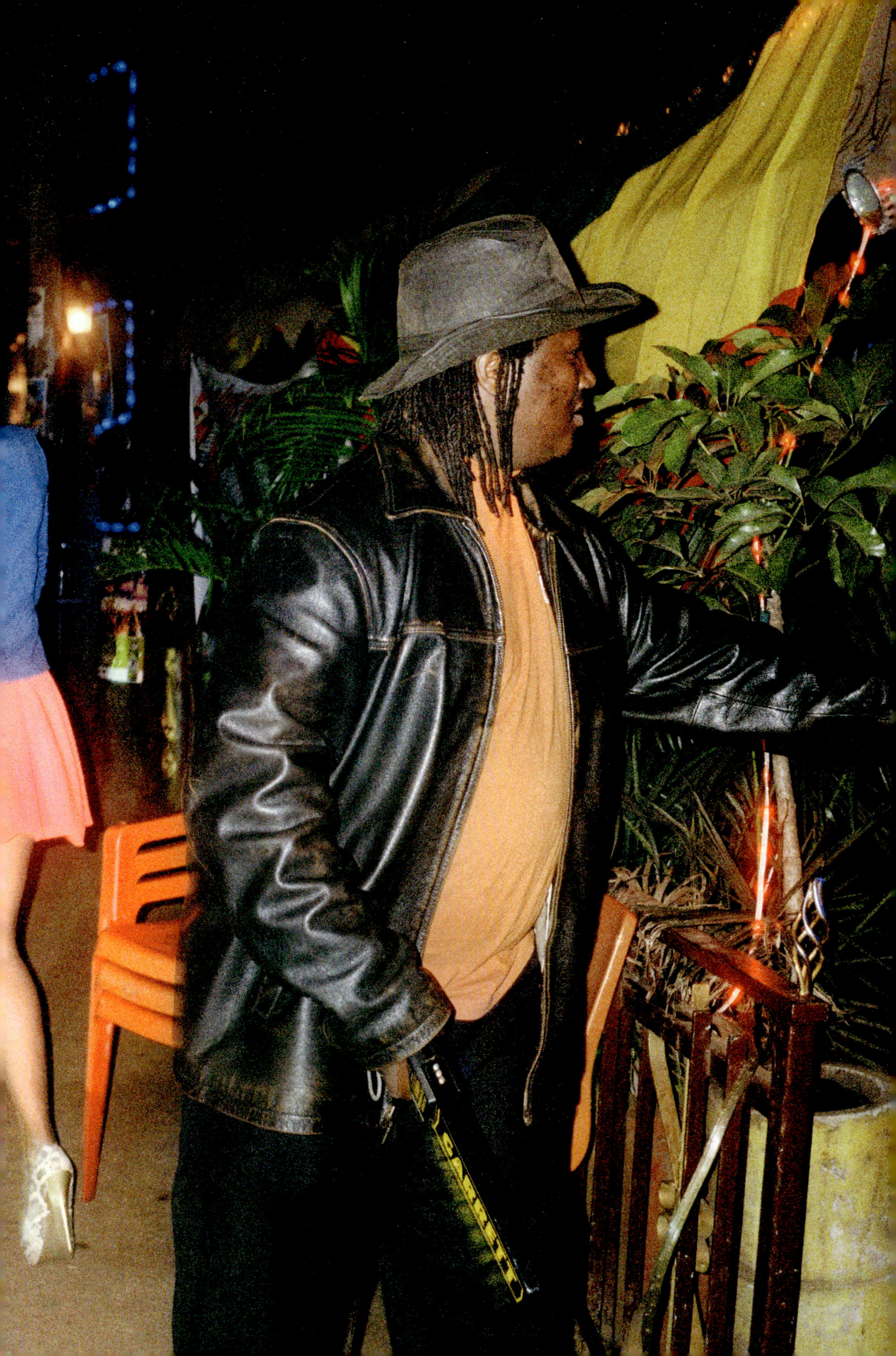

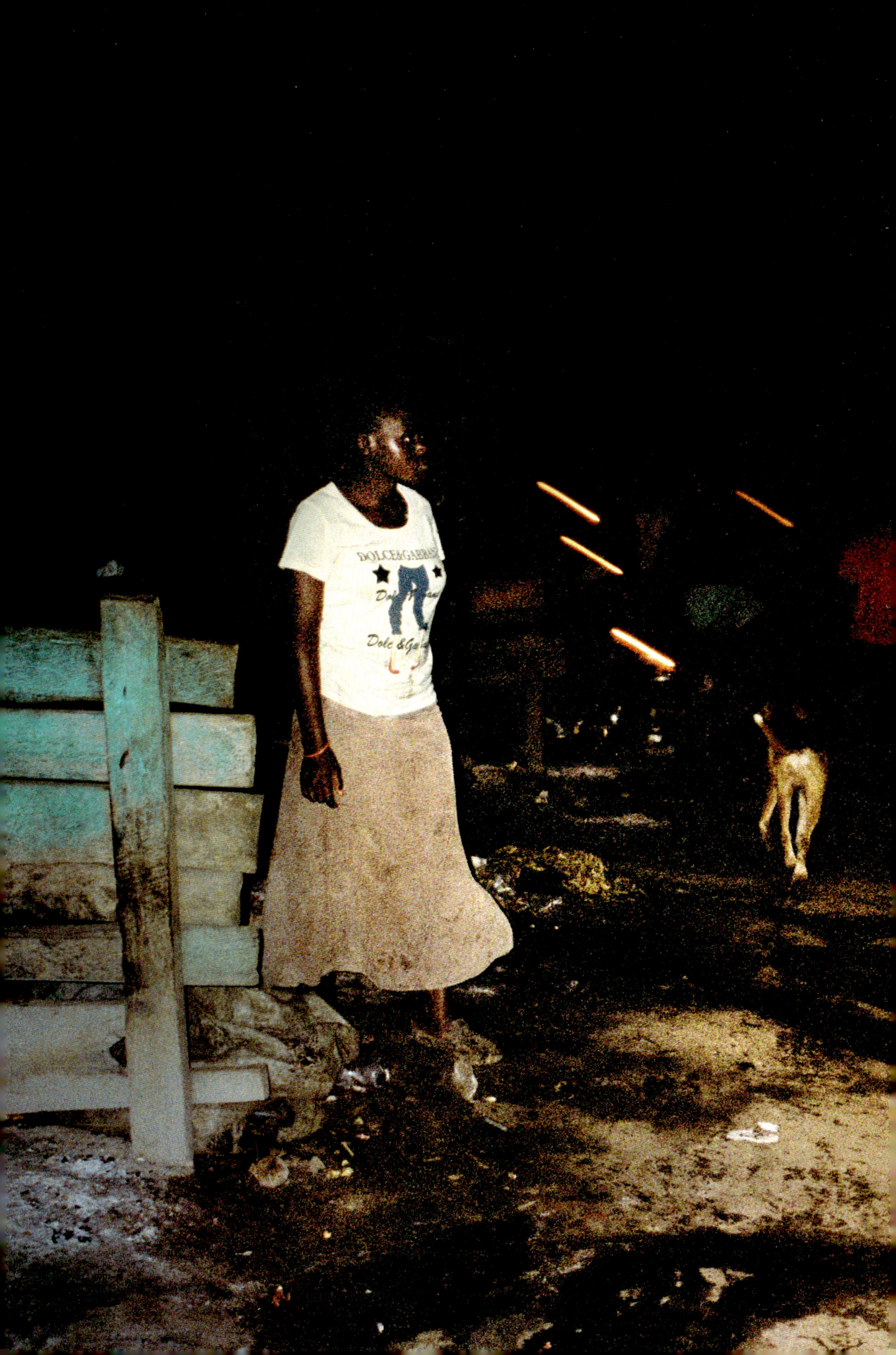

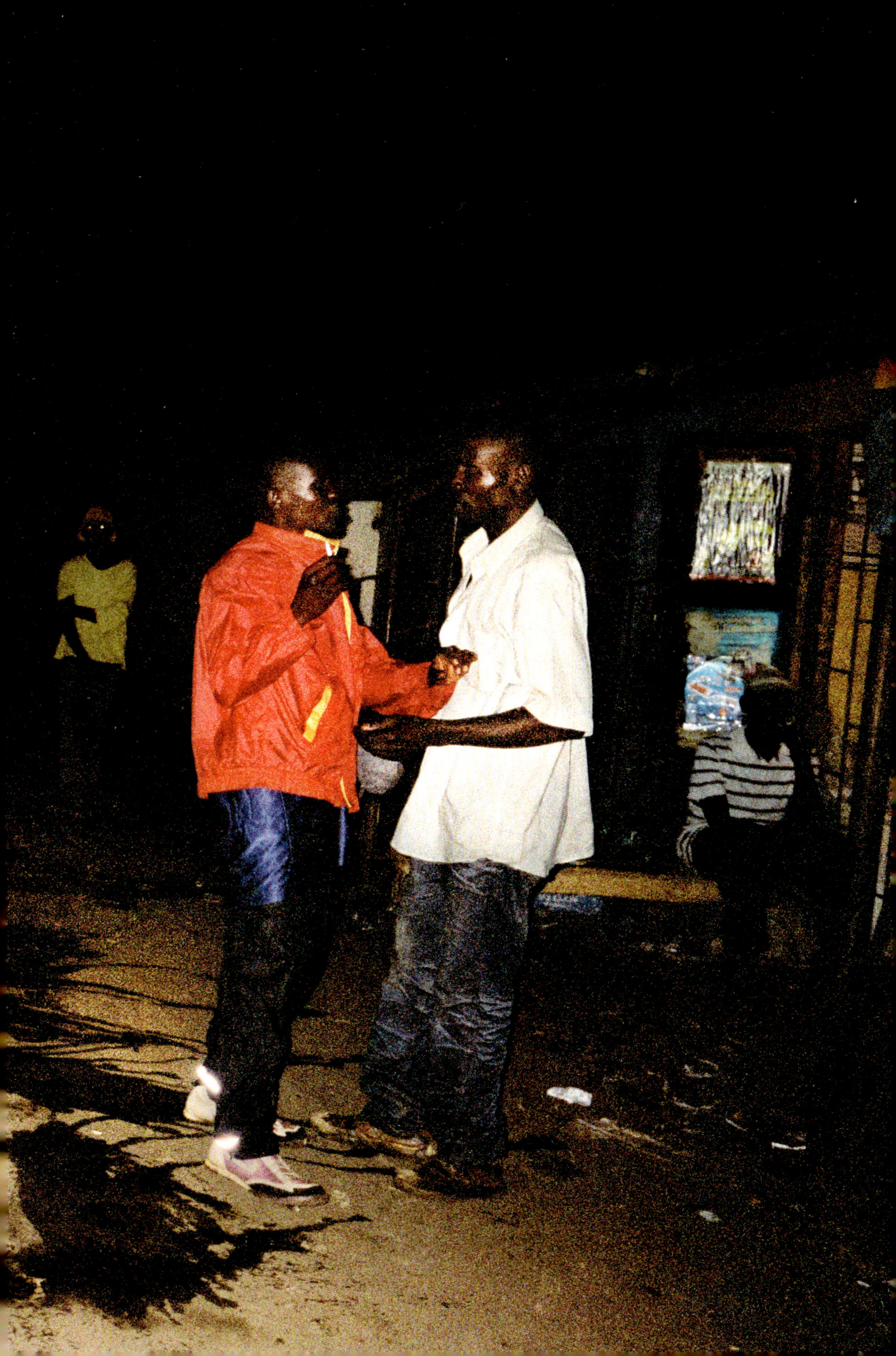

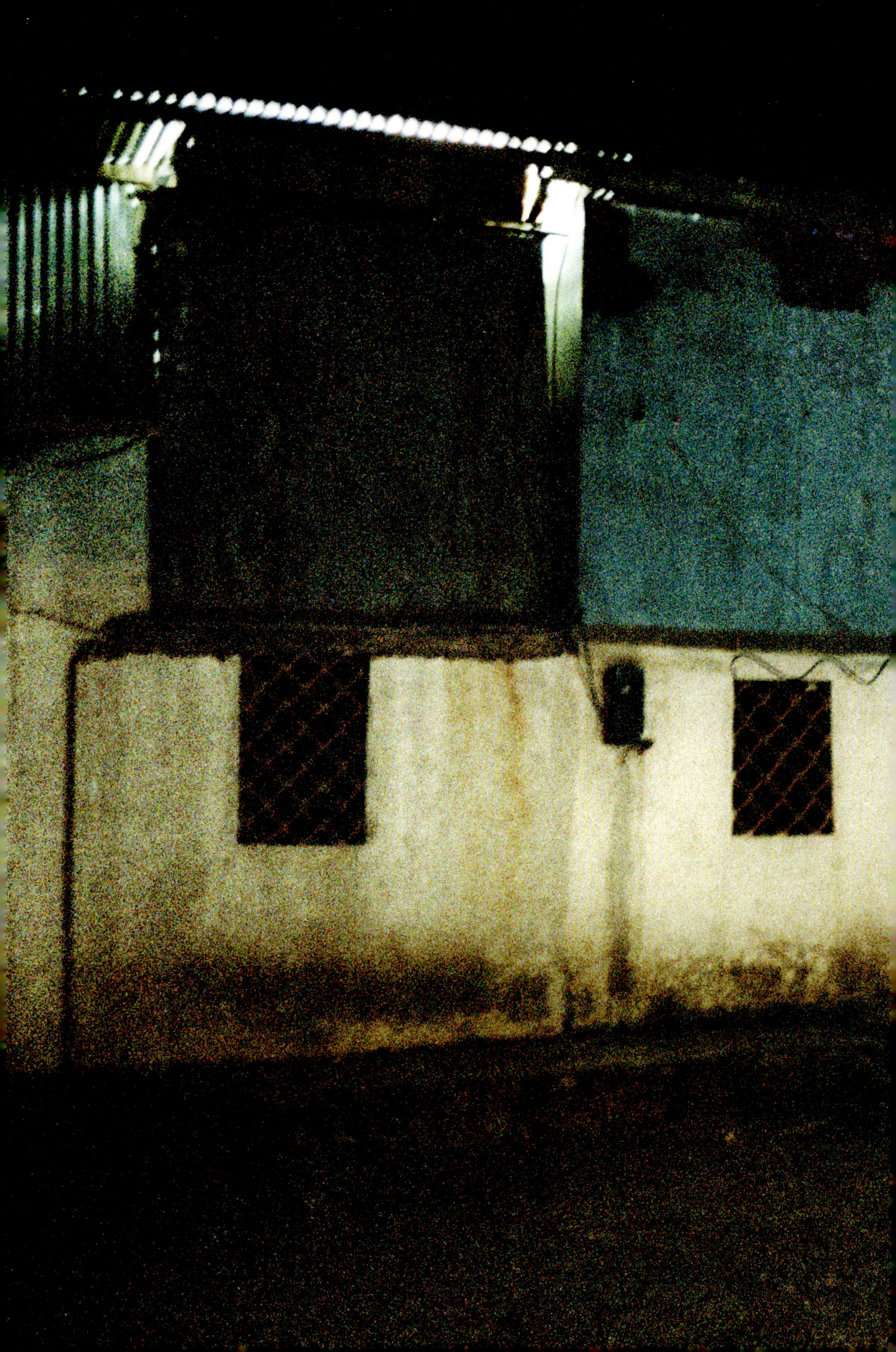

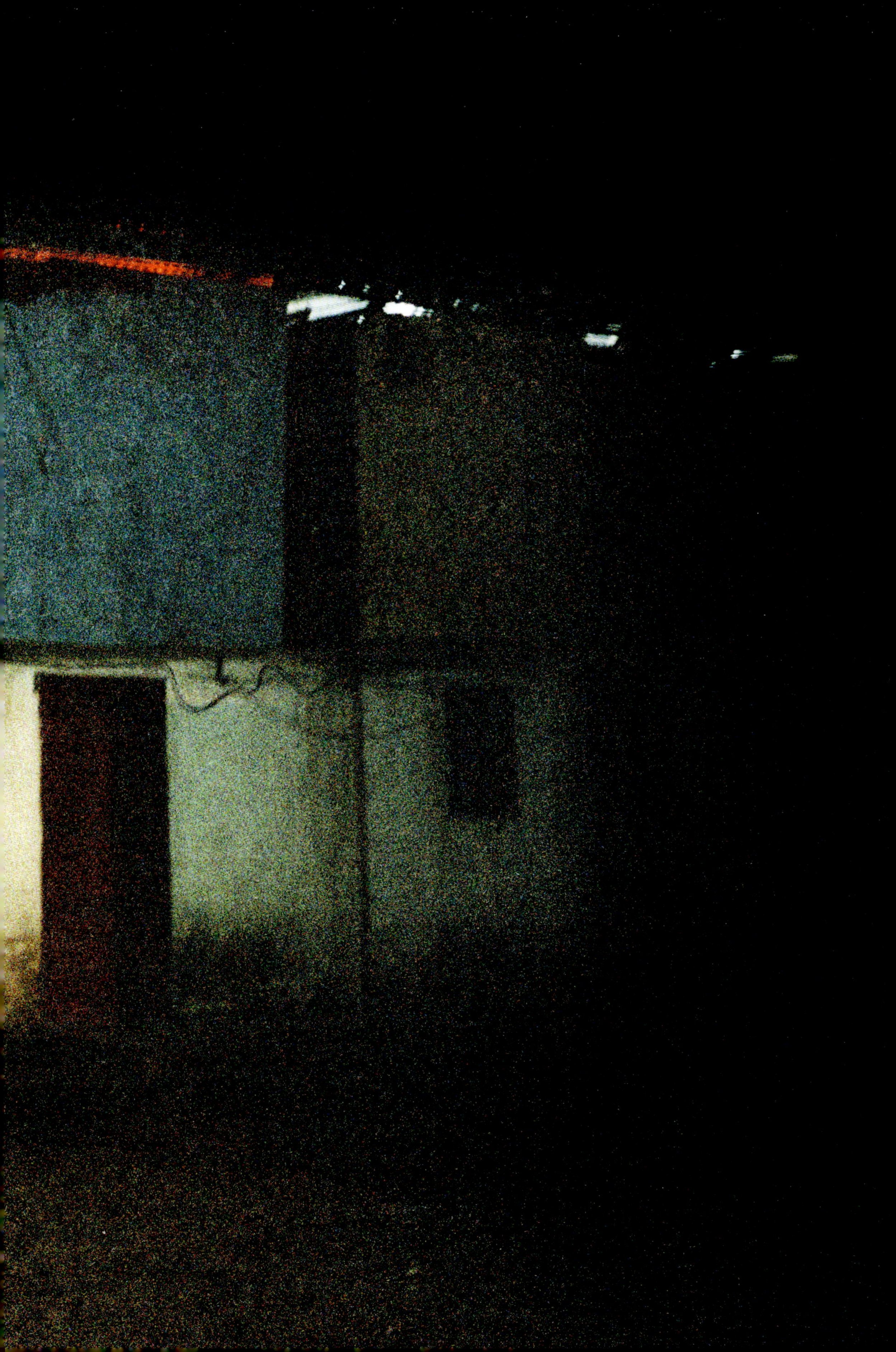

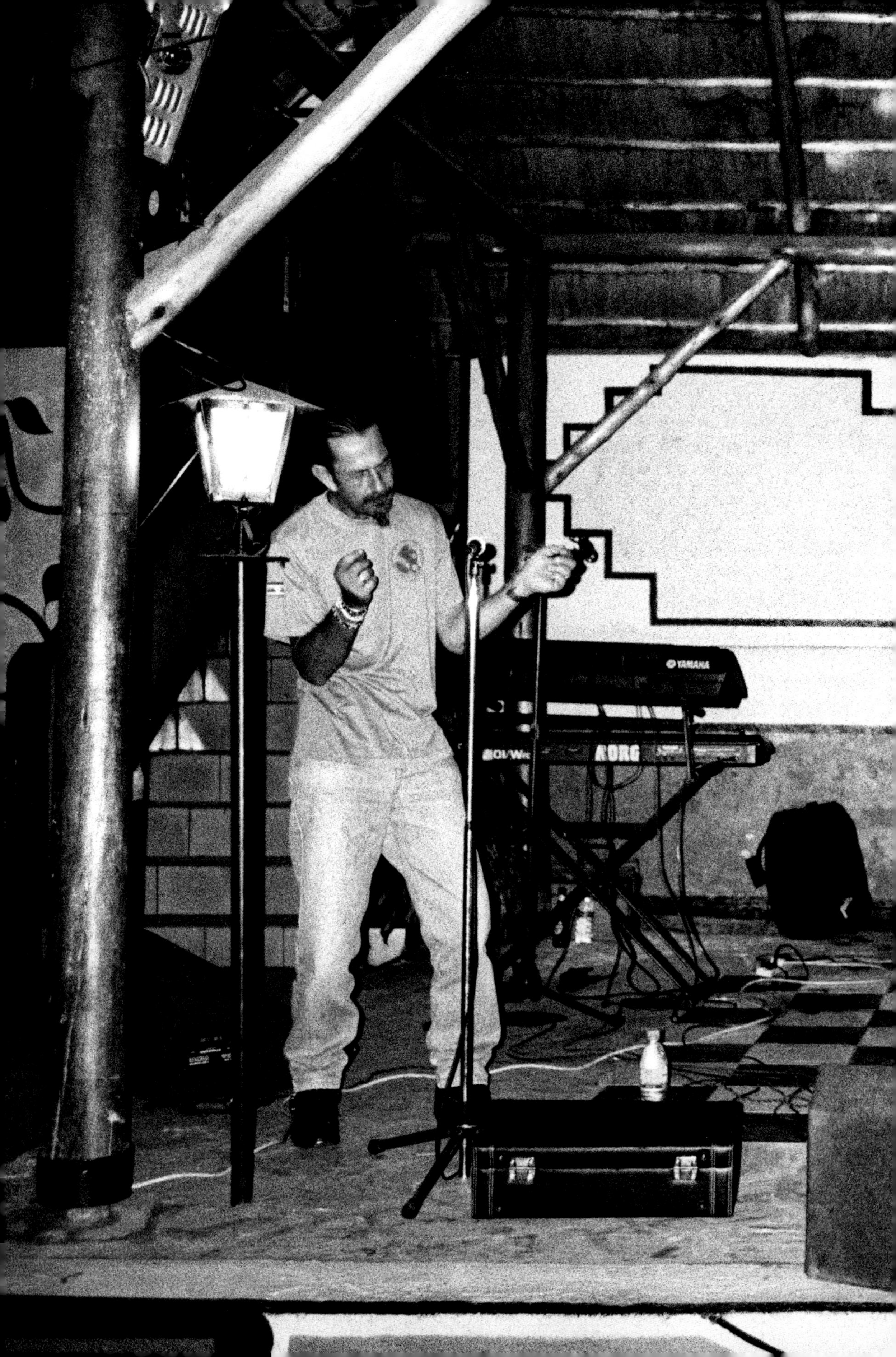
YAMAHA
KORG

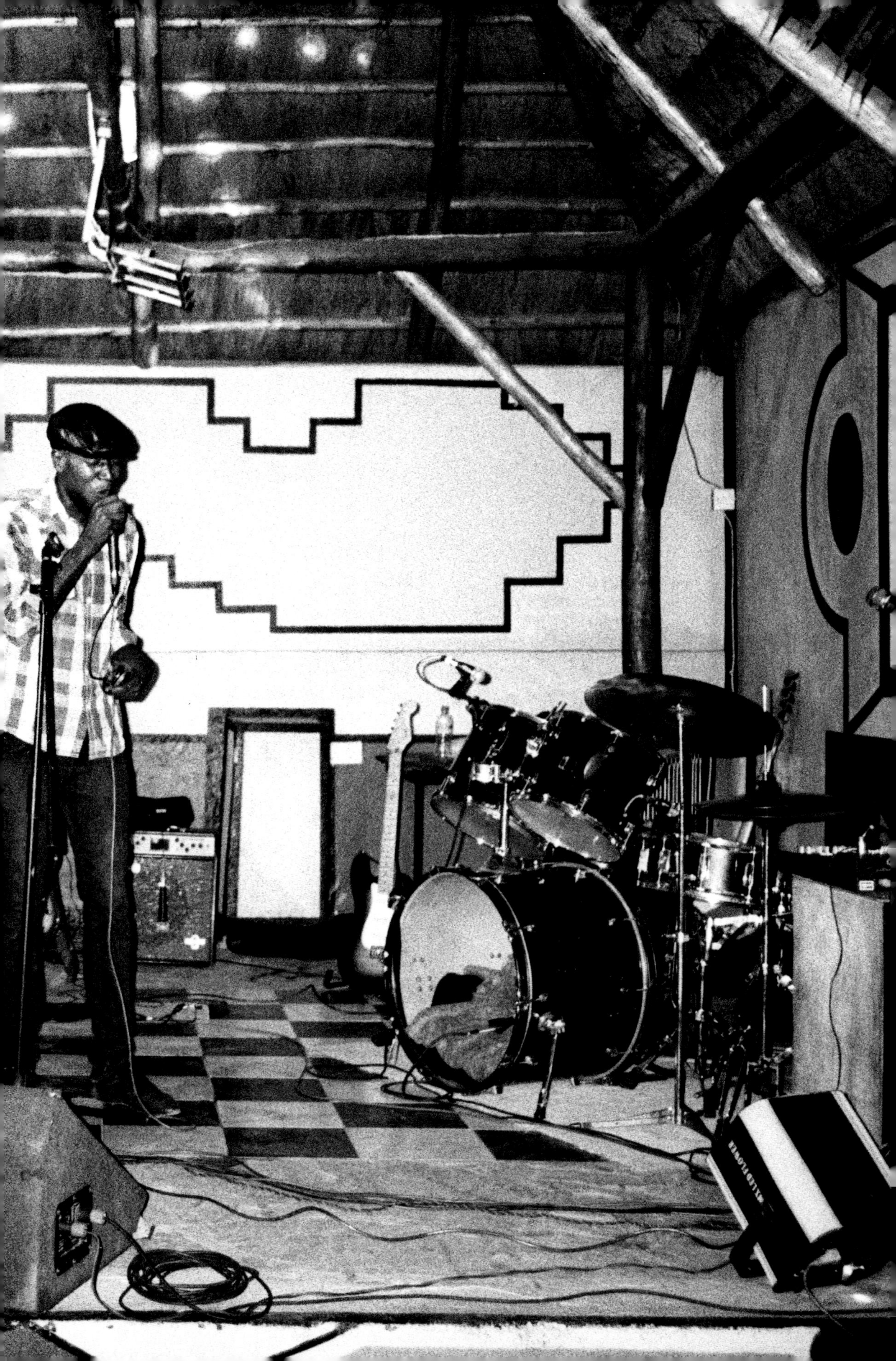

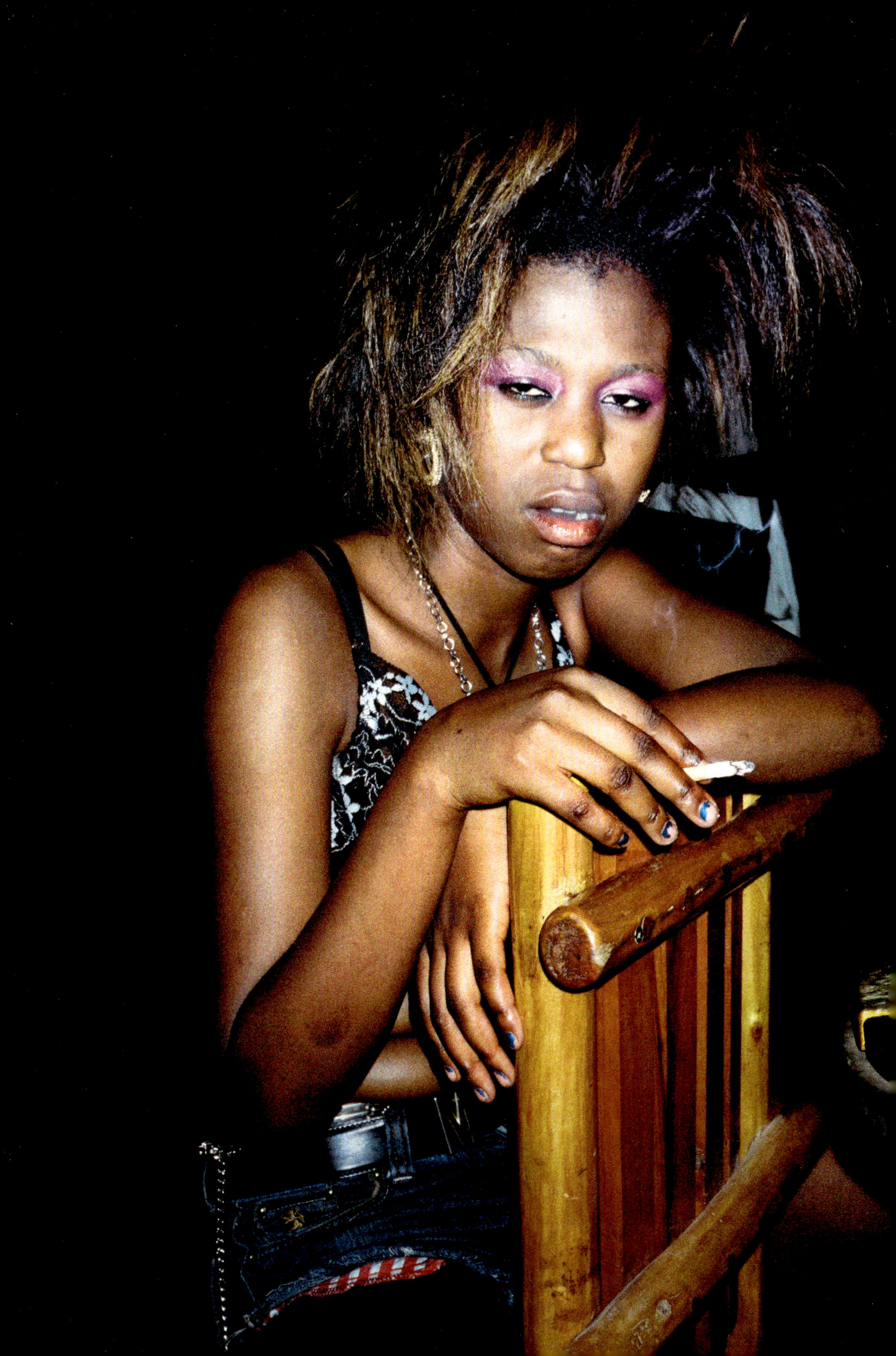

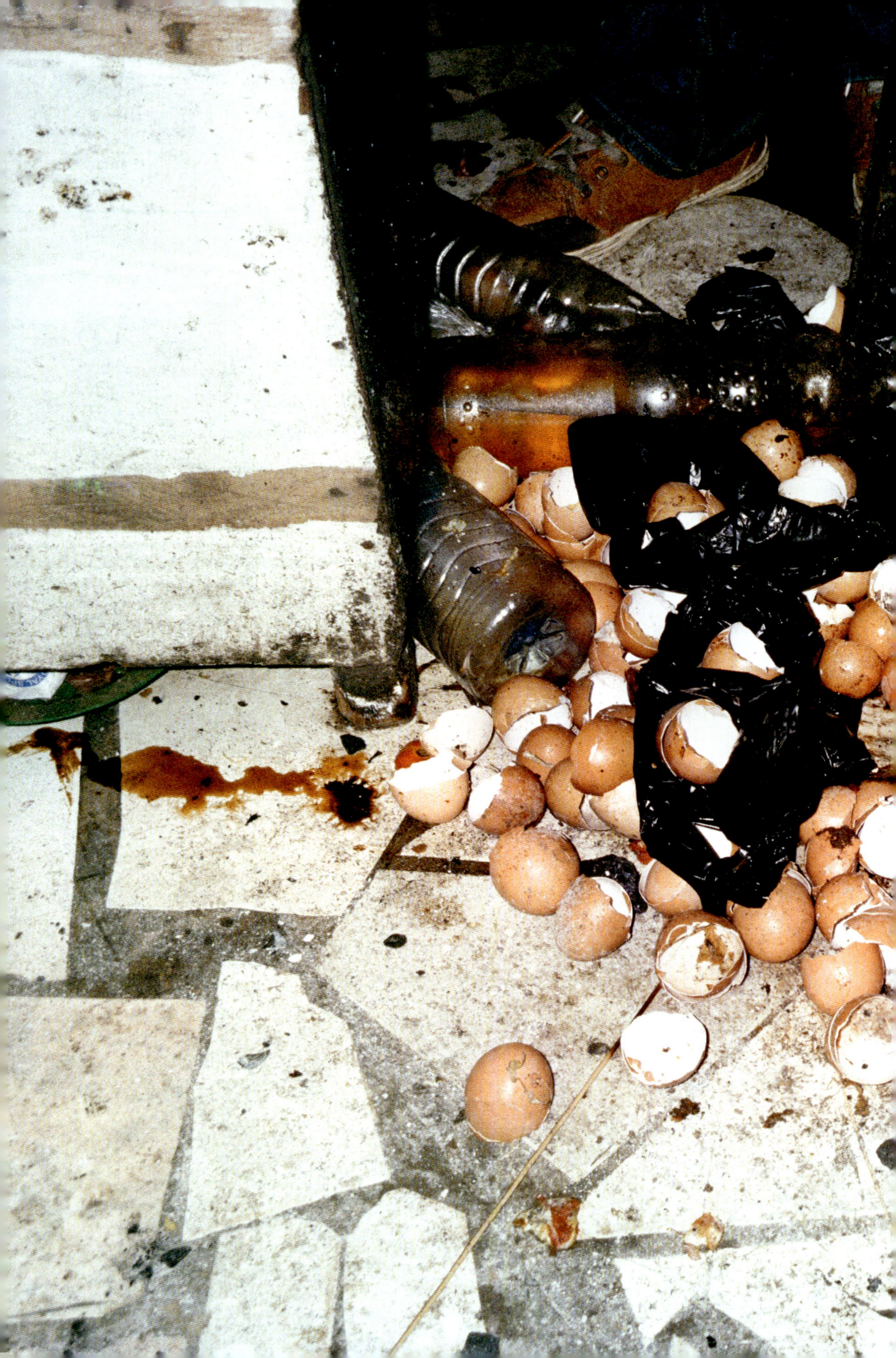

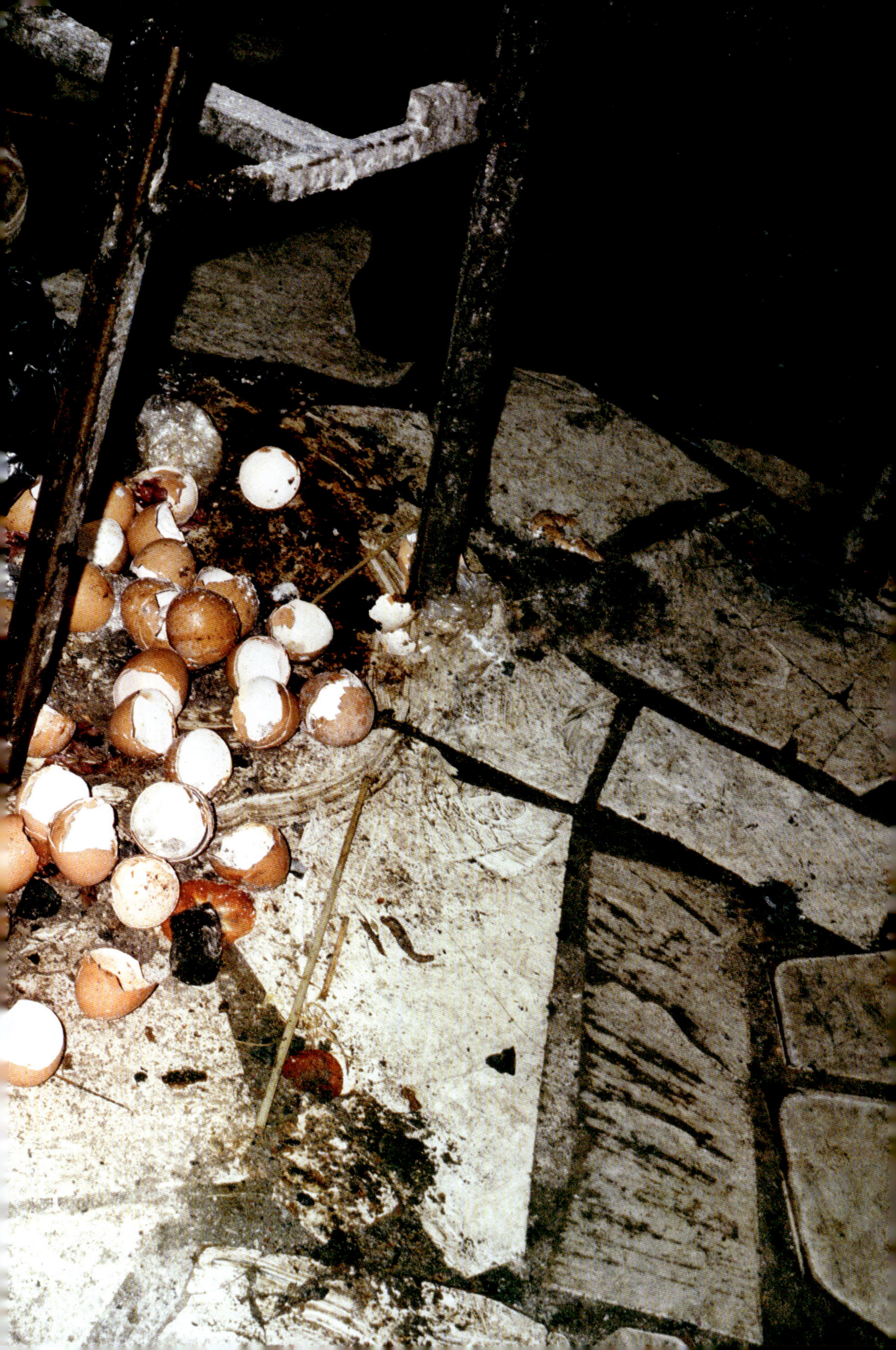

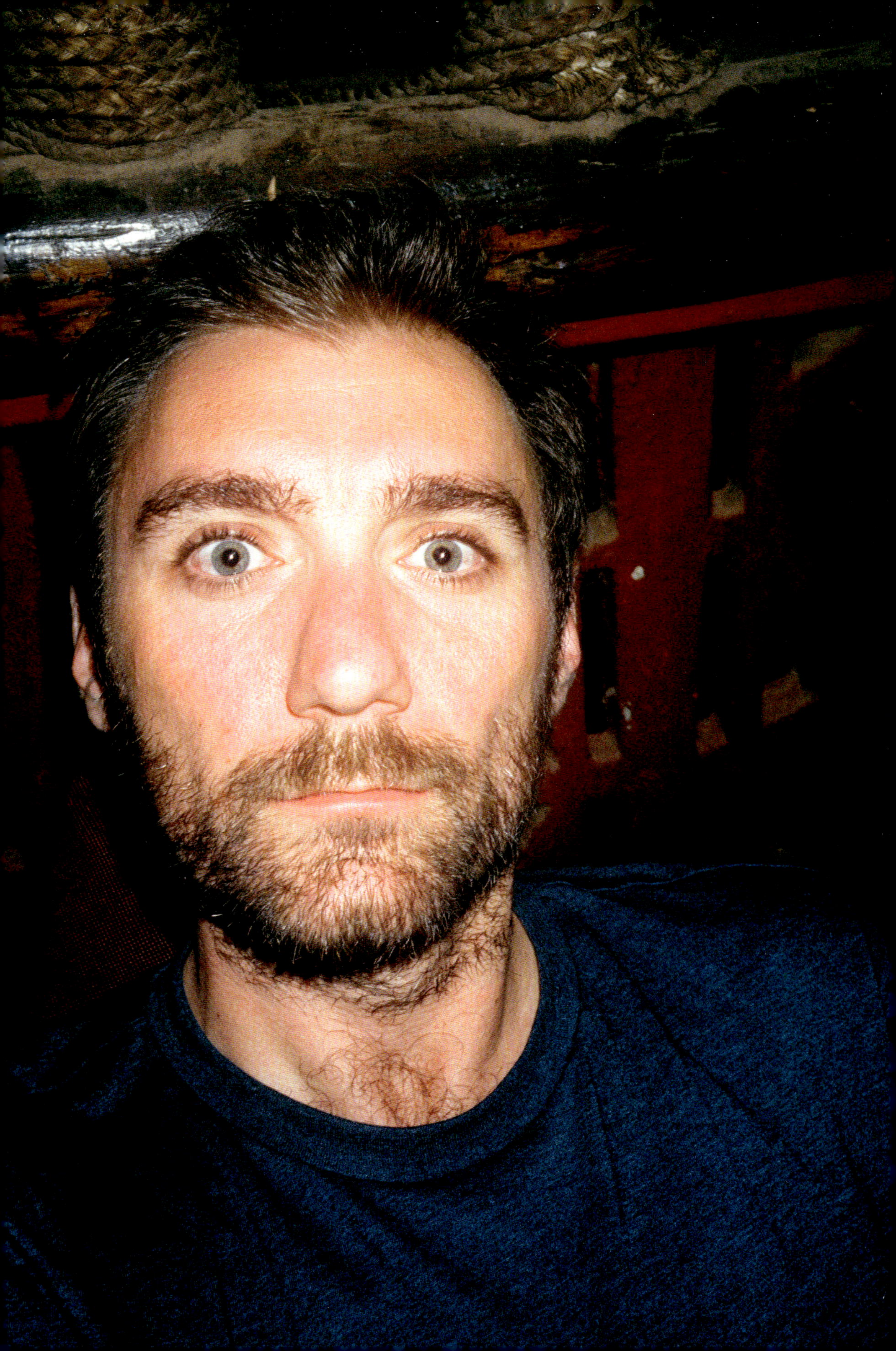

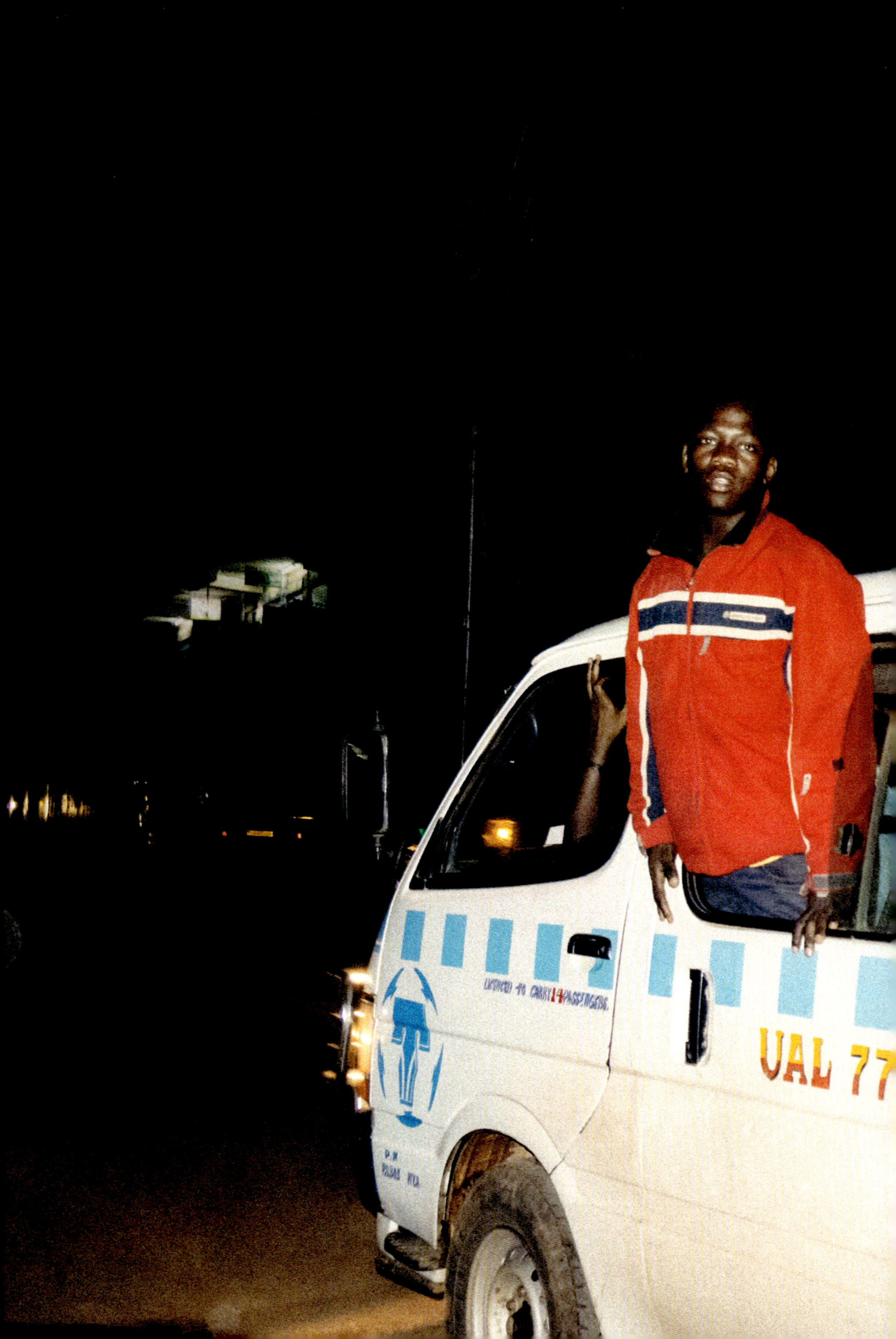
UAL 77

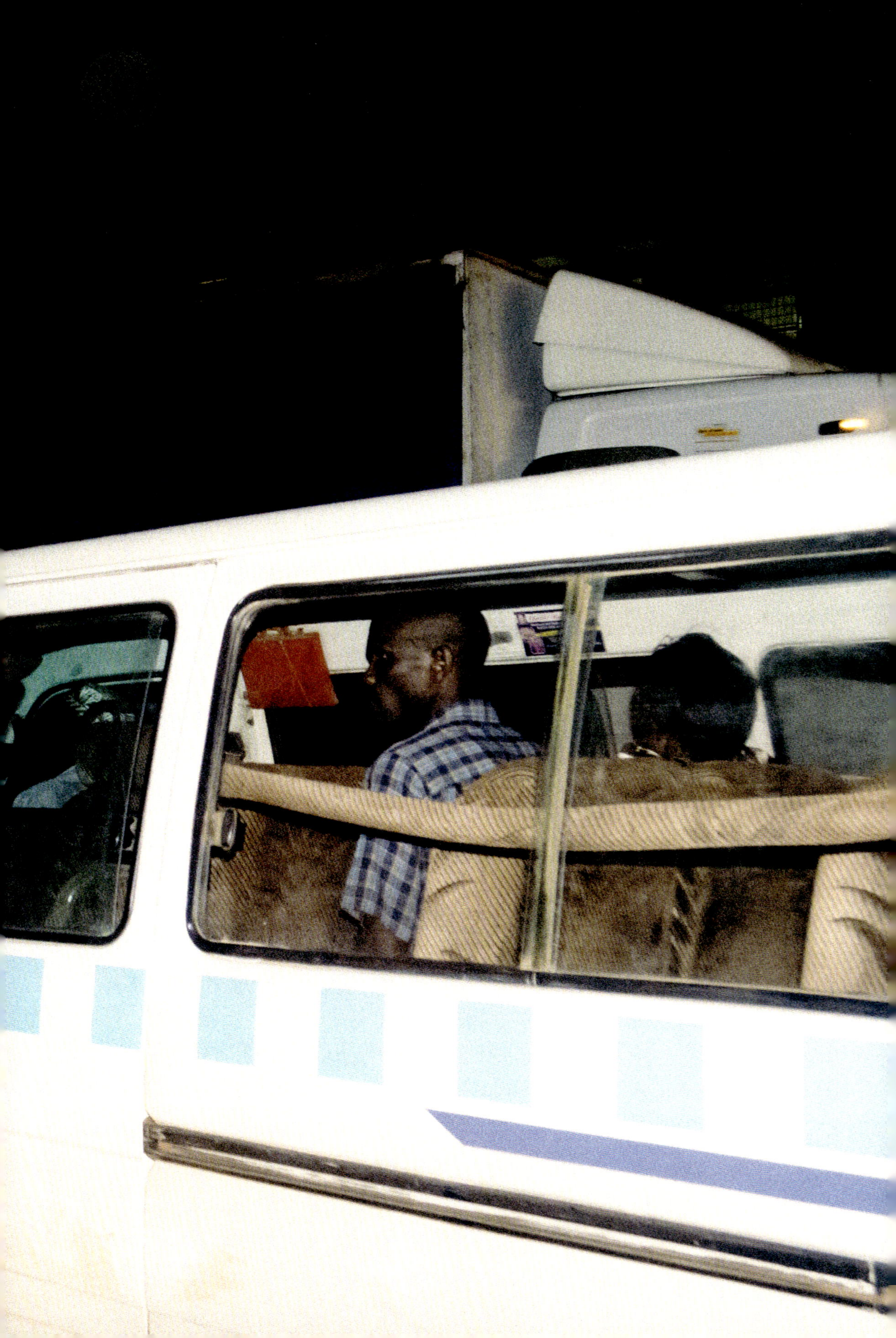

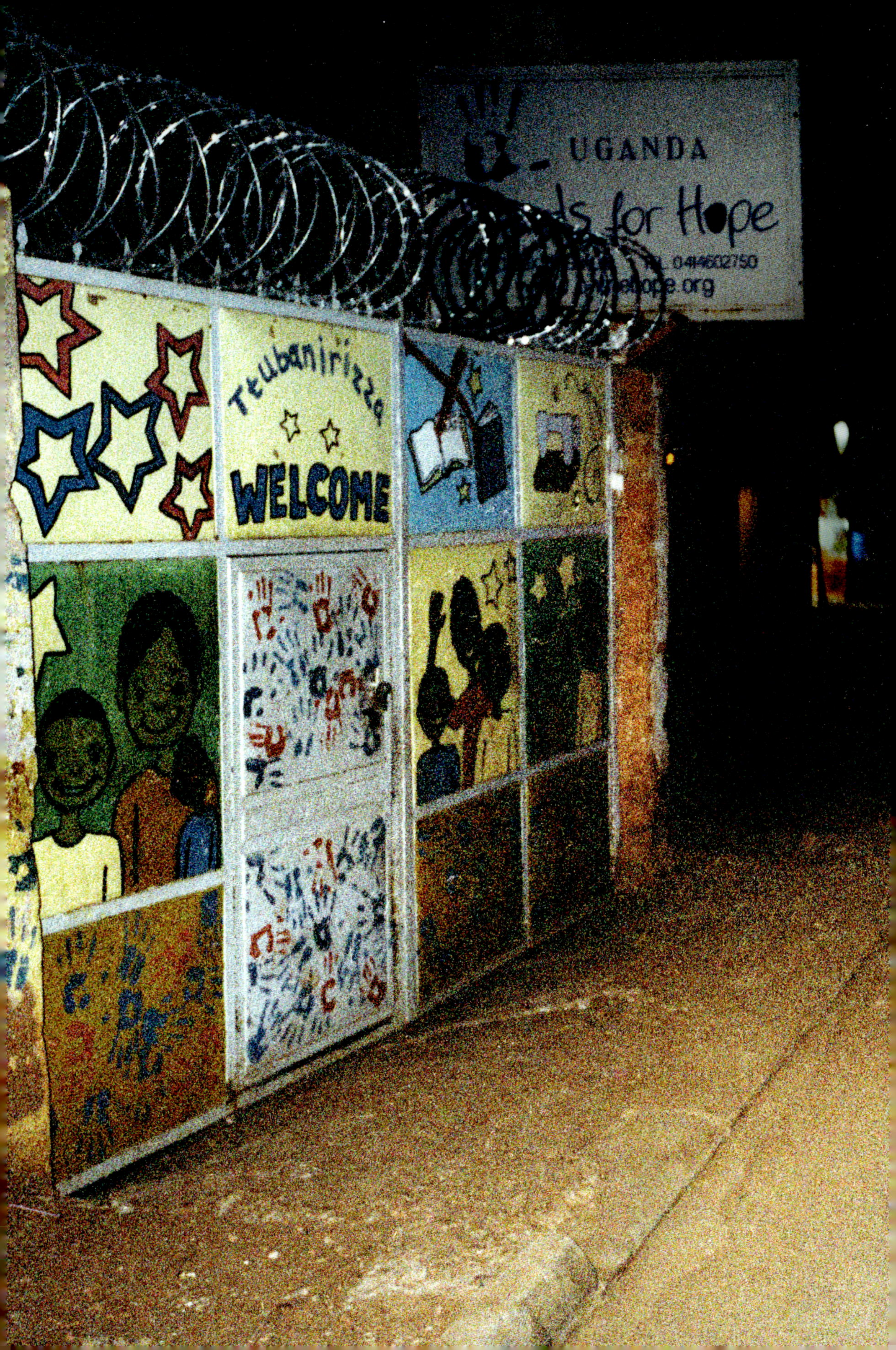
UGANDA
for Hope
0414602750
WELCOME

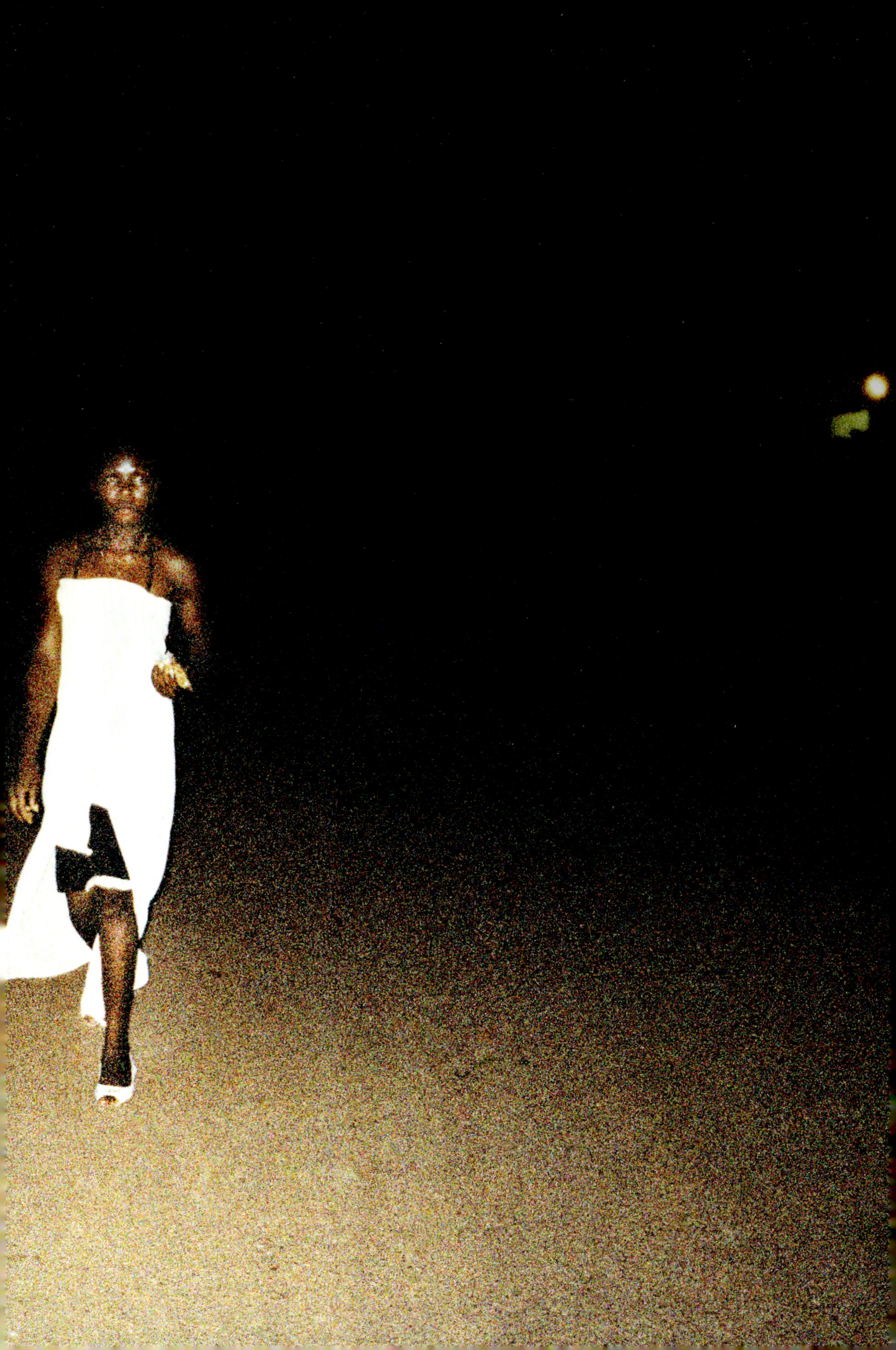

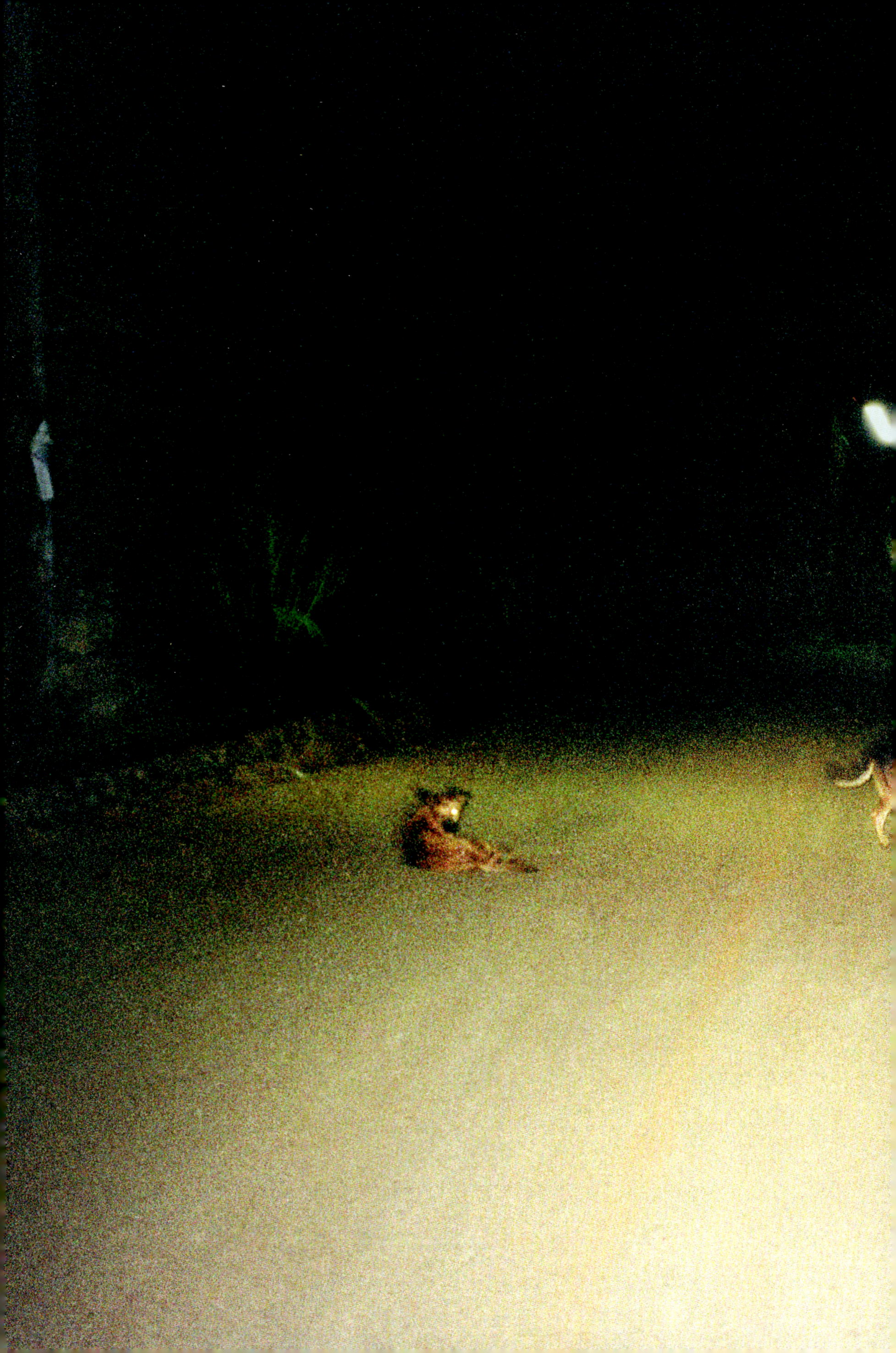

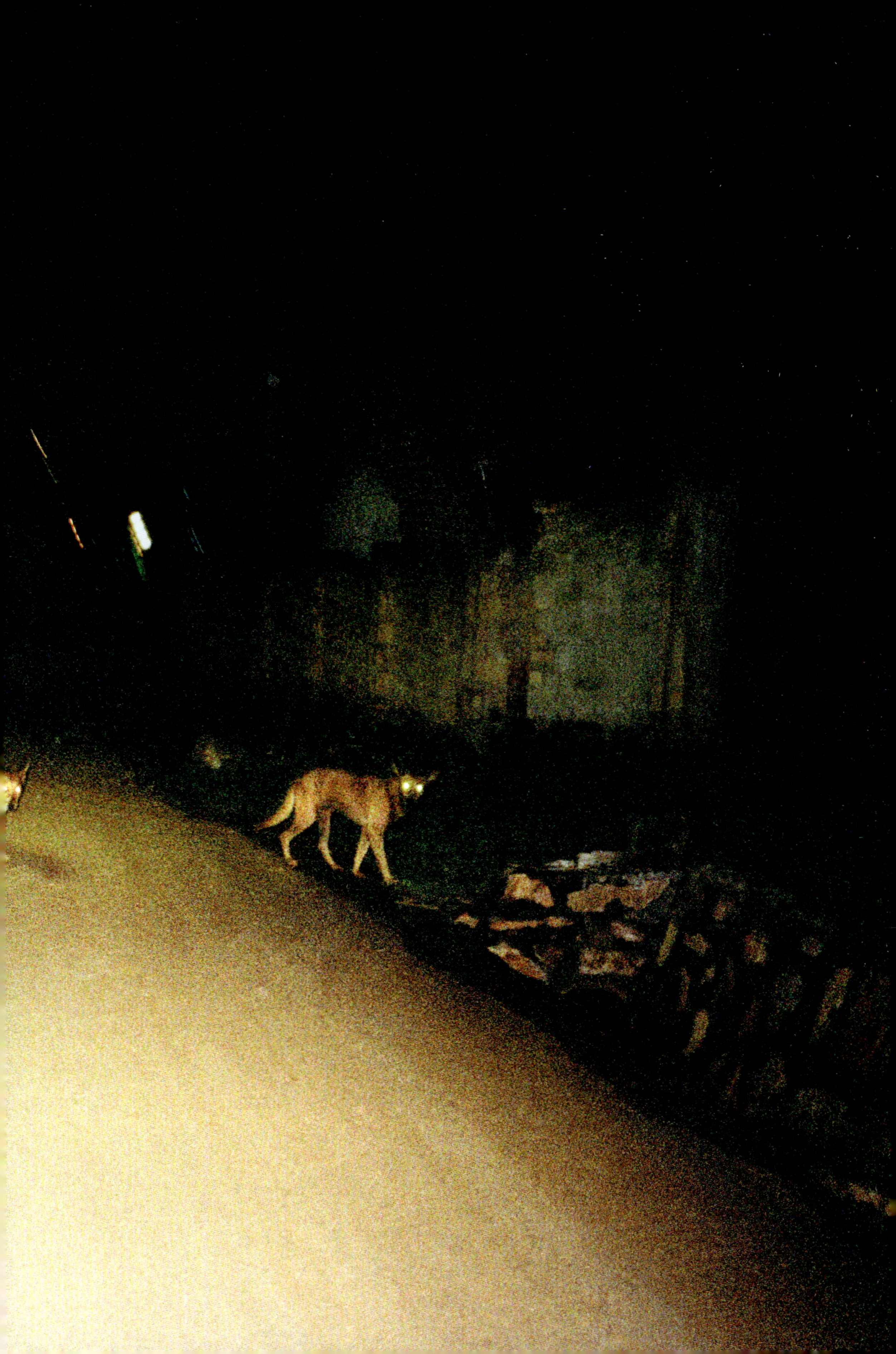

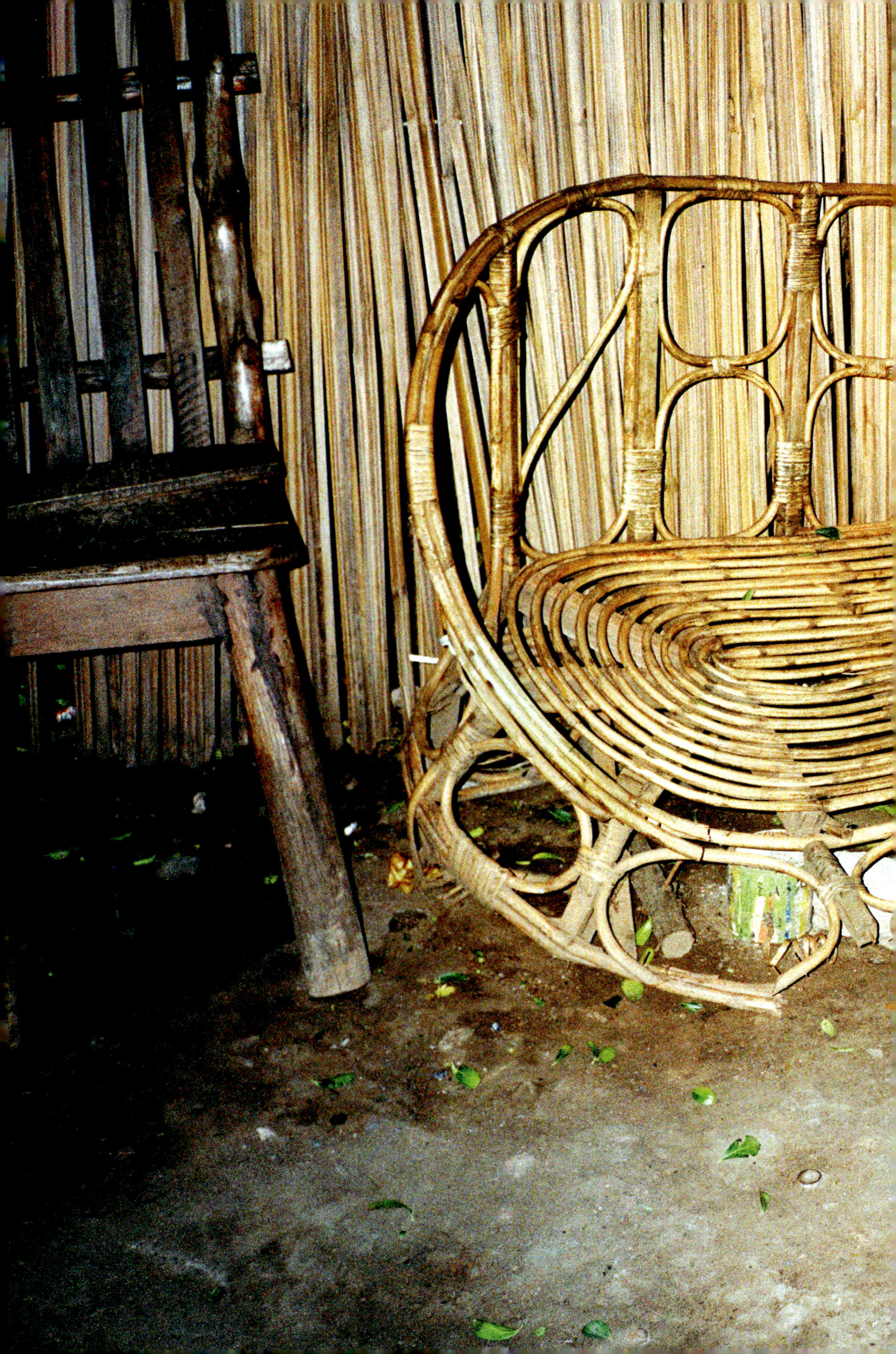

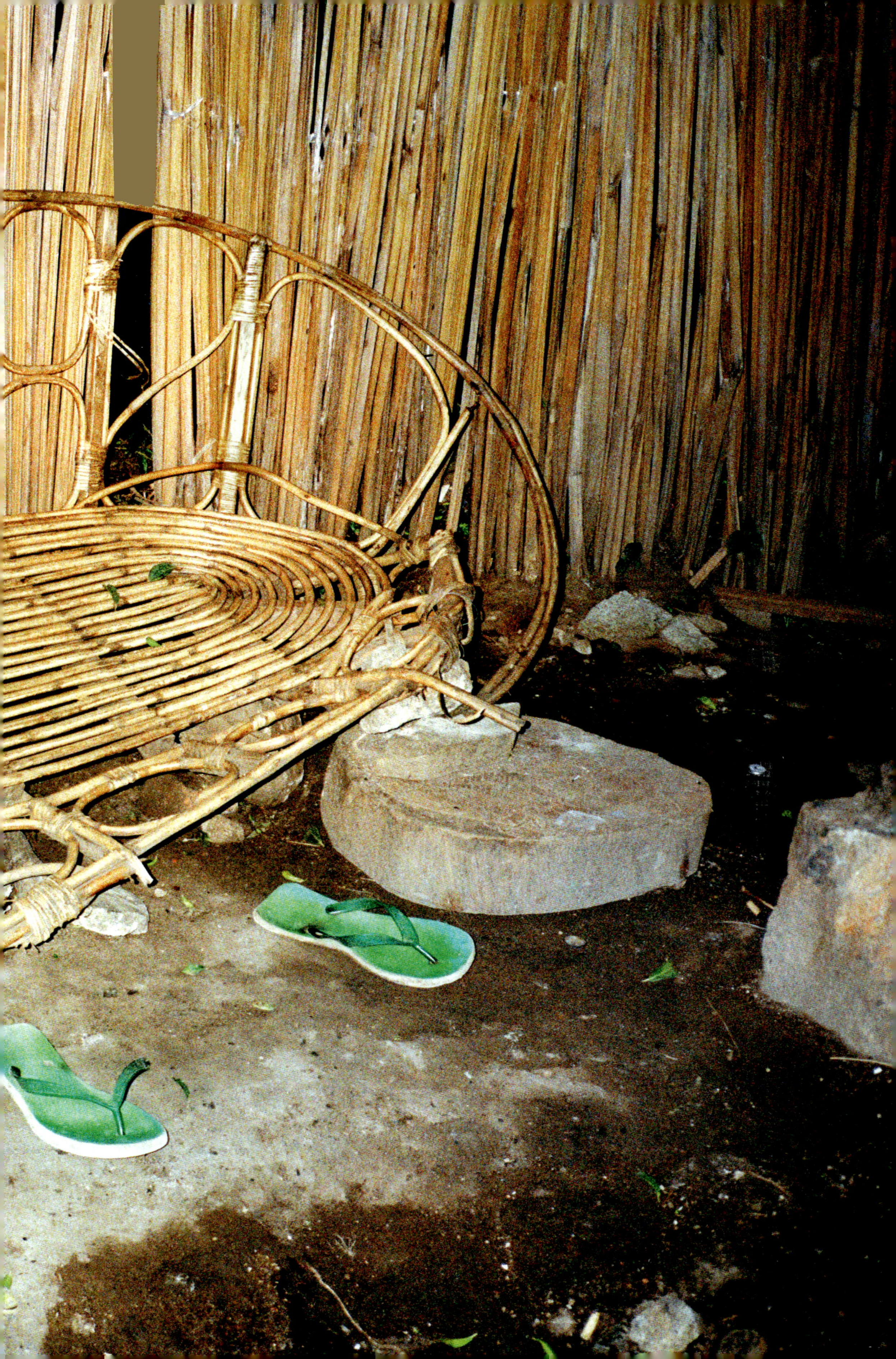

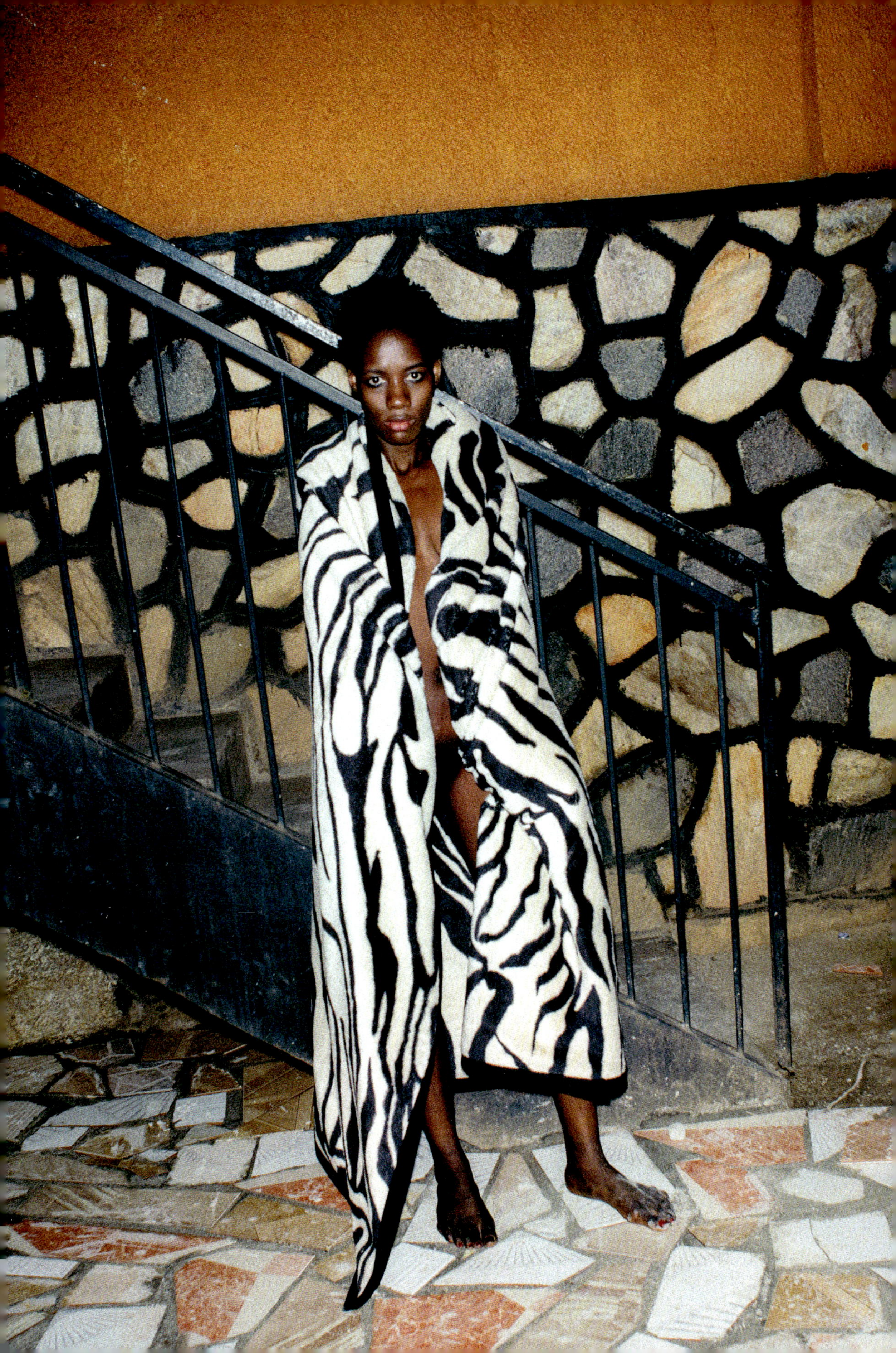